THE PEARL BUYING GUIDE

Second Edition

Text & Photographs

by

Renée Newman GG

International Jewelry Publications

Los Angeles

International Jewelry Publications
P.O. Box 13384
Los Angeles, CA 90013-0384 USA

(Inquiries should be accompanied by a self-addressed, stamped envelope).

Printed in the United States of America and Singapore

Library of Congress Cataloging in Publication Data

Newman, Renée.
   The pearl buying guide / text & photographs by Renée Newman. -- 2nd ed.
      p. cm.
   Includes bibliographical references and index.
   ISBN 0-929975-22-7 : $19.95
   1. Pearls--Purchasing.   I. Title
TS755.P3N49 1994   93-43758
639'.412--dc20   CIP

Cover photograph by Renée Newman
The necklace is courtesy of the
Josam Diamond Trading Corporation, Los Angeles
It is made of 9 1/2 to 10mm Akoya pearls, one South
Sea pearl, a 17.52-carat sapphire, 2.69 carats of diamond
baguettes and 6.78 carats round brilliant-cut diamonds.

Contents

Contents

Acknowledgements

I would like to express my appreciation to the following people for their contribution to *The Pearl Buying Guide*:

Ernie and Regina Goldberger of the Josam Diamond Trading Corporation. This book could never have been written without the experience and knowledge I gained from working with them. Some of the pearls pictured in this book are or were part of their collection.

Charles Carmona, Pin P. Chen, Louise Harris, Susan B. Johnson, Betty Sue King, Peter Malnekoff, Henri Masliah, Lynn Marie Nakamura, and Charles Ueng. They have made valuable suggestions, corrections, and comments regarding the portions of the book they examined. They are not responsible for any possible errors, nor do they necessarily endorse the material contained in this book.

A & Z Pearls Inc., Adachi America Inc., Albert Cohen Co., Gladys Evans, Jye's International Inc., Overland Gems, Inc., Shima Pearl Company Inc., Timeless Gem Designs, and Marge Vaughn. Their pearls or clasps have been used for some of the photographs.

Albert Asher South Sea Pearl Co., Assael International Inc., Gemological Institute of America, Hikari Southsea Pearl Co, Inc., Cultured Pearl Association of America, Inc., Mikimoto Co. Japan Pearl Exporters' Association, King's Ransom, Frank Mastoloni & Sons, Inc, Alan Revere Jewelry Design, and Shogun Trading Co. Inc. Photos or diagrams from them have been reproduced in this book.

Ion Itescu, Carl Addicott, Lisa Bishoff, Cheryl Haab, Maria Johnson, Dawn King, and Monique Truchet. They have provided technical assistance.

Patricia S. Esparza. She has spent hours carefully editing *The Pearl Buying Guide*. Thanks to her, this book is much easier for consumers to read and understand.

My sincere thanks to all of these contributors for their kindness and help.

Suppliers of Pearls & Accessories for Photographs

Cover Photo: Josam Diamond Trading Corporation, Los Angeles, CA

Color Photos:

3a & 3b Hikari Southsea Pearl Co., Inc., Los Angeles, CA

3c & 3e A & Z Pearls, Inc., Los Angeles, CA

3d King's Ransom, Sausalito, California.

4a & 4b Jye's International, Inc., San Francisco and Shima Pearl Co., Inc., Los Angeles, CA.

5a Jye's International, Inc., San Francisco, CA

5b Shima Pearl Co., Inc. Los Angeles, CA

9a Hikari Southsea Pearl Co., Inc., Los Angeles, CA

9b Albert Asher South Sea Pearl Co., Inc., New York, NY

10a-10c Assael International, Inc., New York, NY

10d Shima Pearl Co. Inc., Los Angeles, CA

10e King's Ransom, Sausalito, CA

11a Overland Gems, Inc., Los Angeles, CA

11b & 11c A & Z Pearls Inc., Los Angeles, CA

11d Gemological Institute of America, Santa Monica, CA

11e & 15a A & Z Pearls Inc., Los Angeles, CA

15b Shima Pearl Co., Inc., Los Angeles, CA

15c & 15e Alan Revere Jewelry Design, San Francisco, CA

15d Hikari Southsea Pearl Co., Inc., Los Angeles, CA

Black & White Photos

Chapter 3

Figs. 3.1 - 3.4, 3.6. 3.7 All from the A & Z Pearl, Inc., Los Angeles, CA

Chapter 4

Fig. 4.1 Jye's International, Inc., San Francisco and Shima Pearl Co., Inc., Los Angeles, CA

Chapter 9

Fig. 9.2 Albert Asher South Sea Pearl Co., New York, NY

Chapter 10

Fig. 10.1 Albert Asher South Sea Pearl Co., New York, NY
Fig. 10.4 Assael International, Inc., New York, NY

Chapter 11

Fig. 11.3 A & Z Pearls Inc., Los Angeles, CA
Fig. 11.4 Shogun Trading Co., Inc. New York, NY
Fig. 11.7 Shima Pearl Co. Inc., Los Angeles, CA

Chapter 14

Fig. 14.1 - 14.3 Albert Cohen Co., Los Angeles, CA
Fig. 14.4 & 14.8 Timeless Gem Designs, Los Angeles, CA
Fig. 14.5 A & Z Pearls, Inc., Los Angeles, CA
Fig. 14.6 Frank Mastoloni & Sons, Inc., New York, NY
Fig. 14.7 Shima Pearl Co., Inc., Los Angeles, CA

Chapter 15

Figs. 15.1 - 15.15 A & Z Pearls Inc., Los Angeles, CA
Fig. 15.7 (The pearl shortener) Timeless Gem Designs, Los Angeles, CA
Fig. 15.14 (The mabe pearl enhancer) Shima Pearl Co., Inc., Los Angeles, CA

1

Why Read a Whole Book
Just to Buy Some Pearls?

Annemarie turned on the television. A man was advertising a strand of pearls.

"Folks, feast your eyes on this gorgeous strand of pearls.
So lustrous!
So magnificent!
In the stores, you'd be lucky to find these pearls for $900. Even at a half-price sale they would go for $450. But you won't believe your ears when I tell you my give-away price.
Yes, believe it or not--just $139.
Quantities are limited, so don't delay. Mail in your check today. At this price, jewelers will be ordering these strands by the dozens."

Annemarie had been wanting a strand of pearls and this sounded like a fantastic buy, so she sent away for them. When they arrived, they didn't look as lustrous as she had expected. Two weeks later, she took them to her appraiser. He told her it wouldn't be worth getting a written appraisal for them. At best, they might retail for $150. Then he showed her how their pearl coating was peeling off around the drill holes. Once it all peeled off, she would have nothing but a $5 or $10 shell bead necklace.

Annemarie decided to call the phone number on the sales receipt to see how she could return the pearls and get her money back. An operator came on the line. "The number you have dialed has been disconnected."

Joe's grandmother had passed away and his family was having a backyard estate sale. In her jewelry box, there were a lot of cheap-looking pieces that no one figured were worth much. One lady picked out a pair of pearl earrings and asked what their price was. Since they looked better quality than the rest of the jewelry, Joe told her $20 and the lady handed him a twenty-dollar bill. A month later as Joe was going through his grandmother's papers, he discovered an appraisal for a pair of natural pearl earrings valued at $13,000.

Louise was on a Circle Pacific tour that started in Tahiti and ended in Hong Kong. She was shocked at the high prices in Tahiti. The food was expensive enough, but what amazed her most was that black pearls were being sold for $500 apiece.

When Louise arrived in Hong Kong, she saw that she could get a whole strand of black pearls there for $500. She ended up buying three strands.

After Louise returned home, she commented to a jeweler-friend, Maria, about how expensive the black pearls in Tahiti were compared to Hong Kong. Maria told her it was because the pearls in Tahiti were naturally colored instead of dyed like the ones she'd bought in Hong Kong. Maria added that some naturally-colored black pearls had been sold at auction in the United States for over $30,000 apiece.

Louise wished she had known about black pearls before her stay in Tahiti. She would have paid more attention to them and bought a pendant set with one. It would have been an ideal souvenir, unlike anything sold in her hometown.

Adam was in the Orient attending a convention and he wanted to get his wife a nice souvenir. While browsing in a jewelry store near his hotel, his eyes were drawn to a pearl pendant with a strong pink color. Susie, the owner, told him it was a rare Burmese pearl worth over $10,000. She was selling it, though, for just $900. Adam figured this pendant would be a great investment--plus his wife loved pink--so he bought it.

When he returned home, Adam had the pendant appraised. According to the appraisal, the pearl was a dyed mabe pearl--one which is hollowed out, filled with a paste, then covered with a piece of mother of pearl. The retail value of the pendant--$175.

Suppose Adam had had a book which described mabe pearls and discussed dyeing. It would have helped him realize that the pendant was overpriced and that such a strong pink color was probably the result of dye.

Suppose Louise had had a book which explained how black pearls were valued. It would have helped her understand the difference between the pearls she saw in Tahiti and those in Hong Kong.

Suppose Joe had had a book that described how natural pearls were valued and identified. It would have prevented him from practically giving away his grandmother's pearl earrings.

Suppose Annemarie had had a book that showed the quality differences between cheap and valuable pearls. It would have made her question the quality of the advertised pearls since she'd realize that nobody in the jewelry industry can sell their inventory below cost and stay in business. Armed with that knowledge, she would have rightfully suspected that the $900 retail comparison price was overinflated.

If you glance at the table of contents of *The Pearl Buying Guide*, you'll notice a wide range of subjects relevant to buying pearls. There is no way a brochure could cover these subjects adequately. For example, a leaflet can advise you to pay attention to quality differences such as nacre (pearl coating) thickness. But this is not sufficient. You should also know what an acceptable nacre thickness is and how you can determine it. *The Pearl Buying Guide* has the space to provide you with this information.

Besides understanding how to detect quality differences among pearls, you should know how to choose a knowledgeable salesperson. But how do you spot such an individual? Membership in jewelry organizations, extensive sales experience, and gemological credentials do not necessarily indicate that a person has a good knowledge of pearls. (Gemology-diploma courses tend to focus on diamonds and colored stones rather than pearls.) You should judge jewelry professionals by what they know and by their willingness to share this knowledge with you--in other words, by their candor. There are many people from a variety of backgrounds who are well-qualified to sell and appraise pearls. But to determine who these people are, you have to know something about pearls yourself. A book on judging pearl quality not only helps you select pearl jewelry, it also helps you find a good jeweler and appraiser.

What This Book Is Not

♦ It's not a guide to making a fortune on pearls. Nobody can guarantee that gems will increase in value and that they can be resold for more than their retail cost. However, understanding the value concepts discussed in this book can increase your chances of finding good buys on pearls.

♦ It's not a price guide. Pearl prices vary greatly depending on the dealer, the harvest, the rate of currency exchange, and the location where they are sold. Therefore, price lists can be misleading and quickly outdated. Price examples are given, though, to show pearl pricing relationships.

♦ It's not a ten-minute guide to appraising pearls. There's a lot to learn before being able to accurately determine the value of pearls. That's why a book like this is needed on the subject. *The Pearl Buying Guide* is just an introduction, but it does have enough information to give consumers a good background for understanding price differences.

♦ It's not a scientific treatise on the anatomy of a pearl oyster or the chemical, physical, and optical characteristics of a pearl. The material in this book, however, is based on technical research. The appendix lists the properties of pearls; and the chapters on identifying imitation, cultured, and natural pearls refer to these properties. Technical terms needed for buying, grading, or identifying pearls are explained in everyday language.

♦ It's not a discussion about pearl farming or the historical importance of pearls throughout the world. Good books about these subjects have already been written and are included in the bibliography.

♦ It's not a substitute for examining actual pearls. Photographs do not accurately reproduce color, nor do they show the three-dimensional nature of gems very well. Concepts such as luster, orient, and over-tone color are best understood when looking at real pearls.

What This Book Is

♦ A guide to judging the quality and value of the various types of pearls.

♦ An aid to avoiding fraud, with tips on detecting imitation, treated, and assembled pearls.

♦ A handy reference on pearls for laypeople and professionals.

♦ A collection of practical tips on choosing and caring for pearl jewelry.

♦ A challenge to view pearls through the eyes of gemologists and pearl dealers.

How to Use This Book

The Pearl Buying Guide is not meant to be read like a science fiction thriller or a romance novel. Some laypeople may find this book overwhelming at first. It might be advisable for them to start by looking at the pictures and by reading Chapter 2 (Curious Facts about Pearls), Chapter 17 (Finding a Good Buy), and the Table of Contents. Then they should learn the basic terminology in Chapter 3 and continue slowly, perhaps a chapter at a time.

Skip over any sections that don't interest you or that are too difficult. This book has far more information than the average person will care to learn. That's because it's also designed to be a reference. When questions arise about pearls, you can avoid lengthy research by having the answers right at your fingertips.

To get the most out of *The Pearl Buying Guide*, you should try to actively use what you learn. Buy or borrow a loupe (jeweler's magnifying glass) and start examining any pearls you might have at home both with and without the loupe. This will help you learn to distinguish real pearls from imitations and detect quality differences. Take the quizzes that you'll find at the end of many of the chapters. Look around in jewelry stores and ask the professionals there to show you different qualities and types of pearls. If you have pearl appraisals, study them carefully. If there is something you don't understand, ask for an explanation.

Shopping for pearls should not be a chore. It should be fun. There is no fun, though, in worrying about being deceived or in buying pearls that turn out to be a poor choice. Use this book to gain the knowledge, confidence, and independence needed to select the pearls that are best for you. Buying gems represents a significant investment of time and money. Let *The Pearl Buying Guide* help make this investment a pleasurable and rewarding experience.

2

Curious Facts About Pearls

An Apology from the Pearl Family.

We pearls want to express our remorse for the suffering we have brought on to pearl oysters and mussels around the world. Unfortunately, many are not around to receive our long overdue apology.

Consider the pearl oysters in Venezuela and Panama, for example. Five-hundred years ago, these oysters were abundant and had a fairly tranquil life in this area. Then Christopher Columbus and Vasco de Balboa arrived and discovered pearls. Until the development of the gold and silver mines in Mexico and Peru, we pearls were the New World's biggest export. In fact, the value of pearls exceeded that of all other exports combined; and in Spain, the Americas became known as "The Lands that Pearls Come From." One of the most famous members of our pearl family, La Peregrina ("The Incomparable"), was found in the Americas. A pear-shaped pearl about the size of a pigeon's egg, La Peregrina is particularly noted for its beauty. Among its owners have been Philip II of Spain, Mary Tudor of England, Napoleon III, and Elizabeth Taylor. According to one story, the slave diver that found it was rewarded with his freedom and his master with a plot of land and a position as mayor.

Nowadays the number of oysters producing pearls around Venezuela and Panama is insignificant. One reminder of what an important source of pearls this area once was is the name of an island off the Venezuelan coast, the Isle of Margarita. "Margarita" means pearls. Incidently, if your name is Margaret, Peggy, Marjorie, Margot, Maggie, Gretchen, Gretel, or Rita, it also means "pearl," which in turn signifies purity, innocence, humility, and sweetness.

The overfishing of oysters has not been limited to areas around South and Central America. Pearl oysters and mussels in parts of Europe, North America, and East and West Asia have also either disappeared or been drastically reduced in number.

Besides feeling guilty about the disappearance of so many oysters and mussels, we pearls regret the discomfort we cause to them when they are alive. It might be easier for you to understand what we mean by discomfort if we explained how we originate.

We pearls owe our existence mostly to certain types of saltwater oysters and freshwater mussels. If we are **natural,** then we are usually formed as the mollusk secretes layers of a protective, pearly substance called **nacre** (pronounced NAY-ker) around an irritant. This irritant, which is our **nucleus,** accidentally enters the mollusk and can be a minute snail, worm, fish or crab, or a particle of shell, clay or mud. Experimentation and pearl slicing, however, have led some pearl researchers to believe that most natural round pearls are caused by the accidental entry of a parasitic worm into a mollusk. There aren't many natural pearls produced anymore for them to study. The pearls that are sold today are usually cultured.

If we are **cultured,** then the irritant is intentionally introduced by man. In the case of most freshwater pearls, pieces of mantle (a membranous tissue that secretes nacre and lines the inner shell surface of mollusks) are inserted into a mussel or oyster. Saltwater cultured pearls, however, usually originate from the insertion of a shell bead nucleus along with a bit of oyster mantle tissue into an oyster. In both cases, the shape and size of the resulting pearls depends to a large degree on the shape and size of the implanted irritant.

Sometimes people are surprised to discover how small oysters are for the pearls they host. Japanese pearl oysters grow to only about 10 centimeters (4") in diameter. Imagine what it would be like if you had to carry around a baseball inside of you. This will help you understand why we feel bad about oysters having to put up with us. Besides being a source of irritation, we also lead to their premature death. Many cultured pearl oysters die when a nucleus is inserted or when pearls are later removed.

As we pearls take this occasion to apologize for the miserable fate that we have brought on to the pearl oysters and mussels of this world, we would also like to express our gratitude for their hospitality. Were it not for the oyster and mussel, we pearls would not have the chance to exist.

The Pearl Oysters' Response

We oysters don't harbor any grudges against pearls. They have made our lives worthwhile. Pearls are not responsible for killing off pearl mollusks. Man is. Consider the mussels in Lake Biwa, Japan. They used to be plentiful. Now, due to pollution, the few that are left are struggling to survive.

Consider too the oysters in the Persian gulf. They used to be renowned for producing the world's finest natural pearls. Overfishing plus the discovery of oil and industrialization of the gulf have disrupted the oyster beds there.

As for the pearls' concern about irritating us or causing us pain, their worries are exaggerated. Our nervous system is very simple. Consequently, we don't have the same sense of feeling that humans do.

The fame and prestige that pearls have brought to us oysters has more than made up for the minor discomfort it has caused. Maybe you find it hard to understand how something as plain as a pearl could elevate our status. Some background information on it might help explain why.

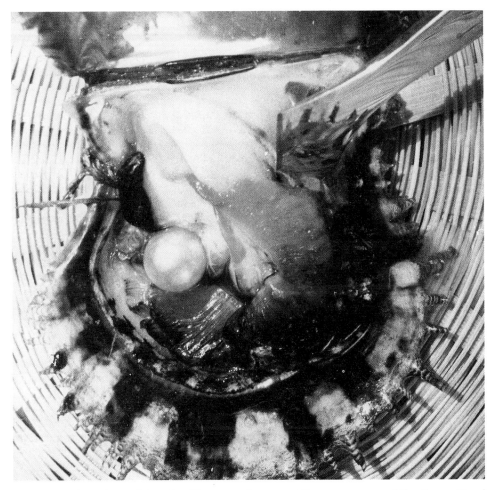

Fig. 2.1 Cultured pearl in a freshly opened oyster. Photo courtesy of the Japan Pearl Exporters' Association.

The pearl is the oldest known gem, and for centuries it was considered the most valuable. To the ancients, pearls were a symbol of the moon and had magical powers which could bring prosperity and long life.

Throughout history, pearls have been considered divine gifts especially suited for royalty. Women who wanted to gain the favor of a king would offer him pearls. In Persia, crowns with double circlets of pearls were the symbol of royal and divine birth. This became a custom elsewhere as well. When Julius Caesar became emperor of the Roman empire, he claimed descent from the gods and was crowned with a pearl diadem.

Pearls, too, have been considered ideal wedding gifts due to their symbolism of purity and innocence. In the Hindu religion, the presentation of an undrilled pearl and its piercing has formed part of the marriage ceremony.

Some cultures, such as the Chinese, have used pearls medically to cure a variety of ailments--indigestion, fever, heart disease. Pearls have also been prescribed as a love potion and tonic for long life. Today, the main component of pearls, calcium carbonate ($CaCO_3$), is used as an antacid and a dietary supplement. Calcium manganese carbonate is an important heart medicine. At the age of 94, Mikimoto, the founder of the cultured pearl industry stated, "I owe my fine health and long life to the two pearls I have swallowed every morning of my life since I was twenty."

The unique qualities of the pearl were particularly well described by George Kunz and Charles Stevenson in 1908 in *The Book of the Pearl* (page 305).

> Unlike other gems, the pearl comes to us perfect and beautiful, direct from the hand of nature. Other precious stones receive careful treatment from the lapidary, and owe much to his art. The pearl, however, owes nothing to man...It is absolutely a gift of nature, on which man cannot improve. We turn from the brilliant, dazzling ornament of diamonds or emeralds to a necklace of pearls with a sense of relief, and the eye rests upon it with quiet, satisfied repose and is delighted with its modest splendor, its soft gleam, borrowed from its home in the depths of the sea. It seems truly to typify steady and abiding affection, which needs no accessory or adornment to make it more attractive. And there is a purity and sweetness about it which makes it especially suitable for the maiden.

Had it not been for the pearl, we oysters would have probably been scorned as lowly, slothful creatures. Instead we're recognized as the creator of an extraordinary gem--one symbolic of all that is pure and beautiful. Therefore we'd like to take this occasion to thank all pearls for the esteem they have brought to our species. We oysters are proud to be their hosts.

3

Pearl Types & Shapes

When you think of a pearl, what's the first shape and color that comes to your mind? Probably round and white. But if you lived in Tahiti, you might initially think of a dark grayish pearl and it wouldn't necessarily be round. If you lived in China, you might first think of a crinkled irregularly shaped pearl. Pearls come in a wide range of shapes, types, and colors; and it is the aim of this chapter to define the various types and to explain the role that shape plays in determining the value of a pearl.

Pearl Types

The difference between natural and cultured pearls was explained in Chapter 2. Technically the term **pearl** should only refer to a natural pearl. Nevertheless, cultured pearls are so common now and natural ones so rare that "pearl" normally refers to a cultured pearl (One exception is in certain Arab countries where cultured pearls tend to be frowned upon. Pearls there are generally considered a special gift from God that should be entirely a product of nature.) In this book, for the sake of brevity, cultured pearls will often be labeled as "pearls." When shopping for pearls, you may come across the term **semi-cultured**. It refers to imitation pearls. Many members of the trade consider it a deceptive term designed to trick buyers into thinking they are getting cultured pearls when they aren't. According to *National Jeweler Magazine* (Nov. 1, 91), some in-flight duty-free magazines have been advertising "semi-cultured" pearls.

Pearls can additionally be classed as saltwater or freshwater. People tend to be most familiar with **saltwater pearls**, which come from oysters in oceans, seas, gulfs, and bays. The best-known example is the Akoya pearl shown in figure 3.1 and discussed below.

Fig. 3.1 Japanese Akoya pearls (cultured saltwater pearls)

Freshwater pearls are found in mussels or oysters in rivers and lakes and tend to be more irregular in shape and more varied in color than pearls found in saltwater oysters (fig. 3.2, & color photos 3c, & 3d. Chapter 11 provides more information on freshwater pearls.

Pearls are further classified into the categories below:

Oriental Pearls   Natural pearls found in oysters of the Persian Gulf or those that look like pearls found there (according to the USA Federal Trade Commission). Sometimes this term is used to designate either any natural saltwater pearl or else more specifically, any natural saltwater pearl found in the West Asia Area, e.g. in the Red Sea, the Persian Gulf, or the Gulf of Mannar off the west coast of Sri Lanka.

A more precise definition of "Oriental pearl" is given by the respected pearl researcher, Koji Wada, in *Pearls of the World* (pg. 69)--natural pearls from one kind of sea-water pearl oyster called the wing shell.

Akoya Pearls   Saltwater pearls from the Akoya oyster (Pinctada fucata martensii), which are usually cultured. These pearls are typically roundish, and their natural colors normally range from pink, to white, to yellowish. (fig. 3.1 and color photo 3a). The chapters on pearl quality in this book focus on Akoya pearls.

Even though they are often called Japanese pearls, they can also be found in oysters outside Japan. Shohei Shirai in his book *Pearls* (pg. 9

& 10) points out that Japanese Akoya oysters also inhabit the tropical seas. His research and on-site surveys have shown that Korea, China, Hong Kong, and Sri Lanka are already culturing pearls using the Akoya oyster. Currently, most Akoya pearls found in jewelry stores are cultured in Japan, but soon China may become the major producer of Akoya pearls less than 7mm in size.

South Sea Pearls As a general term, it can signify any saltwater pearl found in the area extending from Burma and Indonesia down to Australia and across to French Polynesia. It's often used more specifically to refer to large white pearls cultured in the Pinctada maxima oyster--a large oyster found in the South Seas, which is also called the silver-lip or gold-lip oyster depending on the color of its shell lip (color photos 3b, 9a, & 9b).

South Sea pearls tend to range from 9mm to 16mm, whereas Akoya pearls usually range from 2mm to 9mm. A more detailed discussion of South Sea pearls is found in Chapter 9.

Biwa Pearls Freshwater pearls cultivated in Lake Biwa, Japan's largest lake (fig. 3.2 and color photos 3c, 11b, & 11e). Sometimes other freshwater cultured pearls are called Biwas in order to impress buyers. Lake Biwa was one of the first freshwater culturing sites and it has been noted for its high quality pearls. Due to pollution, production has come to a standstill.

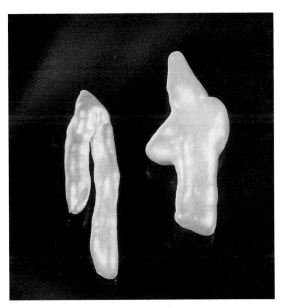

Fig. 3.2 Left: Chinese freshwater pearl, right: Biwa pearl (Japanese freshwater pearl)

Black Pearls

Dark-colored pearls of natural color (not dyed) from the black-lip (Pinctada margaritifera) oyster (color photos 10a-c). Some people use the term "black pearl" to refer to any dark colored pearl. Chapter 10 provides more information about them.

Blue Pearls

Dark-colored pearls found in oysters such as the Akoya or silver-lip oysters. The color is due to foreign contaminants in the nacre or between the nacre and shell bead nucleus unlike black pearls whose color is an inherent characteristic of the pearl nacre. (Hisada and Komatsu, *Pearls of the World*, page 88 and Robert Webster, *Gems*, page 506).

Mother of Pearl

The smooth, hard pearly lining on the interior of a mollusk shell, which is used to make decorative objects, buttons, and beads. Cultured pearls are a lot more expensive than mother-of-pearl beads even though pearl nacre and mother of pearl are composed of basically the same pearly substance ($CaCO_3$ and a little water and conchiolin, a binding agent). Mother of pearl, however, generally has a slightly higher percentage of water and conchiolin than pearl nacre.

Half Pearls

"Whole pearls that have been ground or sawed on one side, usually to remove blemishes" (as defined in *The GIA Jeweler's Manual*). If about 3/4 of the pearl remains, it's called a **three-quarter pearl**.

The term "half pearl" is also used to refer to blister pearls, especially outside the United States.

Blister Pearls

Natural or cultured pearls that grow attached to the inner surface of the oyster or mussel shell. When cut from the shell, one side is left flat with no pearly coating. (Some people apply the term "blister" only to natural pearls of this type.)

Cultured blister pearls are not new. As far back as the 13th century, the Chinese were placing small lead images of the sitting Buddha inside freshwater mussels against their shells. The resulting pearly buddhas were either removed and sold as good-luck charms or else left attached to the shell and used as an ornamental curiosity.

Mabe Pearls

Assembled cultured blister pearls (fig 3.3) (pronounced MAH-bay). The blister pearl is cultured by gluing against the inside of the shell a half-bead nucleus (often of plastic or soapstone). After the mollusk has secreted nacre over the bead, the blister pearl is cut from the shell; and the bead is removed so the pearl can be cleaned to prevent deterioration. The remaining hole is filled with a paste or wax (and sometimes also a bead) and then covered with a mother-of-pearl backing.

Fig. 3.3 Mabe pearls

It can be hard to distinguish between mabe, blister, or half pearls when they are mounted in jewelry. As a consequence, these three terms often end up being used interchangeably.

Despite all the work involved in assembling mabe pearls, they are relatively inexpensive for their large size. This is partly because several can be grown in one oyster and because they are grown in oysters that have rejected a whole nucleus or that are judged unsuitable for producing whole pearls. Also, any type of half pearl will cost far less than if it were whole, no matter what type of oyster it is grown in.

Most large mabe assembled pearls come from the silver-lip or black-lip oysters, but technically the term "mabe" should only refer to pearls cultivated in mabe oysters (Pteria penguin}. The true **mabe-oyster pearls** are known for having a better luster, color, and iridescence than pearls cultured in other oysters and are, consequently, more valuable (color photo 5a). Most of those harvested are 1/2 or 3/4 blister pearls. If a salesperson claims that the jewelry you are buying is made with a mabe-oyster pearl, have him or her write this on the receipt. It's helpful for insurance and appraisal purposes. Information on the culturing of mabe oysters can be found in a write-up by Morimitsu Muramatsu in *Pearls of the World* (pp. 79 to 86).

Fig. 3.4 "Mabe blister pearl" or "blister mabe pearl"

"Mabe Blister Pearls"	An informal term used by some dealers to designate mabe pearls with a nacre rim, making them resemble a fried egg (fig. 3.4). The term "blister mabe" is also used. Technically, though, all assembled mabe pearls originate as blister pearls.
Seed Pearls	Small, natural pearls which measure about two millimeters or less. They usually weigh less than 0.06 carat.
Dust Pearls	Tiny pearls that weigh less than 0.01 carat and that are too small to be useful for jewelry.
Keshi	Pearls that grow accidentally in the soft tissue or the adductor muscle of cultured pearl-bearing mollusks (color photo 15a). "Keshi" is the

term for poppy seed in Japanese. It originated from the minute pearls that were spontaneously formed when a much larger pearl with a bead nucleus was cultured in the Akoya oyster. To the Japanese, these tiny pearls without nuclei resembled poppy seeds, hence the name. After the larger Akoya cultured pearls are removed from the shell, the keshis are collected. Then they are usually exported to countries where the labor costs of drilling and stringing them is low. A high percentage of keshi pearls are ground up and used for medicinal purposes in places such as China, India, and Hong Kong.

Today the term "keshi" also refers to the bigger pearls without nuclei that are spontaneously formed in cultivated South Sea oysters and freshwater mussels (color photo 3b). These can exceed 10mm in width and 10mm in length so they are set in rings, pendants, brooches and earrings and are sometimes made into strands. Fine keshi pearls are noted for their high luster and iridescence and unique shapes. Compared to fine round pearls, their prices are very reasonable.

There is a lot of debate in the trade as to whether keshi pearls should be considered natural pearls. Like natural pearls, they grow accidentally, but they form in oysters that are cultivated by man. The question of whether keshi can properly be called natural has not yet been resolved. However, many Arabs have already made up their mind. They are among the largest buyers of keshi and prefer to regard them as natural.

Mikimoto pearls
Pearls produced and marketed by the Mikimoto Co. Even though Mikimoto pearls come in a range of qualities, they are known for having a higher luster and fewer flaws than the average Akoya pearl. The Mikimoto Co. estimates that only a small fraction of the pearls produced meet the requirements for carrying their trademark clasp. Other companies, too, produce and market pearls of the same high quality standards as those of the Mikimoto Co. Only the name is different.

Consumers should be aware that the Mikimoto name has been misrepresented in some jewelry stores and some discount places. Therefore, **don't assume that pearls with a label saying "Mikimoto" are Mikimoto pearls. Look at the clasp.** Only those pearls which have an 18-karat-gold Mikimoto signature clasp are true Mikimoto pearls. Either a pearl or a diamond will be in the center of it. Also, when you buy Mikimoto pearls, ask the jeweler for the Mikimoto certificate of authenticity that should come with them.

The founder of Mikimoto Pearls, Kokichi Mikimoto, was a pearl farmer, researcher, and merchant who brought respectability to the cultured pearl. In essence, he is the founder of the cultured pearl industry. He is also credited with inventing most of the techniques of oyster farming used today. Using some of Mikimoto's methods, Tatsuhei Mise and Tokichi Nishikawa in 1907, each became the first to invent techniques for culturing round pearls.

In the early 1900's when round cultured pearls were first sold to the public, they were considered by some as fraudulent imitations. In 1921, suits were filed in London and Paris to prevent Mikimoto from selling his cultured pearls. Mikimoto responded by filing suit to stop people from selling imitation pearls as cultured, and he persuaded the French Customs Bureau to charge the same import duty on both natural and cultured pearls. Cultured pearls had previously been classed as costume jewelry. Mikimoto also spent a great deal of time worldwide educating the jewelry trade and the general public about cultured pearls. As a result, cultured pearls became a desirable commodity and are no longer considered imitations. And Mikimoto, son of a poor noodle vendor, came to be known as "The Pearl King."

Pearls Produced by Snails

A hundred years ago, pearls were often broadly defined as any gem grown by a shell animal to protect itself from an irritant. Today, gem laboratories such as the GIA Gem Trade Lab are more strict and would not classify the conch "pearl," for example, as a true pearl. This is because it lacks layers of nacre. This book is about pearls found in oysters and mussels. However, for the sake of interest, it briefly describes the following snail "pearls" because they are sold as pearls.

Abalone "pearls" Found in abalone off the coast of New Zealand, California, Mexico, Japan, and Korea, these "pearls" are known for their colorful, almost opal-like appearance (color photo 3d). They may be any combination of green, blue, pink, or yellow and usually have an irregular shape, sometimes resembling a tooth or a cone. The finest-quality abalone "pearls" are collectors items and may sell for between $5,000 and $15,000.

The September 1991 issue of *Modern Jeweler* reported that about 20,000 saleable cultured abalone "pearls" had been harvested in Korea in 1990. These "pearls" sold in Singapore for as much as $385 per "pearl."

Conch "pearls" Also called "pink pearls"--though many are brownish or white--they are found in the great Conch, a large marine snail found throughout the Caribbean. They may have distinctive flame-like surface markings and the best ones tend to be symmetrical in shape and often oblong. Fine conch "pearls" may cost between $1000 and $10,000 and tend to be most appreciated by Europeans and Arabs.

Fig. 3.5 Osmena or nautilus "pearl"

Osmena "Pearls   "White or gray "pearls" which, according to sellers, are grown in the
chambered nautilus snail from the Philippines (fig. 3.5). Like mabes,
these "pearls" are filled with a kind of paste and then covered with a
backing. Occasionally, they can be found on sale at gem shows for
prices as low as $5 and $10. They may be used as pendants or
earrings. Commercially, osmena "pearls" (also called nautilus
"pearls") are not important.

Judging Shape

Shape plays a major role in determining the price of pearls. Throughout history, round
has generally been considered the most valuable shape for a pearl. Perhaps this was because
pearls were considered a symbol of the moon. Nevertheless, the most famous and valuable
pearls are often not round. That's because factors such as size, luster, and origin are also
important.

Pearls can be divided into four basic shape categories (fig. 3.6):

◆ **Round**
◆ **Off-Round**   Slightly flattened or ovalish (fig. 3.7)
◆ **Semi-Baroque**   Obviously not round. Pear, drop, egg & button shapes are examples.
◆ **Baroque**   Very distorted and irregular in shape (fig. 3.9). Often the surface is

very uneven. They occasionally resemble familiar objects such as teeth, cacti, tadpoles, mushrooms, or snails.

Fig. 3.6 Top to bottom--round, slightly off round, semi-baroque, and baroque shapes

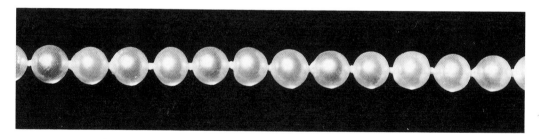

Fig. 3.7 Example of an Akoya strand with off-round pearls

Sometimes additional categories are added for evaluating shape. For example, the sub-categories of "mostly round" and "slightly off-round" are used along with the four basic ones above in the pearl grading system of the GIA (Gemological Institute of America).

Akoya pearl prices are generally based on round pearls. When the pearls deviate from the round shape, they are discounted. Adachi America, a pearl company that has developed a "master set" pearl grading program, has the following discount schedule for their Akoya pearls:

Semi-round	10 to 25% less than round
Semi-baroque	25 to 55% less than round
Baroque	55 to 80% less than round

Midwest Gem Lab, who also offers a master-strand pearl grading system, has another discount schedule, which is based on a survey of some Akoya pearl dealers:

Off-round	0 to 10% less than round
Semi-baroque	10 to 30% less than round
Baroque	70 to 80% less than round*

    *   This is only a general indication. For more exact pricing of baroques, quotes should be obtained from dealers.

The following conclusions can be drawn when comparing these two discount schedules:

◆ Shape can have a significant effect on the price of pearls.
◆ Pearl pricing can vary from one dealer to another.
◆ The upper and lower boundaries of each shape category need to be clearly defined and illustrated (so far this has not been done in the trade). It appears, for example, that the dealers Midwest Gem Lab surveyed had a fairly restricted interpretation of "baroque." Perhaps these dealers and Adachi price baroques alike, but to know this, we need to see what range of shapes each dealer classifies as baroque.

When judging pearls for shape, take into consideration the type of pearl you are looking at. For example, expensive natural pearls are typically baroque, whereas cheap cultured pearls with thin nacre (pearl coating) are generally round. That's because natural pearls don't contain a round nucleus bead, and cultured pearl beads that are hardly coated with nacre don't have much of a chance to grow irregular. The typical shapes of five pearl types are described below to help you know what degree of roundness to expect of pearls. They are listed from the most commonly round to the most commonly baroque.

Akoya pearls with thin nacre	Often round
Akoya pearls with thick nacre	Frequently off-round, but round ones are available too. Baroque Akoya pearl strands are considered low quality.
South Sea cultured	Rarely perfectly round. The larger the pearl, the more it will tend to deviate from round. Baroques are often regarded as a good alternative to the more expensive symmetrical shapes when ones budget is limited.

Natural saltwater	Usually baroque or semi-baroque. Round ones are extremely rare.
Freshwater, cultured & natural	Usually baroque, especially if they are natural. Baroque freshwater pearls are considered desirable. Cultured off-round freshwater pearls are available. They are normally more affordable than saltwater pearls of similar quality and size.

Another grading factor to consider when judging off-round and especially semi-baroque pearls is their **degree of symmetry** (perfectly round pearls are always symmetrical and baroque pearls are by definition unsymmetrical). If for example, you are buying a teardrop pearl pendant for someone special, one with two equal sides would probably be the most desirable. Lopsided pearls can be interesting but they are considered less valuable than those which are symmetrical.

Even though dealers agree round is the most expensive shape, there is no standardized system for determining how shape affects pearl prices. As previously mentioned, the way pearls are discounted for shape variation can differ from one dealer to another. Do not let this lack of standardization lead you to ignore pearl shape as a value factor. Consider it important, and keep in mind when judging pearl prices that it's best to compare pearls of the same shape as well as the same size, color, type, and luster.

Quiz (Chapters 2 and 3)

Select the correct answer.

1. A mother-of-pearl bead is:

a. as valuable as a pearl
b. less valuable than a pearl
c. more valuable than a pearl
d. another name for a pearl

2. Which of the following types of pearls is most likely to be round?

a. A cultured South Sea pearl
b. A natural South Sea pearl
c. An Akoya pearl with very thin nacre
d. An Akoya pearl with very thick nacre

3. Mikimoto pearls:

a. come from a special kind of oyster trademarked by the Mikimoto company.
b. have more flaws than most pearls.
c. come in a range of qualities.
d. are natural pearls.

4. Baroque pearls:

a. originate from Europe.
b. have irregular shapes.
c. are freshwater pearls.
d. are those set in ornate mountings.

5. Mabe assembled pearls may come from:

a. The mabe oyster
b. The white South Sea pearl (silver-lip) oyster
c. The black pearl (black-lip) oyster
d. All of the above

6. Semi-cultured pearls:

a. are imitation pearls.
b. are half natural and half cultured.
c. have a cultivation period which is half as long as that of a cultured pearl.
d. grow in oysters which are bred in a laboratory.

7. High-quality keshi pearls are noted for their:

a. high luster
b. unique shapes
c. iridescence
d. all of the above

8. A salesperson shows you a pearl necklace which he says is Mikimoto promotional-quality. It does not have an 18-karat gold Mikimoto clasp. Which of the following is true?

a. The pearls are probably of high quality.
b. The salesperson is misrepresenting the pearls and misusing the Mikimoto name.
c. The Mikimoto company forgot to put their trademark clasp on the necklace.

True or false?

9. Cultured pearls are imitation pearls grown by man in the Akoya oyster.

10. A pearl must be round to be valuable.

11. Freshwater pearls are those which are cultivated in non-polluted waters.

12. Valuable natural pearls have been found in North, South, and Central America.

13. Cultured round pearls were first produced and marketed in the early 1900's
.
14. Natural pearls are produced by implanting shell beads in oysters which breed naturally.

15. Nacre is the pearly substance secreted around an irritant by an oyster or mussel.

16. When judging prices consumers should try to compare pearls of the same shape and type.

Answers:

1. b

2. c

3. c

4. b

5. d

6.   a

7   d

8.   b

9.   F   They are not imitation pearls.

10. F

11. F

12. T

13. T

14. F

15. T

16. T

4

Judging Luster & Nacre Thickness

"PEARLS--HALF OFF!"

Does this indicate a bargain? Who knows? It might even mean "Nacre--Half Off." No matter what their price, pearls aren't much of a bargain if they're dull-looking or their nacre (pearl coating, pronounced NAY-ker) peels away.

Normally thin nacre means low luster, but there are thin-nacre pearls with good luster and thick-nacre pearls with low luster. Consequently, it's best to treat luster and nacre thickness as two separate value factors.

What is Pearl Luster?

The noted gemologist, Robert Webster, defines **luster** as the surface brilliancy of a gemstone, which depends on the quality and quantity of the reflected light. When the term "luster" is applied to pearls, it tends to have a broader meaning. It also refers to the light reflected off the internal layers of nacre. In other words, a lustrous pearl has more than just a shiny, reflective surface. It also has a glow from within.

Compare, for example, the pearl to a highly polished gold bead. The gold bead will usually have sharper surface reflections than the pearl, but that doesn't mean it's more lustrous. In fact, it's more conventional to describe gold as shiny, bright, or metallic. Brilliant pearls, on the other hand, are more frequently termed lustrous.

Pearls with a very high luster will generally show the following characteristics when viewed under a bare light with the naked eye.

- Strong light reflections
- Sharp light reflections
- A good contrast between the bright and darker areas of the pearl

(Many pearl experts would also list iridescence as a characteristic because lustrous pearls not only reflect light, they break it up into different colors. On round pearls the iridescence tends to be very subtle, and a pinkish tone may result. On high luster baroque pearls, you may see flashes of rainbow colors. Since iridescence is a color phenomenon, this book has it listed as a quality factor in the chapter on color.)

The evaluation of luster will be discussed in a later section. But first, it's helpful to know why pearls vary in luster.

What Determines Luster?

The luster of a pearl depends on the quality of the nacre--it's transparency, smoothness and overall thickness as well as the thickness of each of the microscopic layers of nacre. Under an electron microscope, the nacre crystals of lustrous pearls have a strong hexagonal form and are regularly distributed, whereas the crystals forming the nacre of lifeless pearls lack a clear outline, are thinly scattered, or are irregularly deposited (from *The Retail Jeweller's Guide*, page 90, by Kenneth Blakemore).

The quality of the nacre, and in turn the luster, is affected by a variety of factors such as:

♦ Cultivation techniques used
♦ Cultivation place
♦ Health of mother oyster
♦ Length of time pearl is in oyster
♦ Time of year when pearl is harvested
♦ Pollution
♦ Abnormally wide variations in temperature
♦ Natural disasters such as earthquakes and typhoons
♦ Type of oyster used. For example, the mabe oyster (found mainly in the tropical seas of Southeast Asia) can produce a pearl with a higher luster than those of the South Seas silver-lip oyster. The Akoya oyster is also noted for its capacity to produce pearls of high luster.

High luster is not merely the result of leaving a pearl in an Akoya oyster for an adequate length of time. As one can infer from the above list, cultivating a lustrous pearl is a complex process, and it involves skill and chance.

Judging Luster

Suppose we could line up all the pearls in the world according to the quality of their luster. We would notice that a very low percentage of the pearls would be at the end of the line with the best luster. We would also notice that the pearls would very gradually change in luster as we went down the line. In other words, there would be no distinct luster categories.

We could, however, divide the line of pearls into any number of equal ranges (categories) of luster. Then we could assign a luster name to each category such as **very high, high, medium, low and very low**. Luster categories like this are found in the GIA (Gemological Institute of America) pearl grading system. Pearl dealers have their own in-house grading systems, which often combine various value factors. However, many dealers might feel that the terms **"gem quality"** or **"AAAA"** should only be applied to pearls having an exceptionally high luster. Don't assume, though, that a pearl strand labeled "AAAA" or "Gem" is necessarily top quality. It's a common practice to misuse grades by applying high ones to lower quality goods.

Very high luster pearls have sharp, intense, almost mirror-like light reflections, and there is a high contrast between their bright and dark areas. Such pearls are not always easy to find. In fact, you may be lucky to find a store in your area that has them in stock. Expect to pay premium prices for these pearls. For example, strands of very-high-luster, round, white pearls over 6 1/2 mm won't be priced in the hundreds of dollars. They will be in the thousands of dollars. The actual cost of the strands will be determined by a variety of factors.

Very low luster pearls are easy to spot. They look very milky or chalky, and seem more like a white bead than a pearl. This is due to the low contrast between the light and dark areas of the pearls. Some jewelers won't stock this type of pearl, but others will. This is also the type of pearl a mail order place might be tempted to sell. The customer doesn't see what he's getting. He only sees the super low price listed in the catalogue.

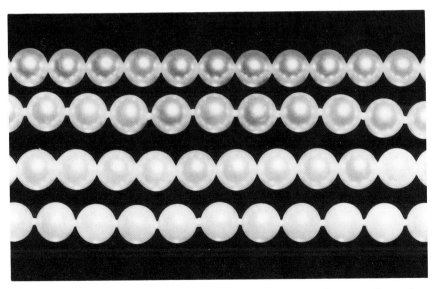

Fig. 4.1 Top to bottom: high luster, medium luster, low luster and very low luster. Note how the dark areas become lighter as the luster decreases.

The majority of the pearls sold in stores probably fall in the low and medium luster ranges. Many fine-quality jewelry stores also stock high-luster pearls. The best way to learn to recognize high-, medium-, and low-luster pearls is to look at strands representing these luster ranges. Some jewelers may show you short master strands illustrating these or similar categories, but they may use different category names such as "bright," "commercial," "AAA," etc. Top-quality pearl salespeople are eager to help you see luster differences so you'll know what you are getting for your money. They don't want their prices unfairly compared to stores offering low-quality "bargain" pearls.

As you shop for pearls and examine them for luster, keep in mind that the pearl industry has not yet adopted a standardized system for grading pearls. What one jeweler considers low luster another might call high. Therefore, **don't rely just on word descriptions of pearls.** What your eyes see is what counts most. Verbal descriptions are merely guides. If you have any strands of pearls at home, it's a good idea to take them along and use them as a basis for comparison. Even pearl dealers rely on comparison strands when buying pearls.

Also keep in mind the following tips when shopping:

♦ Examine the strands on a flat white surface, e.g. a white cloth, board, or paper). Luster can be hard to judge when pearls are suspended or on a dark surface.

♦ If possible, examine the pearls directly under a bare light instead of away from the light. This helps bring out their luster. (Lighting is discussed more in detail in the next section).

♦ Look for the brightest and darkest areas of the pearls. Then compare the contrast between the two. The lower the contrast and the milkier the pearl, the lower the luster. This is one of the quickest and easiest ways to spot low and very low luster. Milky-looking pearls are sometimes sold in "high quality" stores. Be aware that their luster is low.

♦ Examine the light reflections on the pearls. Usually, the less sharp and intense they are, the lower the luster. Sometimes, however, a lack of sharpness is due to surface flaws, rather than the overall luster.

♦ Compare the lusters of the individual pearls on the strand. They will almost always vary somewhat in luster. The luster quality of a strand is determined by its overall appearance, not just by one pearl. High-luster strands, however, should not have low- and very-low-luster pearls. If you find a strand you like that happens to have a pearl or two with an obviously lower luster than the rest of the strand, ask the salesperson to have them changed when they are strung with a clasp.

♦ Roll the pearls slightly so you can see their entire surface. The luster not only varies from pearl to pearl. It varies on each pearl.

♦ Try the pearls on and check if you can see the highlighted spots on them from a distance (say 10 feet/3 meters). You'll be able to if the pearls are of good quality.

♦ If possible, lay the pearls alongside other strands and compare the lusters. This is most effective when you already know the relative quality of the comparison strands. Keep in mind that your impression of a strand will be affected by the pearls it is compared to. A strand will look better when viewed next to lower-luster strands than next to those of higher luster.

Sometimes buyers get so involved in examining the shape and blemishes of pearls that they overlook their luster. The Japan Pearl Exporters' Association would consider this a big mistake. According to their booklet *Cultured Pearls*, "The most important value point in pearls of equal size is luster because that is what gives a pearl its beauty."

How Lighting Affects Luster

Gemologists and appraisers normally grade pearls under standardized lighting conditions. When shopping for pearls, you will encounter various lighting situations. You need to understand, therefore, how lighting affects the appearance of pearls in order to avoid being misled.

The main thing to remember is the stronger and more direct the light, the more lustrous the pearls will look. Ask yourself:

♦ Is the lighting diffused? For example, is the light covered with a white shade? Is the light coming through curtains, clouds, or translucent glass? The more diffused the light is, the lower the luster will appear to be. Bare lights or direct sunlight, on the other hand, will bring out the luster of pearls (figs. 4.2 to 4.4).

♦ How intense is the light? In the case of sunlight, is it early morning or midday? Midday sunlight will bring out the luster more. In the case of light bulbs, are they 60 watt or 150 watt? The higher the wattage, the more lustrous your pearls will look.

♦ How close is the light to the pearls? The further the light is from the pearls, the smaller and less intense the reflections become and the less the pearls seem to glow (figs. 4.2 & 4.3).

If it's possible for you to carry or wear comparison strands of pearls, do so. You'll be able to compare known strands with unknown ones under equal lighting conditions, and it will be easier for you to tell the effect of the lighting on both.

Judging Nacre Thickness

If you were to cut a 7-mm Akoya cultured pearl in half, you would see a large core inside. It would be a bead probably cut from an American mussel shell. The outside of the

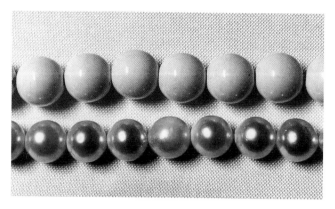

Fig. 4.2 Shiny white plastic beads and pearl strand with a fluorescent desk lamp lighting them from 1 yard (1 meter) away. Even though the surface reflection is sharper on the beads, the pearls are more lustrous because of their stronger glow. Note the low luster of the center pearl and how little contrast there is between its darker and lighter areas.

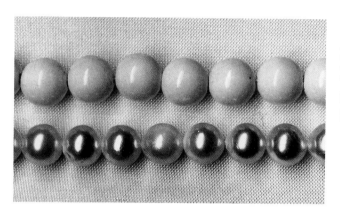

Fig. 4.3 Same beads and pearls with same light 10 inches/ away. The light reflection is larger than figure 4.2, which can make it appear to have a stronger glow.

Fig. 4.4 Same beads and pearls with same light covered with a white cloth (diffused lighting). The light is about 14 inches from the pearls. Note the lower luster appearance and the lower contrast between the darker and lighter areas of the beads and pearls.

bead would be encircled with a pearly layer of nacre. If the pearl had been left in the oyster for just six months, the layer would be very thin, too thin to be very durable or lustrous.

Before about 1960, Japanese Akoya pearl farmers left the pearls in the oyster for at least two and a half years. Mikimoto left his in for over three years for maximum nacre thickness. Then many farmers dropped the time to one and a half years. Around 1979, pearl harvesting started to be done just after six to eight months. The result--a lot of inexpensive, low-quality pearls on the market. And they are still out there, being offered at rock-bottom prices. The buyers end up with shell beads and hardly any pearl. Fortunately, better pearls with thicker nacre are also available, but rarely as thick as those cultured before the 1960's. The goal of this section is to help you determine if the nacre thickness of the pearls you look at is acceptable or not.

The GIA, in their pearl grading course, has defined five levels of nacre thickness for Akoya cultured pearls. They are:

Very thick At least 0.5 mm on all the pearls of the strand

Thick At least 0.5 mm on most pearls of the strand

Medium 0.35 - 0.5 mm on most pearls

Thin 0.25 - 0.35 mm on most pearls

Very thin 0.25 mm or less on most pearls

Pearl dealers don't need to measure the nacre to determine if it's thin or very thin. They know just by looking at the pearls. Some clues are:

◆ The pearls usually have a low or very low luster and may look milky. Some thin-coated pearls, however, may show a decent medium luster.

◆ The nacre coating has cracks.

◆ Areas are visible where the nacre has peeled off.

◆ Layers of the shell beads are slightly visible when the pearls are suspended and light shines through them. These layers look like curved lines, stripes or wood grain. Usually the thinner the nacre, the easier it is to see the lines. Figure 4.5 is an example of what the shell layers look like in a thinly-coated pearl with light shining through it. If you can't see any shell layers, this does not mean that the nacre is thick. There are lots of thinly-coated pearls that don't show these layers. However, if you can see them, the nacre is probably too thin.

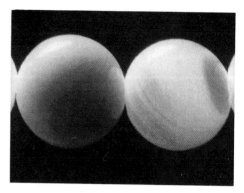

Fig. 4.5 Thin-nacre cultured pearl with light shining through it. Note shell nucleus layers.

Fig. 4.6 Light and dark views of mother-of-pearl shell beads

♦ As the beads are rolled, some may look light and then dark as the light shines through them. This is because the shell beads may have mother-of-pearl layers that block the light. This phenomenon is called "blinking" and can sometimes be seen in thinly coated pearls. Figure 4.6 is an example of two shell beads with no nacre. One in the light position and one in the dark position. When rotated, each of these pearls "blinks." Pearls with thick nacre should not blink.

A more accurate way of judging nacre thickness is by examining the drill holes of the pearls, preferably with a 10-power magnifier such as a hand loupe (fig. 4.7). (If you are ser-

iously interested in gems, you should own a fully-corrected, 10-power, triplet loupe. You can buy them at jewelry supply stores. Plan on paying at least $25 for a good loupe. Examining drill holes with a loupe will also help you detect dyes and imitations). The drill-hole method is too slow to be practical for dealers, but it is a good way for less-skilled people to estimate nacre thickness. It also allows appraisers to give a more objective measure of nacre thickness. Figures 4.8 - 4.11 give you an idea of what drill holes look like under magnification.

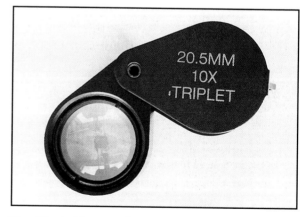

Fig. 4.7 A 10-power loupe

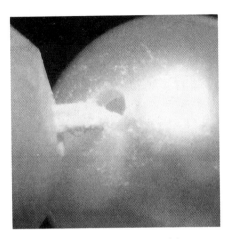

Fig. 4.8 Pearl with acceptable nacre thickness. Note the dividing line between the lighter nacre and the darker nucleus.

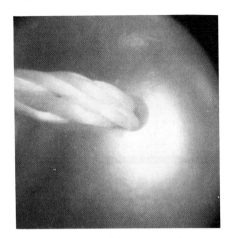

Fig. 4.9 Pearl with acceptable nacre thickness. Often the drill hole is small, so it's hard to see the dividing line.

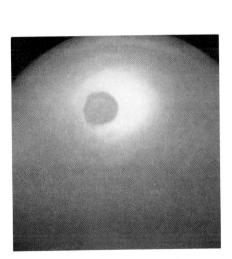

Fig. 4.10 Pearl with nacre that is too thin

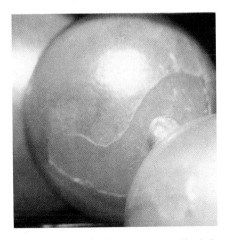

Fig. 4.11 Pearl with nacre so thin it is peeling off

If you have some pearls at home, try examining their drill holes with a loupe under a good light. Find the dividing line between the nacre and the bead. Then look at a millimeter ruler with the loupe to get a visual image of a 0.35-mm thickness. Compare this thickness to that of the nacre. If it is less, this is a sign your pearls are too thin. Seeing actual examples of thin, medium, and thick nacres is an easier way to learn to tell the difference, but examples of each may be hard for you to find.

This book suggests 0.35 mm as a minimum because the GIA uses it as a dividing point between thin and medium nacre and because it has been mentioned in the trade as a minimum. For example, Hiroshi Komatsu of the Tokyo Mikimoto research lab is quoted as saying, "Our tests show the best luster and color occur with at least 0.35 mm of nacre, and Mikimoto pearls are always thicker" (as quoted by Fred Ward in the August 1985 issue of *National Geographic*). Keep in mind that the nacre thickness may not be the same throughout a pearl. Nacre measurements can also vary depending on the measuring instrument used and the person doing the measuring. So consider the 0.35-mm minimum as an approximate thickness.

Nacre thickness has been one of the most discussed issues in the pearl industry. In their December 1991 quarterly bulletin, the Gemmological Association and Gem Testing Laboratory of Great Britain announced they have started issuing nacre thickness reports. This is due to requests from the British Association of Cultured Pearl Importers. They have been concerned about the low-quality, very-thin-nacre pearls that are flooding the market and don't want the reputation of the trade to be tarnished.

When you have your pearls appraised, be sure to ask if nacre thickness is indicated on the report. Also ask how the appraiser's nacre-thickness categories are defined in terms of millimeter thickness. A term such as "thin" can vary from one person to another, so definitions are necessary.

Also make sure that the millimeter thickness is of the radius of the pearl, not of the diameter, which would be twice the nacre thickness along the radius. If someone tells you the average nacre thickness of an Akoya pearl is 1 mm, figure they have doubled it. Today it's hard to find Akoya pearls with even a 0.5-mm thickness.

It's not deceptive to sell thin-nacre pearls as long as the thin nacre and its consequences are disclosed to buyers. Ideally, consumers could choose from a wide range of nacre thicknesses and know exactly what they were getting for their money. Since this ideal does not currently exist, it's to your advantage to pay attention to nacre thickness and to learn to detect thin nacre yourself.

Is Nacre Thickness Important and Does it Affect Pricing?

As you shop, you may encounter pearl salespeople who claim nacre thickness is unimportant and has no effect upon price. Beware. All their pearls may be of low quality. Ask them, "Why is something which affects the beauty and durability of pearls unimportant?"

As for price, it has to be affected by nacre thickness. It naturally will cost a farmer progressively more to culture pearls for 6 months, 1 1/2 years and 2 1/2 years. The additional cost must be passed on to the buyers.

Often the effect of nacre thickness on price is linked to that of luster. Thicker nacre usually means higher luster, and both bring higher prices. An example of this linkage is found in the pearl pricing system of the Adachi America Co. They don't list nacre thickness as a separate factor on their price guides; but whenever it is lower than the luster grade indicates, they'll downgrade the luster and sell the pearls for less. To them nacre thickness is important.

The Mikimoto Company thinks it is important too. One of their advisors, Shigeru Miki, made the following statement in the August 1985 National Geographic article by Fred Ward. "The most important quality of a cultured pearl is thickness of the nacre. It gives color, luster, and appearance. Pearls are among the softest of all gems, and normal body fluids, as well as contact with perfumes, hair sprays, and acids reduce nacre. A thinly coated pearl won't last many years."

Golay Buchel, a company with branches in Europe, North America and the Orient, discusses luster and nacre thickness in its booklet *Pearls*. They are listed as separate value factors and both are described as important. Golay Buchel's advice to consumers (p. 34): "Remain flexible with regards to colour, size, shape and light surface markings, but **never** make concessions regarding the thickness of the coating."

Chapter 4 Quiz

Select the correct answer.

1. A jeweler says his pearls are AAA quality. You should conclude:

a. The pearls are of high quality.
b. The pearls may be of any quality
c. The pearls are not graded properly because the highest possible grade is A+.
d. The pearls have a high luster. Quality factors such as shape and color also need to be indicated.

2. A large percentage of the Akoya pearls sold today:

a. have a very high luster.
b. have thick or very thick nacre.
c. have thin or very thin nacre.
d. none of the above.

3. You have a written appraisal that states your pearl necklace has very thick nacre. You should assume:

a. Your pearls have a nacre thickness of exactly .5 mm or more on all the pearls
b. Your pearls have a nacre thickness of approximately .5 mm or more on all pearls.
c. Your pearls have a nacre thickness of approximately .5 mm or more on most pearls of the strand
d. Nothing if the appraiser has not defined his/her nacre-thickness grades somewhere on the appraisal.

4. Which type of lighting will make pearls look the most lustrous?

a. a bare 100-watt light bulb
b. candlelight
c. daylight on a rainy day
d. a fluorescent light covered with a translucent plastic shade

True or False?

5. Today, cultured pearls tend to have thicker nacre than they did in the 1950's.

6. When the judging luster of a strand, you should roll the pearls slightly on a flat, white surface.

7. If a cultured pearl is left in an Akoya oyster for at least three years, it will have a high luster.

8. Pearls with very low luster are easy to spot because they look more like white beads than pearls.

9. There's no point in paying $35 for a loupe when you can find brand new ones for $10.

10. If a pearl has thick nacre, it will have a high luster.

Answers:

1. b There's no standardized pearl grading system, so a jeweler can assign whatever meaning he wants to a grade. Even standardized grades such as those for diamonds are misused and inflated by some salespeople. Therefore it's best to base your judgement of a gem on what it looks like rather than on a grade assigned to it.

2. c

3. d The grading of nacre thickness is not standardized. "Very thick nacre" can have a variety of meanings depending on which appraiser or jeweler is using the term.

4. a

5. F

6. T

7. F Not necessarily. Improper cultivation techniques, disease, and pollution are a few of the factors that can lower the luster of a pearl even though it is left in an Akoya oyster for a long period of time.

8. T

9. F A $10 loupe will generally distort what it magnifies. A 10-power, fully corrected loupe is an ideal gem magnifier. Unfortunately, it will cost more than $10 brand new.

10 F Not necessarily. South Sea pearls usually have thicker nacre than Akoya pearls, yet their luster tends to be lower. The quality of the nacre is just as important as its thickness. A pearl with very thick nacre can have a very low luster.

5

Judging Color

If you were buying Swiss cheese and you had a choice between some that was white and some that was slightly yellow or cream color, which would you choose? Most likely the cream color because the average person has been conditioned to expect Swiss cheese to have a yellowish tint. If when you bought Swiss cheese, you happened to discover that pieces with large holes often tasted better than those without, you might also develop a preference for Swiss cheese with big holes.

People's expectation of what pearls should look like have been conditioned in a similar manner. Many expect pearls to be white because that is what they are accustomed to seeing. Plus pearls are associated with the moon, weddings, purity--which, in turn, are connected to the color white.

Within the jewelry trade, it was also noticed that Akoya or Persian Gulf pearls with high luster often had a pinkish tint. So, a lot of people developed a preference for pearls with a slight pink tint. To meet the demand for such pearls, producers bleached their pearls and dyed them pink.

Coloring foods to enhance their appearance is an accepted practice, so is bleaching pearls. Dyeing pearls, however, has not been as well accepted, especially if the resulting color is unstable. Sometimes higher prices are charged for dyed pearls. Some people are opposed to this practice.

This chapter discusses factors to consider when choosing the color of pearls. The topic of color will also be addressed in the chapters on freshwater, black, and South Sea pearls. The Akoya pearl is the main focus of this chapter.

Pearl Color

Pearl color is complex. It's a combination of the following:

Body Color   The predominant basic color of the pearl. When pearls are lying on a white surface, body color can be best viewed on the outer edge of the pearl.

Overtone

The one or more colors that overlie the body color. On black pearls these colors are easiest to see in the lighter areas of the pearl (color photo 10c). On white pearls they are easier to see in the darker areas (color photo 5a).

For example, lay some white pearls on something white, and look at them under a strong, direct light (midday sun is ideal but a light-bulb will do). The outer rim area of the pearls, which is reflecting the white background, will be lighter than the center of the pearls if they are of decent quality (except for the bright reflection of the light). If you look closely, you should see a slight pink, green, blue, and/or silver color in the central dark areas of the pearls. This is the overtone. Generally you will see more than one overtone color in a strand of pearls (color photo 5b). You may also see more than one on the same pearl. For example, the South Sea pearl on the front cover of this book has both pink and green overtones. In color photo 5a, some pearls have both pink and blue overtones.

Iridescence

A play of lustrous colors. They may be like those of the rainbow, or they may be a subtle combination of colors such as pink, blue, green, and silver as seen in the blister mabe pearl of color photo 15b. The colors of this pearl change when you move it in your hand.

Orient is another term that is used to refer to pearl iridescence. In a handout from their pearl grading course, the GIA specifies that "orient has 6 colors: violet, blue, red, green, yellow, orange, all the colors of the rainbow." Some dealers, however, employ the term more loosely to also mean a combination of overtone colors. Other dealers and many books written in the past use the term "orient" to refer to luster because iridescence and luster are interconnected. Since "orient" may be interpreted in various ways, this book tends to use the term "iridescence" instead.

When you shop for pearls, you may come across terms such as **white rosé**. This means white pearls with a pink overtone. "Rosé" is the French word for pink. **Pink rosé** means that most of the pearls have a light pink body color and a pink overtone. White pearls with a silver overtone may be described as **silver(y) white**. Often salespeople don't specify the overtone but they just say one color such as "pink" which describes their overall impression of the pearls.

Judging Pearl Color

When deciding what color pearls to buy, your primary concern should be what looks best on you. But you will also want to know how the color affects their price.

The overall body color can play a significant role in determining the price of Akoya pearls. Five main **body color categories** for pearls are:

Light pink (pink) Usually the highest price category, but some dealers price light pink and white pearls alike. A few dealers make a distinction between pearls with subtle pink tints and those that look artificial and obviously dyed. They may refuse to stock the latter. Incidently, jewelers often have no way of knowing if their pink pearls are dyed because suppliers are not required to disclose this. Naturally-colored pink pearls, however, typically have a light pink rather than pink body color.

White   Equal to or less than pearls with a light pink body color. Some people in the trade have a negative view of "white pearls" because they associate them with the very thin-nacre pearls that look milky white and have no overtone. It's not the white body color that makes these pearls appear low-quality; it's the absence of overtones, as seen in the middle strand of color photo 5b. Lustrous, valuable pearls normally have silver, pink and/or blue overtones.

Light Cream   Usually cost less than white. The higher the quality of the pearls, the greater the price difference will probably be between light cream and white. In low qualities there may be no difference.

Cream   Usually cost less than light cream. In cream colors, the general tendency is the darker the color, the lower the price. Cream-color pearls are sometimes termed **champagne pearls**.

Dark Cream,   May be priced about 40% or more lower than white pearls. The darker
Yellow or Golden   the cream or yellow color, the greater the price difference.

When judging color, keep in mind that there is no standardized system of communicating or grading color in the pearl industry. What one dealer calls light cream, another might call cream. Nevertheless, there is an awareness of the concept "cream color" and general agreement that cream-color Akoya pearls tend to cost less than those which are pink and white.

Overtone color(s) may or may not affect the price. The three most common overtones are--pink, green, and silver. If the color of the overtones has an effect on price, it will generally be as follows:

Pink overtones   Can increase the price

Silver overtones   Usually no effect

Green overtones   Sometimes may decrease the price slightly

Blue overtones are associated with top-quality pearls. Some Japanese dealers describe the color of the most valued Akoya pearls as a bluish-pink, which in essence is a light-pink body color with blue and pink overtones. These pearls, which are very rare and difficult to find in America, are sometimes classified by the Japanese as "hanadama quality."

There is no general agreement in the trade as to how overtones affect price. Most dealers, however, would probably concede that Akoya pearls with pink overtones tend to be more highly valued than those with green ones. This explains why pearls are often dyed pink but not green. What counts most about overtone is how it affects your overall impression of the color and luster of the pearls. Pearl dealers would agree, too, that the presence of overtones is highly desirable. Their absence is a sign of low luster and thin nacre.

The third color component of pearls, **iridescence**, is rarely obvious on round Akoya pearls. It tends to be very subtle combination of pink, blue, and green. A more obvious iridescence--flashes of rainbow colors--is more likely to be seen on freshwater pearls and baroque shapes. Iridescence is always considered a positive value factor.

When examining pearls for color remember the following tips:

◆ Judge the color of pearls against a non-reflective white background. Pearls not only reflect the color of the background, they also absorb it. Afterwards, place the pearls on your hand or around your neck to see how they look on you.

◆ Take into consideration the lighting (see next section). If possible look at the pearls under different types of light sources--daylight near a window, fluorescent, and incandescent (light bulbs). You'll probably be wearing the pearls under a variety of light sources.

◆ It's a lot easier to compare color than to remember it. If possible, wear or take along some comparison pearls. Otherwise, compare the color to other pearls in the store. Even using white and cream-colored papers as color references is better than relying on color memory.

◆ When pearl strands are exactly adjacent, their color may seem to bleed from one strand to another. Therefore, also compare them slightly separated from each other.

◆ Every now and then, look away from the pearls at other colors and objects. When you focus on one color too long, your perception of it becomes distorted.

◆ Consider how evenly distributed the color is on the pearl(s), especially if it's one major pearl on a ring or pendant. A uniform color is more highly valued than a blotchy one.

◆ If you are trying to decide between white and pink pearls of the same quality but the pink pearls cost more. Look in a few of the drill holes with a 10-power magnifier. If you can see red or pink stains on the nacre layer or a pink line between the nacre and the nucleus, they are dyed (color photo 5d). Seeing positive indications of dye may influence your decision. By the way, even if you don't see evidence of dye, the pearls may still be dyed.

◆ Make sure you're alert and feel good when you examine pearls. If you're tired, sick, or under the influence of alcohol or drugs, your perception of color will be impaired.

How Lighting Affects Color

Just as luster is affected by lighting, so is color, but in a different way. If you were to take a photograph indoors under a light bulb with daylight film, the picture would be orangy or yellowish. If you took it under fluorescent light, the picture would look greenish. Even though, unlike cameras, your eyes can adjust to changes of color from lighting, you are still influenced by them. Consequently, your perception of pearl color will depend on the lighting the pearls are viewed under.

The whitest, most neutral light is at midday. Besides adding the least amount of color, this light makes it easier to see various nuances of color. Consequently, it's best to judge pearl color under a daylight-equivalent light. Day-light fluorescent bulbs approximate this ideal, but some of these lights are better than others. One that is often recommended for color grading gems is the Duro-Test Vita Lite. This light, however, is not as effective as true sunlight for seeing detail. For example, it is normally easier to read very fine print in sunlight than in artificial light. The intensity of the light from the sun has a lot to do with this.

When you shop for pearls, your choice of lighting will probably be limited. Use the information below to help you compensate for improper lighting.

Type of light	Effect of Light
Light bulbs up to 150 watts candlelight	Add red or orange, so pearls may look pinker or more yellowish
Fluorescent lights	Depends on what type they are. Some have a neutral effect. Others add green which may make the pearls look greenish or grayish.
Light under overcast sky or in the shade under blue sky	Adds blue so pearls may look grayish or a bit bluish
Sunlight	Depends on the time of day, the season of the year, and the geographic location. At midday it normally has a neutral effect on the color. Earlier and later in the day it adds red, orange, or yellow so the pearls may look pinker or more yellowish.

Emphasis on proper lighting when viewing gems has not been restricted to modern-day times. In 1908, in *The Book of the Pearl* (p. 370), Kunz and Stevenson wrote:

"At great receptions, large and apparently magnificent pearls are frequently seen, which are really of inferior quality, and yet owing to the absence of pure daylight, they can easily be mistaken for perfect specimens by any one not especially familiar with pearls. Indeed, if the royalties of Europe should wear all the pearls belonging to the crown jewels at the same time, in a palace or hall lighted with candles, gas, or even with some types of electric light, they would seem to have a quality which many of them do not and never did possess. It is, therefore, essential for the buyer to use every precaution in reference to the light in which he examines his purchase."

What Causes Pearl Color?

A lot of pearl farmers wish they had the full answer to this question. Then they could control the color of the pearls they cultivated. Now they have only part answers or clues. Some of the determinants of pearl color seem to be:

♦ The type of host oyster. Oysters vary in their potential to produce certain colored pearls. For example, black pearls are cultivated in the black-lip oyster because other oysters don't produce pearls of the same type. Even though pearl farmers know the black-lip oyster is essential to the cultivation of black pearls, they don't know yet how to consistently make it produce a specific color. The pearl may end up being white or a variety of shades of gray as well as black, bronze, greenish or purplish.

♦ The quality of the nacre. If the nacre is very thin, the color will look milky and lack overtone tints. Besides being affected by the number of layers of nacre, pearl color is affected by the thickness of each layer. In *Pearls of the World* (p. 71), researcher Koji Wada states, "The reason why the pearl made by the Akoya pearl-oyster has a better pink tone than pearls made by other mollusks is that it has layers of equal thickness."

♦ The environment they are grown in. It's theorized that there may be trace elements in the water that affect the color. For example, cream-color pearls are typical of natural pearls from the Ohio River, but not of those found in other American Rivers.

♦ The color of the tissue that is inserted with the bead nucleus. (Tissue from another oyster's mantle, the part of the oyster that secretes pearl nacre, has to be implanted with the shell bead for a cultured pearl to grow.) Koji Wada has found that if the tissue inserted in Akoya oysters is yellow, cream-colored pearls tend to form. If white, white pearls result (*Modern Jeweler*, September 1990, pp. 42-44, David Federman).

What Color is Best for You?

Most pearl experts agree that a buyer's color choice should be primarily based on what will look good on the person who will wear the pearls. Some salespeople, though, give color advice by suggesting what's popular in specific geographic areas. One fairly consistent statement, for example, is that South Americans prefer cream- or golden-colored pearls.

When shopping in the United States, the color listed as the number one choice may vary from one salesperson to another. Perhaps it's a matter of what the store has in stock. Quite often it's claimed that the most popular pearl color in America is pink. The US, however, is a diverse nation. Consequently, pink is not the color that looks best on all Americans. Picking a color on the basis of its popularity might lead to a poor choice.

Determining the colors that flatter you most is not always easy. Carole Jackson, in her book, *Color Me Beautiful*, provides some guidelines with color illustrations. She points out on page 28, for example, that olive-skinned people and most blacks and Orientals look radiant in clear, vivid, cool colors (pink, white, blue, red) but sallow in warm colors (cream, orange, beige, mustard). Warm colors, however, are very flattering to people with peach or golden complexions (Redheads and blondes often have this skin coloring).

Some people in the trade recommend white and pink pearls to Asians and Anglos and cream or golden pearls to blacks and olive-skinned customers. This is because cream colors look whiter on a dark-skinned person than on someone with lighter skin.

One easy way to determine which pearl colors will compliment you is to put on white, light pink, and cream-colored clothing and see what looks best next to your face. It's helpful to get the opinion of family and friends. Often, two of the colors look equally attractive, but it's rare that all three will. The final test will be to put the pearls on your hand or around your neck and see how they look. Consider, too, if you want people to notice the pearls when you wear them. If you do, then choose a color that contrasts with your skin tone. Pearls that blend in too closely won't be very striking.

When you are buying for others, they probably won't be able to try on the pearls. So beforehand, observe what color clothes they like to wear and look good in. If they don't like beige or cream-colored clothes and these colors don't flatter them, you would be better off avoiding cream-colored pearls.

Two other considerations when choosing pearl color are versatility and price. If you would like to wear the pearls as often as possible, then select a color that will go well with most of your wardrobe. If your budget is limited and you are trying to choose between light or dark cream pearls, the dark cream pearls could be the ideal choice. Don't buy them, though, if cream colors make you look washed out. The purpose of jewelry is to enhance your appearance, not detract from it. So put some thought into your color choices. It will pay off in the end.

Chapter 5 Quiz

Select the correct answer.

1. Which of the following body colors is considered the most valuable for an Akoya pearl?

a. gold
b. light pink
c. cream
d. champagne

2. Which of the following overtone colors is the most valued on an Akoya pearl?

a. green
b. silver
c. gold
d. pink

3. You look in a drill hole of pearl and you see a dark pink line between the nacre and the bead nucleus, this means:

a. The pearl comes from the pink-lip oyster.
b. Nothing in particular. It's an inherent characteristic of pearls with pink overtones.
c. The pearl has been dyed.

4. When judging the color of pearls, you should examine them

a. on a black background.
b. on a white background.
c. on a background the same color as their body color.
d. hanging in the air.

5. Which of the following can affect your perception of pearl color?

a. The color of the room you are in
b. The lighting
c. Alcoholic beverages
d. All of the above

Answers:

1. b
2. d
3. c
4. b
5. d

6

Judging Flaws

Imagine that you're buying a bouquet of roses for a special friend. If you were to look closely at each rose, you would probably notice some brown spots, small holes, or torn edges. Yet it's doubtful that any of these flaws would keep you from getting the bouquet. You would select it on the basis of its overall attractiveness.

However, if you were buying just one rose for somebody, you would most likely examine it more closely and expect it to have fewer flaws than the roses in a bouquet. Judging pearls is much the same. Our standards of perfection for a single pearl are normally higher than for a strand. But whether we are dealing with roses or pearls, we should expect nature to leave some sort of autograph.

When discussing flaws in diamonds or colored gems, the jewelry trade uses the term **clarity**. This refers to the flaw grade or the degree to which a stone is flawed. In the pearl industry, a variety of terms is used. For example:

Blemish	Spotting
Cleanliness or Cleanness	Surface
Complexion	Surface appearance
Flawlessness	Surface perfection
Purity	Texture

There are also a variety of synonyms for the term flaw:

Blemish
Imperfection
Irregularity
Spot
Surface characteristic
Surface mark or marking

When dealing with diamonds and colored stones, gemologists limit the term "blemish" to surface flaws such as scratches and bumps. The term "inclusion" refers to flaws that extend below the surface such as cracks and holes.

"**Blemish**" takes on a different meaning when used with pearls. It means any kind of flaw, internal or external. This book normally uses the term "flaw" because it's short and easily understood by the trade and general public. For the sake of variety, some of the other terms are used as well.

Flaws can be positive features. They serve as identifying marks that a gem is ours and not somebody else's. They help prove that it is real and not imitation. Flaws can lower the price of gems without affecting their overall beauty. Perfection does not seem to be a goal of nature. In fact, the longer a pearl is in an oyster, the more likely it is for irregularities to occur. Therefore, when shopping for pearls, there's no need to look for flawless ones. You just need to know what types of flaws to avoid. This chapter will go into that, but first you should know what flaws are found on pearls.

Pearl Flaws

A standardized terminology has not been developed for pearl flaws. The terms found below are based mostly on those listed in the GIA (Gemological Institute of America) pearl grading course. These flaws are usually judged without magnification.

♦ **Bumps and Welts:** Raised areas which are found alone or in groups (fig. 6.1 & 6.6). They may sometimes cover most of the surface area of the pearl. If bumps or welts are very large, they can put the pearl into the off-round category. Occasionally pearls have a wrinkled appearance. This is due to groupings of welts (figs. 6.3 and 6.8).

♦ **Discolorations:** Spotty areas often caused from concentrations of conchiolin, a protein substance that holds nacre crystals together. Discolorations are not frequently seen because pearls are typically bleached to even out their color.

♦ **Chips, Holes, and Patches of Missing Nacre:** Flaws which may occur on any type of pearl but that are particularly common on those with thin nacre (figs. 6.2).

♦ **Pits and Pinpoints:** Tiny holes on the surface which are normally hardly noticeable and, therefore, not serious (figs. 6.4 & 6.7). "Pinpoints" may also refer to tiny bumps since, from a distance, these look about the same as tiny pits.

♦ **Dimples:** Circular depressions or indentations which are often found in groups.

♦ **Dull Spots:** Areas of very low luster due to variations in nacre quality or contact with chemicals, cosmetics, or skin secretions.

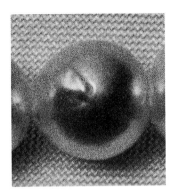

Fig. 6.1 Bump

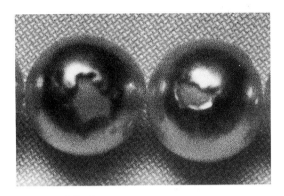

Fig. 6.2 Missing nacre

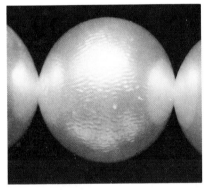

Fig. 6.3 Little welts ("wrinkles")

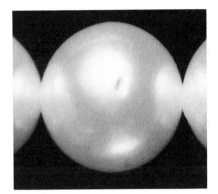

Fig. 6.4 An insignificant pit

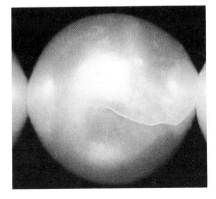

Fig. 6.5 A crack and small scratches

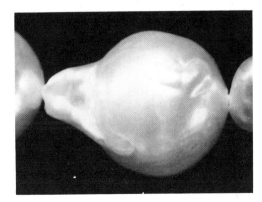

Fig. 6.6 Bumps & welts on a baroque pearl

♦ **Cracks:** Breaks in the nacre and/or bead nucleus (fig 6.5). Small cracks in the bead may look like little hairs trapped under the nacre. Cracks, even when not visible, can threaten the durability of a pearl.

♦ **Scratches:** Straight or crooked lines scraped on the pearl (fig. 6.5). These aren't serious unless the pearl is so badly scratched the luster and beauty is affected.

Determining Which Flaws Are Acceptable and Which Aren't

It's not the presence of flaws that matters. It's the type, quantity, and prominence of the flaws that does. Listed below are flaws which would normally be considered unacceptable:

♦ **Cracks throughout the pearls.** Thick nacre does not crack easily. Thin nacre does. Even if the cracks aren't noticeable, they are a sign that the nacre is too thin and that the pearls won't give you lasting wear.

♦ **Prominent flaws in a single pearl.** When buying pearl earrings, pendants, pins, or rings, pay closer attention to the flaws. For example, the pearl with the bump in figure 6.1 would not be acceptable as the featured pearl of a jewelry piece, but it would be okay in a strand. If you are buying a large expensive pearl and you want to compromise on price, try to select one whose flaws can be hidden by the setting.

♦ **Patches of missing nacre.** Just as diamonds with big chips are considered unacceptable, so are pearls with chunks of missing nacre. Both the beauty and durability of the pearl are affected.

♦ **Obvious discolorations throughout the pearls.** For the sake of beauty, try to select pearls with a uniform color. There are plenty of them available.

Fig. 6.7 A group of minor pits

Fig. 6.8 A group of tiny welts

♦ **Flaws which cover the majority of the surface of the pearl.** They can cause a viewer's attention to be directed more at the flaws than at the pearls. Figures 6.7 and 6.8 are examples of how groups of minor flaws over a large surface area become more noticeable and therefore less acceptable.

Despite the undesirability of blemishes, if you had to choose between heavily flawed, lustrous pearls and near flawless pearls with very thin nacre and low luster, you would be better off with the flawed ones. At least you would be getting some pearl for your money.

Drawing a line between what's acceptable and what isn't is not always easy. Below are a couple of examples that may help you understand what is meant by "unacceptable quality." Both of these strands are low quality. For many people and occasions, strand A would still be acceptable, whereas it's hard to imagine why anyone would ever want to buy strand B. Nacre has already peeled off of three of the pearls on strand B. The overall luster is very low and two of the pearls seem to have no luster at all. It's obvious, too, from looking at the missing nacre areas that the nacre thickness is very low. In sum, strand B is just made up of shell beads with a bit of an ugly nacre coating.

Fig. 6.9 Strand A: Acceptable or unacceptable quality depending on the buyer's goals

Fig. 6.10 Strand B: Unacceptable quality

Strand A has a fair number of flaws, but they aren't very noticeable, especially when it is worn. It has a medium-nacre thickness, which can be determined by looking in the drill holes. It's luster ranges between medium and low (it looks lower in the photo because of the diffused lighting), and the pearls are fairly round. For somebody with a limited budget, this strand could be a good choice. For someone looking for a fine quality necklace for a special person, Strand A would be unacceptable.

Keep in mind when buying pearls that it's not just their inherent quality that determines their acceptability. Your needs and desires also count. Therefore, it's you that has the final say as to what's acceptable and what's not.

Tips On Judging Flaws

When you shop for diamonds, salespeople may suggest that you look at the stone under magnification so you'll know it's clarity. This won't happen when you shop for pearls. The reason jewelers don't have you view them under a microscope is because pearls are graded and valued on the basis of how they look to the naked eye, not under magnification (except nacre thickness).

When dealing with knowledgeable salespeople that have your interests at heart, you won't need to look at pearls with a loupe (hand magnifier). They will point out the flaws and other quality factors and show you how to compare pearls. But there are times, when it is advisable to use a loupe. Some are:

♦ **When dealing with people you don't know or who may not be trustworthy.** Suppose you are at a flea market or an antique show and you see a pearl piece you'd love to have that you would never find in a jewelry store. Or, suppose you are on vacation abroad and you want a souvenir but you don't know any jewelers and none have been recommended to you. In both cases, it would be advisable to use a loupe and check for flaws, thin nacre, dye, and imitations. The more experience you get at examining a pearl's flaws, surface, and drill holes with a loupe, the easier it will be for you to identify them and judge their quality.

♦ **When the lighting is poor.** Suppose you're an antique dealer or a pawnbroker and you're in a place where the lighting is not ideal. And suppose you have to make a quick decision about whether to buy some pearls and how much to offer. Poor lighting will make it harder to judge flaws and overall quality. Use a loupe as a means of compensating for the lack of proper lighting.

♦ **If you have a hard time reading small print.** It's not any easier to see small flaws with the naked eye than it is to read fine print. When buying top quality pearls, a quick look at them through a loupe could help you make a better choice.

♦ **Whenever pearls are being offered at a price that seems too good to be true.** There's usually a catch somewhere. It will probably be easier to find it with a loupe than with the unaided eye, especially for people who don't deal with pearls on a regular basis.

A few other pointers for judging flaws are listed below:

♦ Besides looking at the pearls against a white background, look at them against a dark one. Certain flaws show up better against black or other dark colors. Also hold the pearls in the air to examine them for flaws. Do not judge luster or color in this way though.

♦ Examine the pearls under a strong light. The more intense the light, the easier it is to see detail. When judging blemish, it's also a good idea to look at pearls under different types of lighting--bare/diffused, fluorescent/incandescent, close/distant. Each type may bring out different details in the pearls.

♦ Roll the pearls. Otherwise you may not see some serious flaws and you won't know what percentage of the pearls is flawed. An anecdote by Kunz & Stevenson in *The Book of the Pearl* (p. 371) illustrates the importance of looking at all sides of the pearls.

> "A pearl necklace valued at $200,000, shown at one of our recent great expositions, was, to all appearances, a remarkably beautiful collection, and it was only when the intending purchaser took them from their velvet bed and held them in his hands that he realized that there was not a perfect pearl in the entire collection. It must have taken more than a week of study for the clever dealer to arrange them so that the best part, sometimes the only good part of each pearl, should be where the eye would fall upon it. After they had been turned in the hands a few seconds, not one perfect specimen was visible."

♦ Keep in mind that it's normal for pearls to have a few flaws. The GIA takes this into consideration in the way they define their "flawless" category for pearls on a strand: "Most appear blemish-free to the unaided eye." It would be abnormal for all of the pearls to be flawless.

Do we need standardized grades to judge flaws?

The diamond industry has a standardized system for grading flaws based on a system developed by the GIA. Ten-power magnification is used. The advantage of having this system is that buyers can communicate what they want anywhere in the world. In addition, written appraisals and quality reports are more meaningful.

The pearl industry does not have such a system. Nevertheless, flaws do affect the price of pearls. Occasionally you will come across grades such as AAA, AA, A. Depending on the supplier or store, these grades may refer to the luster, the flaws, a combination of these two factors, or they may include other factors such as shape and nacre thickness. In essence, pearl grades have no meaning except what the seller assigns to them. Therefore, do not rely on grades to compare pearl prices. (Don't rely on grades to compare diamond prices either because the grades are often misused).

One of the drawbacks of the diamond grading system is that it has sometimes led buyers to become so focused on color and clarity that they overlook brilliance and cut. Some grading documents have also neglected these factors somewhat. They may not mention the proportions of the bottom and top of the diamond (pavilion depth and crown height percentages). Yet these proportions can significantly affect the beauty and value of your diamond.

The lack of standardized flaw grades in the pearl industry has perhaps led to a greater emphasis on brilliance (luster). If so, this is fortunate. The lack of standardization has not kept pearl dealers from judging blemish, nor should it keep you from doing so. You can form your own grading system. For example, it's not hard to evaluate the flaws of the strands in figure 6.11. You may wish to simply describe them as relatively clean, moderately flawed, and heavily flawed. (Remember to view the entire surface of pearls by gently rolling them.)

Fig. 6.11   Top to bottom--relatively clean, moderately flawed, and heavily flawed.

Maybe you'd prefer to assign these strands three grades like A, B, & C. If you are accustomed to the grades A, B, C, D, & F from school, these may be easier to use. Whenever you look at pearls, ask to see a wide range of qualities. Some stores may have master strands indicating different qualities and these will be helpful. Gradually you will be able to create your own mental image of each grade category. Base your set of blemish grades on:

♦ The prominence of the flaws. Visible flaws away from drill holes are more serious than those near the holes. High bumps can be more noticeable than small pits or low bumps.

♦ The type of flaws. Chipped or missing nacre is usually more serious than bumps even though it may be less noticeable.

♦ The percentage of the pearl surface that is flawed. It's a lot more serious if 80% of the surface of a pearl is flawed than if only 10% of it is. You need to roll the pearls to check this factor.

♦ The percentage of pearls on a strand that are flawed and to what degree. This is a factor that doesn't exist in diamond grading. Pearl grading is more complex. It's much harder to develop consistent grades for sets of gems than for single gems.

After you've established your own grading system and can use it consistently, you'll be better able to compare prices than if you just rely on grades written on pearl tags--grades whose meaning changes according to the store or supplier using them. Another benefit of creating your own grading system--the most important one--you will increase your powers of observation and thought. This is what pearl evaluation is all about.

Chapter 6 Quiz

Select the correct answer.

1. Which of the following is the least serious?

a. missing nacre
b. a crack
c. a scratch
d. a large discoloration

2. Which of the following can affect the way you grade the flaws on a strand of pearls?

a. The background the pearls are viewed against
b. The lighting
c. Your eyesight
d. All of the above

3. Which is the least serious?

a. A bump next to a drill hole
b. A visible discoloration on a single pearl
c. A group of welts
d. A cracked bead nucleus

4. Flaws:

a. Can help you prove that your pearls are real and not imitation.
b. Can lower the price of pearls without affecting their overall beauty.
c. Can help you distinguish your pearls from those of someone else.
d. All of the above.

True or False?

5. When checking for flaws on a strand, you should roll the pearls in order to see their entire surface.

6. Pearl flaws should never be examined under magnification.

7. The longer a pearl is in an oyster, the more likely it is to have flaws.

8. The term "pearl blemish" only refers to flaws that are on the surface of a pearl.

9. Pearls with flaws are defective.

Answers:

1. c

2. d

3. a

4. d.

5. T

6. F Even though pearl flaws are graded without magnification, a magnifier can help you compensate for poor lighting or poor eyesight. Also, knowing what pearl flaws look like under magnification can help you determine if "pearls" are imitation or not.

7. T

8. F It can also refer to internal flaws such as cracked nuclei and flaws that extend below the surface such as holes and missing nacre. The term "surface characteristic" can also mean internal flaw when it is applied to pearls.

9. F It's normal for pearls to have flaws.

7

Size, Weight, Length

Size

Suppose you are in a store looking at 3 strands of Akoya pearls that were all bought from the same dealer at the same time. Their sizes and prices are:

a. 3 - 3 1/2 mm --- $350
b. 4 1/2 - 5 mm --- $350
c. 6 - 6 1/2 mm --- $700

Would it be surprising if they were all the same color and quality?

Not necessarily, some dealers do price 3 - 5 mm strands alike in some of their grades. Other dealers would increase the price for all their grades as size gets bigger. But every dealer would show a price increase from 5 mm to 6 1/2 mm, although the degree of increase could vary a great deal. There is no standardized system for determining exactly how pearl size affects price. Nevertheless, pearl dealers would agree that size is a very important price factor.

The size of round saltwater cultured pearls is expressed in terms of their diameter measured in millimeters. One millimeter is about 1/25 of an inch. Since pearl size varies within a strand, a range of 1/2 millimeter is usually indicated, e.g. 7 - 7 1/2 mm. Occasionally, a few of the pearls might fall slightly above or below the size indicated.

The size of non-round pearls can be expressed in terms of their greatest width and length and in some cases depth. The measurements are generally rounded to the nearest half or whole millimeter.

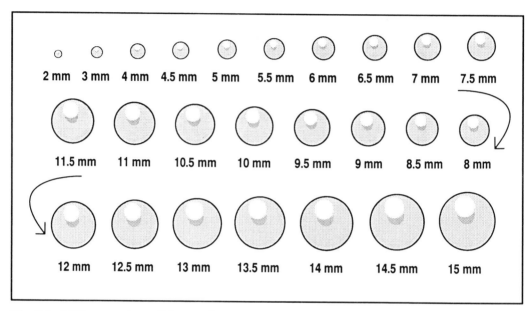

Fig. 7.1 Millimeter sizes. Diagram by Dawn King.

When determining the effect of size on price, keep in mind the following.

♦ Price jumps between pearl sizes tend to be uneven. An illustration of this is the following imaginary price list for grade X pearls.

7 1/2 - 8	$2,500
8 - 8 1/2	$5,000
8 1/2 - 9	$6,000
9 - 9 1/2	11,000

The above price increments are not unusual. Pearl prices tend to jump more as the sizes reach the 8 or 9 mm mark.

♦ Price/size relationships vary from one dealer to another.

♦ The effect of size on price varies from one harvest to another. If too many pearls of one size are harvested, their price will go down.

♦ Size tends to have the least effect on price in sizes below 5 mm.

♦ Demand can have an important impact on the way size affects price. If there's a high demand for a specific size, its price tends to increase. This explains why occasionally smaller pearls sell for more than bigger ones of the same quality.

Weight

When pearl dealers buy large lots of cultured pearls, they are usually charged according to the weight of the pearls. The measure generally used is the **momme**, an ancient Japanese unit of weight which equals 3.75 grams or 18.75 carats. **Kan** is a Japanese unit of weight equalling 1000 momme. Pearls are not sold by the momme or kan in retail stores.

The size of natural pearls is often expressed in pearl grains. One **grain** equals 0.25 carat. Natural American freshwater pearls may be sold according to their carat weight. The **gram** is commonly used to express the weight of cultured freshwater pearls, although carat weight is also used. One **carat** = 1/5 gram. Or in other words 5 carats = 1 gram. Weight equivalences are summarized in Table 7.1. The approximate weight of individual loose pearls can be calculated by referring to both tables 7.1 and 7.2.

Table 7. 1 Weight Conversions

1 carat (ct)	= 0.2 g = 0.007 oz av = 4 p grains = 0.053 m
1 gram (g)	= 5 cts = 0.035 oz av = 20 p grains = 0.266 m
1 ounce avoirdupois (oz av)	= 28.3495 g = 141.75 cts = 565 p grains = 7.56 m
1 pearl grain (p grain)	= 0.05 g = 0.25 ct = 0.013 m = 0.0017 oz av
1 momme (m)	= 3.75 g = 18.75 cts = 75 p grains = 0.131 oz av

Table 7.2 (Based on data from the Shima Pearl Co.)

Size	Pieces Per Momme	Size	Pieces Per Momme
2.5 mm	160 pcs	6.5 mm	9.3 pcs
3 mm	90 pcs	7 mm	7 pcs
3.5 mm	63 pcs	7.5 mm	6 pcs
4 mm	40 pcs	8 mm	5 pcs
4.5 mm	27 pcs	8.5 mm	4.2 pcs
5 mm	19 pcs	9 mm	3.5 pcs
5.5 mm	15 pcs	9.5 mm	3 pcs
6 mm	12 pcs	10 mm	2.5 pcs

Length

When pricing pearls, you should take into consideration the length of the strand as well as the millimeter size of the pearls. The pearl trade has specific names for different necklace lengths. They are as follows:

1. Choker   A 14 to 16 inch (35 to 40 cm) necklace whose central pearl normally lies in the hollow of the throat or just below it. It looks especially attractive with V-neck blouses and dresses.

2. Princess   A 16 to 20 inch (40 to 50 cm) necklace. This slightly longer length is well suited for pearl enhancers (detachable pendants) and can slenderize the neck.

3. Matinee   A 20 to 26 inch (50 to 66 cm) necklace. Some people like to wear a matinee length along with a choker. Or they have it strung with two hidden (mystery) clasps so it can also be worn as a bracelet and shorter necklace.

4. Opera   A necklace about twice the size of a choker.

5. Rope   A necklace longer than an opera length. The defined length will vary according to the jeweler or company using the term.

Courtesy Mikimoto Co.

Pearl necklace lengths are summarized in the following list:

1.	Choker	14 - 16"	35 - 40 cm
2.	Princess	16 - 20"	40 - 50 cm
3.	Matinee	20 - 26"	50 - 66 cm
4.	Opera	28 - 36"	70 - 90 cm
5.	Rope	40" +	1 meter and longer

The preceding lengths are approximate. Definitions of necklace-length terms can vary from one jeweler to another. Keep in mind that pearl strands become slightly longer when knotted and strung with a clasp to form a necklace. The following table will help you determine approximately how many pearls there are in a 14" and 16" strand.

Table 7.3 (Based on data from the Shima Pearl Co.)

Size	Pearls per 14" strand	Pearls per 16" strand
2.5 - 3 mm	130	148
3 - 3.5 mm	110	125
3.5 - 4 mm	97	110
4 - 4.5 mm	83	95
4.5 - 5 mm	76	87
5 - 5.5 mm	70	80
5.5 - 6 mm	63	72
6 - 6.5 mm	57	65
6.5 - 7 mm	53	60
7 - 7.5 mm	50	57
7.5 - 8 mm	46	52
8 - 8.5 mm	43	49
8.5 - 9 mm	41	47
9 - 9.5 mm	39	44
9.5 - 10 mm	36	41

There are some other terms relating to pearl necklaces that consumers might not be familiar with. They are:

Bib   A necklace of 3 or more concentric strands. The lowest strand normally does not fall below a matinee length.

Dog collar   A multi-strand choker-length necklace. The strands may be clasped together in a single clasp. "Dog collars" help conceal neck wrinkles.

Torsade   A multi-strand necklace formed by twisting strands around each other. This is a popular way to wear freshwater pearl strands.

Uniform strand A strand whose pearls are all about the same size.

Graduated strand A strand with pearls of different sizes which gradually get larger towards the center. Graduated strands provide a big pearl look at a lower price than uniform strands.

Fig. 7.2 Dog-collar. Photo courtesy Cultured Pearl Associations of America & Japan.

8

Judging Make

Imagine spending fifteen years collecting over 30,000 pearls just to find the right pearls for one necklace. Someone in Texas took the trouble to do this. A picture of the resulting necklace can be seen in color photo 11d. The pearls on the strand have a variable fair to very good luster, most are round but some are off-round, they range in size from 3.70 mm to 8.15 mm, and their color ranges from brownish to purplish pink with a few pearls being pinkish orange.

This necklace could be classified as having an unusually fine make. Why? Because all of the pearls on the necklace were natural freshwater pearls recovered from lakes and rivers in West Texas. And it's amazing that so many pearls of this type could be so round and blend together so well. When judging make we have to take into account availability of the pearls being graded.

Make is a combination of the following factors:

♦ How well the pearls match or blend together in terms of color, shape, luster, size, and surface perfection
♦ How centered the drill holes are
♦ How smooth the size increase is of pearls in graduated strands

Some dealers charge a premium that may range from 1%-15% for Akoya strands that are of very fine make. Others may discount them if the pearls don't match very well. Premiums of up to 30% or more can be charged for well-matched pairs of large, high quality natural or South Sea pearls. It can take a lot of time and luck to find pearls that match.

Fine make is relative, though, and buyers should be flexible about their expectations. One should not expect South Sea, freshwater, or natural pearls to be as round and match as well as cultured Akoya pearls.

The definitions of what constitutes good, fair, and poor make in Akoya pearl strands can vary from one dealer to another. Some may emphasize color most. Uniform luster, size, and/or shape may be more important to other dealers, even though they would probably all agree that the overall appearance is what counts. An example of what dealers would agree is a poorly matched Akoya strand can be found in figure 8.1. The very-low-luster pearl brings down the grade considerably. Figure 8.2 is an example of a well-matched strand.

Fig. 8.1 Poorly matched strand

Fig. 8.2 Well-matched strand

There are questions that remain unanswered concerning the make of Akoya pearl strands:

♦ Should dyed and non-dyed Akoya strands be graded alike when it is a lot easier to match dyed pearls than those that aren't?

♦ Should a non-dyed pinkish strand be graded as strictly for make as a non-dyed cream-colored strand when cream colors are more plentiful?

♦ Should very-thick-nacre pearls be discounted as much for shape variations as thin- and medium-nacre pearls when pearls that are in the oyster longer have a greater chance of growing irregular?

We need to be careful not to become so concerned about perfect matching that we end up downplaying other quality factors. We also need to make sure that we are realistic about our expectations.

The author recalls being in Tokyo just after taking a pearl grading seminar. Somehow she had formed the idea that if the overtones of pearls in strands didn't match, they were unacceptable. She looked at some of the highest priced Akoya strands in some of most exclusive stores in Tokyo and was quite surprised to find not a single strand whose overtones matched. They all seemed to have a combination of green, pink, and silver overtones, but the strands varied in the percentage of each color. Finally, she realized that she was being unrealistic and that as long as the body color looked uniform and the overtones blended together well and their differences weren't obvious, there was nothing wrong with the pearls.

Judging make requires a balanced perspective. On the one hand, we shouldn't be so lax that we let shoddy workmanship become the norm. On the other, we shouldn't be so perfectionistic that no pearls can meet our standards. When you look at a strand of pearls, consider its overall impact. Your attention should not be drawn away by obviously mismatched pearls. Neither is it desirable for the pearls to be lackluster but perfectly matched. Look at as many different qualities and strands of pearls as often as possible. You will form a sense of what's acceptable and eventually you'll have an appreciation for what is truly fine make.

9

South Sea Pearls

Mallory is puzzled. At the mall, she saw a large pearl ring in a jewelry store window for $4000. Then, in a another store window, she saw what appeared to be a ring of the same size and quality for $400. She went in and asked the salesman if it was a real pearl ring. He told her it was and suggested she try it on. She liked it, and considering the price of the other ring, felt she was getting a bargain, so she bought it. Now she is wondering why there was such a large difference in price between the two rings. Can you think of a possible explanation?

There is one. The pearl in the first ring was a whole **South Sea pearl**--a large whole pearl cultivated in a South Sea oyster. (In this chapter, "South Sea pearl" refers to white or light-colored pearls, not black ones). The pearl Mallory bought was a 3/4 mabe pearl--an assembled pearl, which was also probably from a South Sea oyster. A mabe pearl grows attached to the inner surface of the oyster shell. After it is cut from the shell, the nucleus bead which was inserted to make it grow is removed, and the remaining hole is filled with a paste or wax (and sometimes also a bead). Then it is covered with a mother-of-pearl backing. The resulting mabe pearl has a pearly nacre coating almost the same as a whole cultured pearl. The main difference is that it tends to be thinner. Consequently, some mabe pearls may crack very easily.

Even though the salesman was not wrong about the pearl being a real cultured one, he should have told Mallory it was an assembled pearl, especially since there is a vast price difference between mabe and whole pearls. But people don't always do what they're supposed to do. And some salespeople may not know the difference between a mabe pearl and a South Sea pearl (It should be noted that some people in the trade do not regard mabes as true pearls).

Mabe pearls are commonly shaped like half pearls, which makes them ideal for pendants and pins. They are also grown in 3/4 shapes to make them appear more like whole pearls when set in mountings such as rings. If a mabe pearl is loose, it's easy to tell it's assembled because the mother-of-pearl backing has a different appearance than the pearl nacre (fig 9.1). Plus you can see the line where the backing and pearl dome were glued together. When mounted, however, a mabe pearl may look like a South Sea pearl, particularly if the bottom of the pearl is encased in gold.

Fig. 9.1 Side view of a mabe pearl

Assembled pearls may occasionally be hard for professionals to detect. The winter 1989 issue of *Gems and Gemology* shows an assembled pearl which seemed to be a whole natural pearl when x-rayed (p. 240). But when it was unmounted, it became obvious that two pearl pieces had been glued together. The final GIA Gem Trade Laboratory report concluded "Assembled pearl consisting of two sections of natural pearl or blister pearls cemented together."

Large fine-quality whole pearls of any type are very rare and expensive. In April 1990, Sotheby's sold a strand of 45 cultured South Sea pearls ranging from 16 to 19 mm for $2,200,000. According to Sotheby's, the pearls were perfectly round and matched, and they had rose overtones and an exceptional luster.

South Sea pearls are cultivated in a variety of places--Australia, Burma (now called Myanmar), Thailand, Indonesia, the Philippines. Currently, Indonesia is the most important producer of pearls in the 9 to 11 mm range. The main source of pearls over 11 mm has been Australia. In some seasons, it has produced up to 60% of the world's large South Sea pearls.

(*National Geographic*, December 1991, p. 114 and *Pearls of the World*, p. 179). Australia's first pearl farm was established in 1956 on the Northwest coast at Kuri Bay. Prior to that time, Australia was producing up to 75% of the world's supply of mother of pearl, and pearls were just sold as a byproduct.

The silver-lip (Pinctada maxima) oyster is the main oyster used in Australia to cultivate South Sea pearls. If it's healthy, it can produce up to four pearls inserted at different times. The cultivation period may range from 1 1/2 to 2 years. The oysters that are unsuitable for whole pearls or that reject the bead nucleus are used to culture mabe pearls.

To avoid confusion, the pearl from the mabe oyster (Pteria penguin, penguin wing, or black wing) has not been mentioned in this section. Some people regard it as the only true mabe pearl. However, it is not easy to find mabe-oyster pearls in areas such as North America. Most of the large mabe assembled pearls sold are cultivated in South Sea silver-lip or (sometimes) black-lip oysters and tend to have a lower luster and less iridescence than the mabe-oyster blister pearl. No matter where a mabe originates from, salespeople should never call them South Sea Pearls. Only a large whole pearl merits the price and name of "South Sea Pearl."

Judging Quality

South Sea pearls are judged according to their luster, color, shape, flaws, size, and nacre thickness as follows:

Luster

The higher the luster, the more valuable the pearl. White South Sea pearls have a lower luster potential than Akoya and black pearls. Take this into consideration when evaluating white pearls. For tips on how to judge luster, see Chapter 4.

Color

As is the case with Akoya pearls, choice of color should be based on what will look best on the person who will wear the pearls. The color varies depending on which variety of Pinctada maxima oyster the pearl comes from--the silver-lip or gold-lip. The silver-lip oyster, the main oyster in Australia, tends to produce silvery white pearls. The gold-lip variety, which is more commonly found around countries such as Indonesia, Thailand, and the Philippines, is more likely to produce golden or cream-colored pearls.

The color of South Sea pearls is judged in about the same way as it is in Akoya pearls. White and pink pearls are more highly valued than yellowish pearls. The presence of pink overtones and iridescence is very desirable.

In the past, Burmese pearls were prized for their fine color, largely because of their pink overtones. Pearls from Australia, which were less valued, tended to be white with no pink overtones. Burmese pearls no longer have the same prestige. Recently there was a pearl auction in Burma. One dealer describes the pearls there as "mostly reject quality." This decline started after the departure of Japanese technicians and cultivators.

The quality of Australian pearls, however, has improved, especially their color. Now instead of being greenish or just white, many of their pearls have pink overtones. Consequently, high-quality pearls from Australia now have the prestige that once was accorded to those from Burma.

Fig. 9.2 An Australian South Sea pearl necklace (14.8 x 11.2mm) with two detachable pearl pendants (16.3 x 11.8mm) that can also be worn as earrings. The necklace, which contains 29 pearls, would wholesale for about $250,000. *Photo courtesy Albert Asher South Sea Pearl Co.*

Shape

The more round the pearl the more valuable it is. But round South Sea pearls are very rare, far more rare than Akoya pearls, which are smaller and have thinner nacre. Normally the shape of South Sea pearls ranges from off-round to baroque, with baroque being the most common and least expensive.

Be willing to compromise on shape. This may be necessary due to the high price and limited availability of round South Sea pearls.

Flaws

South Sea pearls are graded for flaws in the same way as Akoya pearls, except with much more leniency. The fewer the flaws the higher the price.

Size

South Sea pearls generally range in size from 9 to 18 mm. The world's largest round South Sea pearl may be 20.8 mm (over 3/4"). A picture of it is in the December 1991 issue of *National Geographic* (p. 115). Baroque pearls can grow larger. The "Nugget of Australia," a pearl belonging to the collection of Golay Buchel, has a length of 25 mm and weighs 90.6 ct. (*Pearls of the World* p. 116). It's their large size that makes South Sea pearls so expensive. As would be expected, the larger the pearl the greater its value.

The size of a cultured pearl is primarily determined by the size of its bead nucleus. The bigger the oyster, the bigger bead it can accept and the bigger pearl it can grow. Consequently, small Japanese oysters which measure 4 inches (10 mm) across, produce smaller pearls than the silver or gold-lip oysters which can measure 12 inches (30 mm) across. Black-pearl oysters, which also produce white pearls grow up to about 8 inches (20 mm) across and produce a pearl in between the size of the silver-lip and Akoya oysters.

Nacre Thickness

Big pearls do not necessarily have thick nacre. As with Akoya pearls, the nacre thickness of cultured South Sea pearls has decreased during the past 30 years. In the April 1971 issue of *Lapidary Journal*, Australian pearl farmer C. Denis George stated that a good cultured South Sea pearl had a nacre thickness double the radius of the bead nucleus. In other words, a 15-mm pearl had about a 5-mm nacre thickness and a nucleus whose radius is about 2.5 mm. If this standard were used today, it would be very hard to find a good South Sea pearl. Judging from standards published by black pearl producers, South Sea pearls today should have a nacre thickness of at least 1 mm of the radius. (See nacre thickness section in Chapter 10).

One millimeter may sound thick compared to the minimum standard this book suggests for Akoya pearls--0.35 mm. Keep in mind, though, that Akoya pearls have a finer-grained nacre than South Sea pearls and they are smaller. A 0.5-mm thickness on a 6-mm Akoya pearl is 1/6 of the radius. A 1-mm thickness on a 12-mm South Sea pearl is also 1/6 of the radius. Therefore, it is reasonable for buyers to expect nacre at least 1 mm thick on their South Sea pearls, especially considering their high cost.

Thin nacre is not as easily detected in South Sea pearls as it is in Akoya pearls. Due to the thicker nacre, the shell layers of the bead do not show up as well and it's harder to see the bead nucleus through the drill hole. In addition, the pearls are often mounted in jewelry so the drill holes are not visible.

To avoid buying South Sea pearls with nacre that's too thin, consumers should select pearls with a good luster and deal with jewelers who consider nacre thickness important. Also they should have their pearls x-rayed by a gem lab when the price of the pearls is high enough to warrant the cost of an x-ray report, which is about $100 to $300. The nacre thickness can be measured in the x-ray photograph.

Like all other pearls, those from the South Seas come in a wide range of qualities and prices. Some sell for over $30,000 and some sell for $100. The price factors above are what determine the value. For example, just take a $30,000 dollar South Sea pearl, make it smaller, add lots of flaws, give it a baroque shape, color it yellow, and give it a dull, drab luster. What can be the result? A $100 South Sea pearl.

Quiz (Chapters 7, 8 and 9)

Select the Correct Answer

1. Which would be the hardest to match?

a. Dyed Akoya pearls with very thick nacre
b. Dyed Akoya pearls with thin nacre
c. Non-dyed Akoya pearls with very thick nacre
d. Non-dyed Akoya pearls with thin nacre

2. Which would be the easiest to match?

a. 9 to 9 1/2 mm Akoya pearls
b. 9 to 9 1/2 mm South Sea pearls
c. 6 to 6 1/2 mm Akoya pearls
d. A graduated strand of South Sea pearls

3. Which of the following necklace lengths is shortest?

a. Opera
b. Matinee
c. Princess
d. Rope

4. Larger pearls can be cultivated in the South Seas than in Japan because:

a. the oysters in the South Seas are exposed to more sunlight.
b. South Sea oysters are larger than the Japanese Akoya type.
c. there are so many tropical fish for South Sea oysters to feed on.
d. none of the above

5. Which country has produced the most South Sea pearls and mother of pearl?

a. Burma
b. Australia
c. Japan
d. The Philippines

6. Which of these units of weight is heaviest?

a. 1 carat
b. 1 gram
c. 1 ounce avoirdupois
d. 1 pearl grain
e. 1 momme

7. Which of the following weighs the least?

a. 1 carat
b. 1 gram
c. 1 ounce avoirdupois
d. 1 pearl grain
e. 1 momme

True or False?

8. It's easier to match natural pearls than cultured pearls.

9. Mabe assembled pearls cost a lot less than South Sea pearls.

10. There's a regular rise in price as pearl size increases.

11. Two matched pearls can cost a lot more than two unmatched ones.

12. Since South Sea pearls are so big, there's no need to be concerned about the thickness of their nacre.

13. The effect of size on price can vary from dealer to another.

Answers:

1. c

2. c

3. c

4. b

5. b

6. c

7. d

8. F   It's a lot harder to match natural pearls.

9. T

10. F   Price jumps tend to be uneven.

11. T

12. F

13. T

10

Black Pearls

Gray. Is this an appealing color for a gem? For a diamond, it wouldn't be, nor would it be for a sapphire. But judging from the prices of "black pearls," pearl connoisseurs find dark gray very appealing. In April 1990, for example, a single strand of 27 black pearls was sold for $880,000 at Sotheby's. This was more than $32,000 per pearl.

Black pearls are not necessarily black. More often than not they range from a medium to very dark gray. Also the colors of pearls that look black may be natural or dyed.

If you go to Hong Kong, for example, you may see strands labeled "black pearls" that sell for a few hundred dollars. They are probably artificially colored Akoya pearls whose natural color was undesirable. In Tahiti, **"black pearl"** can only refer to **a dark-colored pearl of natural color from the black-lip oyster** (Pinctada margaritifera). The jewelers in both areas are correct in their use of the term. In both cases the pearls are dark-colored and they are real cultured pearls. This book, however, uses the Tahitian meaning of "black pearl" because that is the one accepted by the major wholesalers of fine-quality pearls.

Naturally-colored black pearls can also be confused with naturally-colored "blue pearls." Unlike black pearls whose color is an inherent characteristic of the pearl nacre, **blue pearls** derive their color from foreign contaminants in the nacre itself or between the nacre and the shell bead nucleus. Naturally-colored, dark Akoya pearls are good examples of "blue pearls."

They may be blue, black, gray, or brown. Black pearls and "blue pearls" can look the same but due to the difference in the origin of their color, "blue pearls" are worth less. The fact that "blue pearls" might decay or lose their color if holes are drilled through them is another reason for their lower value. (A more detailed analysis of black pearls and "blue pearls" is given by Yoshihiro Hisada and Hiroshi Komatsu of the Mikimoto Co. in *Pearls of the World* (pages 87-94) and Hiroshi Komatsu and Shigeru Akamatsu in the Spring 78 issue of *Gems & Gemology* (pages 7-15)).

Since there can be a great value difference between black pearls, "blue pearls" and artificially colored pearls even though they may look the same, consumers need to be concerned about buying black pearls that are misrepresented. Later in the chapter, some guidelines are given on how to spot pearls that are not really black pearls. Keep in mind, though, that the only sure way to identify a black pearl is to send it to a lab and have it tested.

Fig. 10.1 An array of white and black pearls from the South Seas. The white necklace is Burmese and the black ones Tahitian. The largest pearl in the oyster shell measures 18.2 mm and is from Burma. *Photo courtesy Albert Asher South Sea Pearl Co.*

It's only been within the last 10 to 20 years that cultured black pearls have become commercially important. Most of them are cultivated in Tahiti (French Polynesia to be more accurate) and others are produced in places like Okinawa and Fiji. Natural black pearls, however, became known in Europe after Hernando Cortez and later explorers discovered colored pearls in the Gulf of California. In the late 1700's and early 1800's, La Paz in Baja California became the black pearl center of the world. Natural black pearls in the South Seas were also being fished at this time. Gradually black pearls grew popular especially among European royalty, such as Empress Eugenie of France. But the oyster beds were overfished and black pearls became scarce. Then in the 1940's, a large percentage of the black lip oysters in the Gulf of California died for unknown reasons. Today, even though natural pearls are occasionally found, you should assume that unless otherwise specified, the black pearls sold in stores are cultured. Because of this, throughout the rest of this chapter the term "black pearl" will refer to cultured dark pearls of natural color found in the black-lip oyster.

Judging Quality

A black pearl is judged according to its luster, color, shape, flaws, size, and nacre thickness as follows:

Luster

Black pearls can look almost metallic. You should expect a higher and different luster from them than you would from white South Sea pearls. Dark nacre does not reflect light in the same way that white nacre does. The best way to learn the luster potential of a black pearl is to look at some black pearls ranging from very low to very high in luster. After you compare them, you probably won't be satisfied with a black pearl of low luster. Keep in mind that lighting can affect black pearls in the same way it does white pearls, so compare pearls under equivalent lighting conditions. (See Chapter 4 for discussion of lighting.)

Low luster in black pearls is often correlated with thin nacre, as is the case with white pearls. But thin-nacre black pearls can have good luster and thick-nacre pearls may have low luster. Consequently, it's best to treat luster and nacre thickness as two separate value factors.

Color

Generally the darker the black pearl, the more valuable it is. The finest black pearls also have a green overtone which is called "peacock green. A solid black pearl with no overtone is considered undesirable and may cost as much as 50% less than one of similar quality with green overtones. Pearls with muddy colors are also viewed as undesirable.

Other overtone colors on black pearls are pink, blue, gold, silver, and a reddish purple called "aubergine," which is the French word for eggplant. These overtones may be present in a variety of combinations and are considered a plus factor. Black pearls also have a wide range of body colors--black, gray, blue, green, brown.

There is no standardized system throughout the pearl industry for classifying or valuing the color of black pearls, and considering the complexity of it, there may never be. There is no standard either for determining how dark a pearl must be to be called "black" (black-lip oysters produce pearls ranging in color from white to gray to black). There is, however, general agreement that the most valued color for a black pearl is an evenly distributed greenish black which may or may not have reddish-purple highlights. This is a contrast from Akoya pearls where greenish tints are not highly valued.

Shape

Round shapes are the most expensive. The more perfectly round the pearl, the more valued it is. Pear and drop shapes are the next most expensive followed by button shapes which are flat on one side and rounded on the other. The more symmetrical these shapes are, the more their value. Baroque shapes and circled pearls with ring-like formations around them are the least expensive (figs. 10.2 and 10.3).

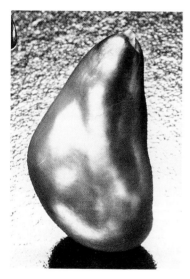

Fig. 10.2 Baroque-shape Tahitian black pearl

Fig. 10.3 Circled black pearl

When you need to cut down on the price of a black pearl, shape is a good category to compromise on. In fact, baroque and circled pearls often make more interesting jewelry pieces than round pearls do.

Size

Naturally the bigger the black pearl the more expensive it is. Black pearls generally range in size from about 9 to 18 mm with their average size tending to be between 9 and

11.5mm. Some baroque black pearls may reach 25 to 30 mm. Size has a great impact on price. A 1 mm increase in the size of medium-quality pearls can raise their price 100 to 200%. In other words, a 14 mm pearl which costs $5,000, might cost $10,000 if it were 15 mm and $30,000 if it were 16 mm.

At the retail level black pearls tend to be described and priced according to millimeter size. Weight may be used as an additional means of identifying them. This is the opposite of round diamonds where the price is based on the weight, but measurements may be given to help distinguish them from other diamonds of the same weight.

On the wholesale level, however, large lots of black pearls are sold according to their weight, which is measured in momme (1 momme = 3.75 grams = 18.75 carats). The pearls are graded into various categories, and each category is assigned a per-momme price.

Flaws

Flaws can decrease the price of black pearls considerably, which is an advantage for consumers. A black pearl can often be mounted in a way that will hide its flaws when worn. This means if you select your pearl(s) carefully, you can have a clean-looking one for a lower price. Remember that blemishes on single pearls tend to be more obvious than on those in strands. Therefore, when buying a loose black pearl, figure out in advance how you will wear it so you can choose one whose flaws won't be noticeable.

Nacre thickness

It should be at least 1 mm (of the radius). The thicker the nacre the more valuable the pearl.

As you are shopping, you may encounter salespeople who claim that all black or white pearls from the South Seas have thick nacre, and that nacre thickness need not be a consideration. Many people who specialize in producing or studying black pearls would disagree.

Dr. Jean-Paul Lintilhac, installer and developer of two black pearl farms in Tahiti, is one example. In his book, *Black Pearls of Tahiti*, he states that jewelers in Tahiti are worried about the thinness of the nacre of some of the pearls offered to them for sale. He goes on to say that certain pearl farmers are in such a hurry to recover their investment that they harvest their pearls prematurely and as a result the nacre is very thin. Then he writes (p. 85):

"Formerly a big pearl meant a good thickness of nacre, but with the supergrafts used today, size is no guarantee. If you are buying a big expensive pearl, you have the right to ask for an x-ray of it which will enable you to see and measure the thickness of the layers of nacre surrounding the nucleus. One millimeter of nacre is a minimum for a good pearl."

Tahiti Pearls, a major black pearl company, also tells consumers in their book *The Magic of the Black Pearl*, that nacre thickness is a criteria used to judge black pearls. They indicate a 1 mm to 1.5 mm nacre thickness as an appropriate range for black pearls.

Hisada and Komatsu of the Mikimoto Co. put nacre thickness at the top of their list of black pearl quality factors (*Pearls of the World* p. 90). They state:

"Nacre thickness is a basic factor in judging the elegance of the pearl. Its beauty and durability depend on the thickness of the nacre, its quality and quantity."

The Mikimoto company, in their leaflet "The Art of Selecting Cultured Pearls," tells consumers: "For beautiful pearls the most important factors are luster and nacre thickness."

Chapter 4 gives guidelines on determining if the nacre thickness of Akoya pearls is acceptable. Unfortunately these techniques do not work as well on black pearls. It's often impossible to see into their drill holes because the pearls may be glued to a jewelry piece such as a ring or pendant mounting. Also the nacre of black pearls may mask the layers of a shell bead nucleus that might be visible in a thin-nacre Akoya pearl.

Usually the best way of determining the nacre thickness of a black pearl is with an x-ray. And, if you are spending thousands of dollars on a pearl piece, it's well worth your money to have a gem lab x-ray the piece to check for nacre thickness and to determine if the color is natural. But what should you do if you are paying, say $500 for a black pearl pendant? An x-ray in a case like this is probably not worth the money. The best thing you can do is to choose pearls with as high of a luster as possible and **buy your pearls from jewelers who consider nacre thickness important.** If they don't think it's important and they don't mention it, this might either mean they have something to hide or they don't take it into consideration when buying pearls for their inventory. And as a consequence, their pearls may not have an adequate nacre thickness.

It's often hard to understand why one pearl may cost $50 and another may cost $1000. But let's consider how the above factors might work together to lower the price. If a pearl costing $1000 decreases 1 mm in size, it's price may drop 50% to $500. If it then changes from a dark greenish grey color to a muddy gray with no overtones, it's price could drop another 50% to $250. Going from a very high to very low luster could bring its price to $125. And then adding lots of flaws to it could bring it down to $50.

Pearl pricing is not as mathematically regular as this example. Nevertheless, the above quality factors can have a similar effect on its price. So take them into consideration as you shop and compare prices. Also, when you look at pearl prices in ads and catalogues, remember that they are meaningless if an adequate description of the pearls is not included.

Natural Color or Not?

Off-color pearls from the Akoya and silver- or gold-lip oysters are sometimes blackened to improve their appearance. Light-colored pearls from the black-lip oyster are occasionally

3a High-quality Japanese Akoya cultured pearls with body colors ranging from light pink to dyed blue and dyed black. *Photo courtesy Hikari Southsea Pearl Co.*

Printed in Singapore

3b South Sea keshi (the two bottom strands) and Australian South Sea cultured pearls. The largest loose pearl at the top is 18mm and is worth $30,000 wholesale. South Sea cultured pearls are produced by oysters which have been implanted with a nucleus. South Sea keshi are formed accidently in oysters cultivated by man and contain no nuclei. (The term "cultured" is often omitted for the sake of brevity.) *Photo courtesy Hikari South Sea Pearl Co.*

3c An impressive bird-of-paradise necklace made from freshwater pearls. The center pearl is from Japan's Lake Biwa and the smaller pearls were cultivated in China. *Photo courtesy A & Z Pearls.*

3d Natural abalone pin/pendant surrounded by moonstones, tanzanite cabs, Japanese Biwa and Chinese freshwater pearls. The abalone is a sea snail and is noted for the vividly-colored nacre it produces. *Photo courtesy of King's Ransom. Photo*

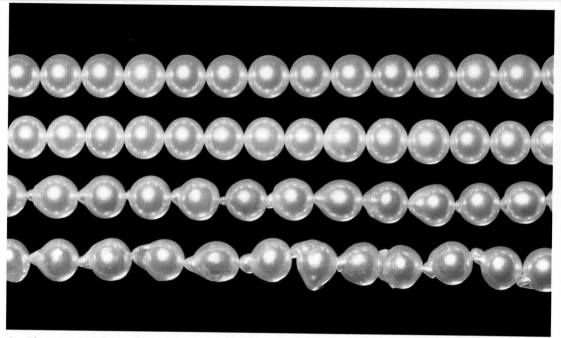

3e Shape comparison photo of Akoya pearl strands. Top to bottom--round, slightly off-round, semi-baroque, and baroque. Round is the most expensive shape type. Baroque costs the least.

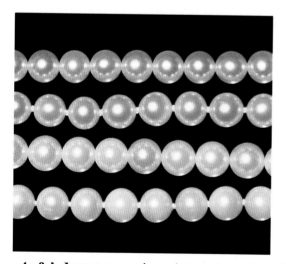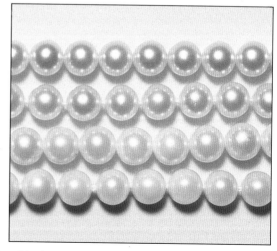

4a & b Luster comparison photos of strands against black and white backgrounds. Top to bottom: High lustre, medium luster, low luster, very low luster.

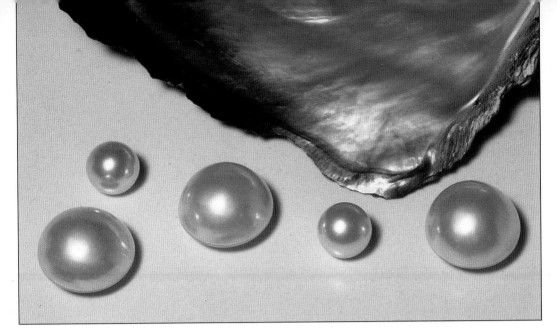

5a Top-quality pearls are colorful, like an oyster shell. These mabe and Akoya pearls have a light pink body color with blue and pink overtones. As you move the pearls, they appear to change color due to their pearly iridescence. The overtone colors are most apparent when the pearls are viewed against a white background under a strong direct light such as a light-bulb. Broad diffused lighting tends to whiten pearls.

These mabe pearls are from the Pteria Penguin (mabe/black-wing) oyster, which is noted for producing a high-quality, iridescent nacre.

light pink---pink overtones

white---pink & green overtones

white---green & silver overtones

low quality white

cream---mostly pink overtones

golden---various overtones

dyed golden

5b Akoya pearls come in a range of colors. Specifying pearl color, however, is not easy. Body color, overtones, and iridescence must all be considered. To complicate matters, the pearls within a strand vary in color.

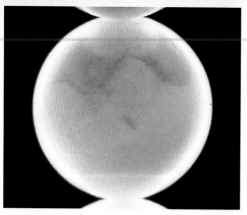

5c Pink dye in pearl cracks

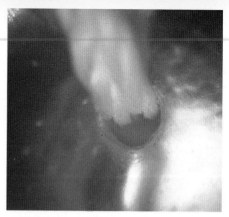

5d Pink dye in pearl drill-hole

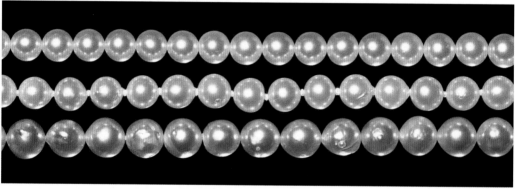

6a Surface comparison photo. Top strand--relatively clean (unblemished), middle strand--moderately blemished, bottom strand--heavily blemished.

6b Enlarged view of same strands

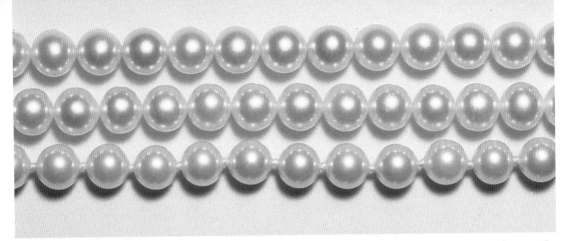

12a Top two strands--cultured pearls, bottom strand--good-quality imitation pearls. Genuine pearls of good quality will typically have either pink, green, silver, or blue overtones; whereas imitations tend to lack these overtones and be more uniform in color. A better way of distinguishing imitation from genuine pearls is to examine them with a 10-power magnifier.

12b Under 10X magnification, the surface of the imitation pearl (top) looks coarse and grainy compared to the smoother-looking surface of the real cultured pearl (bottom).

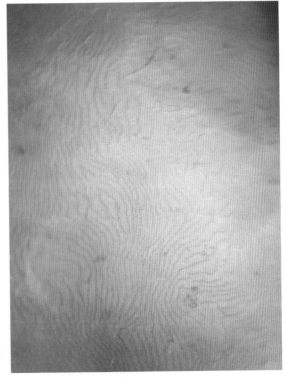

12c Surface of a Tahitian cultured pearl viewed at 64-power magnification. The maze-like patterns prove the pearl is genuine. When rubbed lightly against the biting edge of the front teeth, the pearl feels gritty due to the microscopic surface ridges.

9a Indonesian South Sea pearls (9-10mm). Indonesia is noted for its wide selection of pearls in the 9 to 11mm range. *Photo courtesy of the Hikari South Sea Pearl Co.*

9b An Australian South Sea pearl necklace (17.8 x 13.5mm) with matching pearl and diamond earrings. The necklace has a wholesale value of about $700,000 and the earrings $75,000. *Photo courtesy Albert Asher South Sea Pearl Co.*

10a An exceptional black pearl necklace (13-14mm). The pearls are of natural color and were cultivated in French Polynesia (groups of islands which include Tahiti). This necklace would wholesale for about $80,000. *Photo courtesy Assael International.*

10b Tahitian black pearl button earrings (14mm) with detachable drop pearls. Note their fine luster, symmetry, surface, and green overtones. *Photo courtesy of Assael International.*

10c An example of pink and green over-tones on a Tahitian black pearl button clasp. These overtones are frequently found together on high-quality black pearls. The absence of overtones is a sign of low quality. *Photo courtesy of Assael International.*

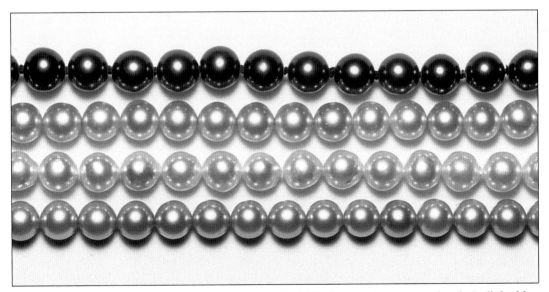

10d Japanese Akoya pearls. Top to bottom--dyed black, gray (non-natural color), light blue (natural color), and dyed blue.

10e Mabes and blister mabes interspersed with tourmaline, aquamarine, citrine, chrysocolla, rose quartz, moonstone, chrysoprase, and tanzanite cabs. *Photo courtesy King's Ransom. Photo by Ron Fortier.*

11a Chinese freshwater pearls (non-dyed)

11b Freshwater Biwa pearl set in 18K gold to form an angel figurine. It is mounted on a lapis base. *Photo courtesy A & Z Pearls.*

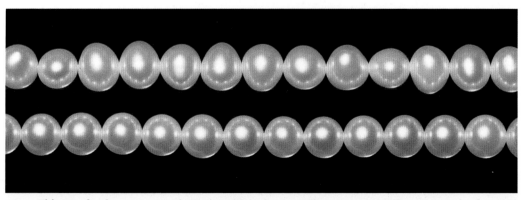

11c Chinese freshwater strand (top), which from a distance resembles a strand of round saltwater pearls (bottom). Off-round freshwater pearls may sell for 1/3 to 1/10 the price of saltwater pearls of similar luster, size, and color depending on their quality category.

11d Strand of natural freshwater pearls from the San Angelo area of West Texas (3.70 to 8.15mm). These pearls were collected over a period of 15 years. *Photo courtesy Gemological Institute of America. Photo by Shane McClure.*

11e Necklace made with 48 Biwa pearls. Finding such a large number of well-matched Biwa is no easy task because these Japanese pearls are now quite rare. *Photo courtesy A & Z Pearls.*

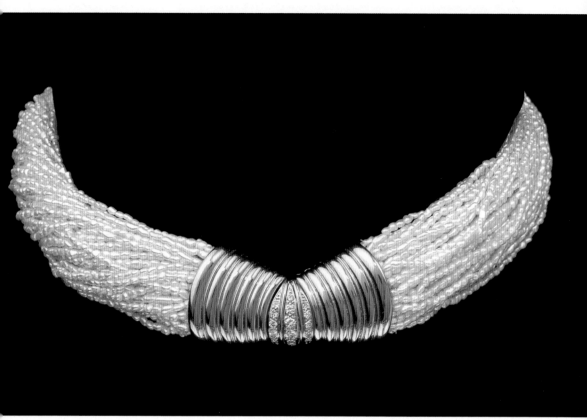

a A 42-strand keshi necklace. Keshi are pearls produced naturally as a by-product of pearl culturing.
oto courtesy A & Z Pearls.

5b Tahitian mabe blister brooch

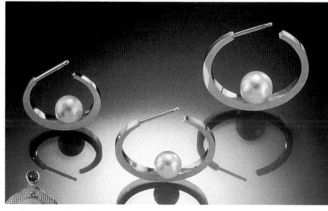

15c Hand-crafted 14K-gold earrings featuring moveable Akoya pearls. *Photo courtesy Alan Revere Jewelry Design*

15d Brooch and earring set with Australian South Sea pearls (12-13mm) and diamonds. *Photo courtesy Hikari South Sea Pearl Co.*

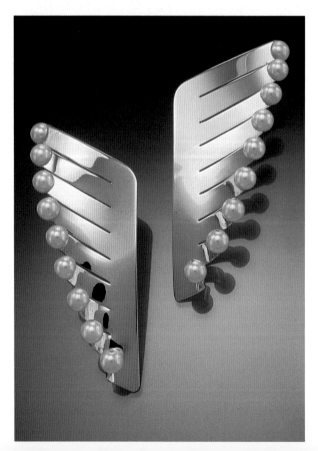

15e Hand fabricated 14K-gold and pearl earrings. *Photo courtesy Alan Revere Jewelry Design. Photo by Ralph Gabriner.*

Fig. 10.4 A Tahitian black pearl necklace with a platinum and diamond ball clasp and matching pearl drop earrings (16 x 12 mm). According to government regulations in Tahiti, all black pearls sold there must be of natural color. This necklace would wholesale for about $100,000. *Photo courtesy Assael International.*

The following methods are used to darken pearls.

♦ **Silver salt treatment**: This is the most common way of blackening Akoya pearls. The pearls are soaked in a weak solution of silver nitrate and dilute ammonia and then exposed to light or hydrogen sulfide gas.

♦ **Irradiation**: This method works best on freshwater pearls, but occasionally off-color Akoya pearls are darkened in this manner. It involves bombarding pearls with gamma rays. This blackens the shell bead nucleus of Akoya pearls and makes their nacre appear dark.

♦ **Dying the bead nucleus**: Occasionally the shell bead nuclei are dyed before they are inserted in the oyster. Afterwards the dark bead shows through the nacre and makes the pearl nacre look dark.

♦ **Plastic coating**: In a few instances, pearls have been darkened with thin plastic coatings. This coating can be easily detected by its strange feel and by bald spots on the pearl where the coating may have worn away.

According to the GIA pearl grading course, the color of irradiated pearls and those colored with silver salts is stable. People who deal in dyed black pearls also state that pearls treated with these two methods do not fade. Occasionally, though, there are reports of dyed black pearls that lose their color. Perhaps this is because the bead nucleus was dyed instead of irradiated or because the irradiation or silver nitrate treatments were done improperly. For your protection, buy dyed pearls from reputable jewelers. That way if there is a problem, you'll be able to return the pearls and get a refund.

As one can see, dyeing is not the only means of coloring pearls. Nevertheless, for the sake of brevity, the term "**dyed**" will be used in the rest of this chapter to describe any artificially colored pearl.

Many people associate the term "dyed" with the terms "cheap" and "fake." However, dyed black pearls were sold in fashionable stores as far back as the 1930's--long before black pearls were being commercially cultivated. Dyed black pearls were considered elegant. They are still in demand. Plus they have the added bonus of being much more affordable than their naturally-colored counterparts. A large percentage of the pink pearls sold in stores have also been dyed and this means there's a wider selection of pink pearls available for consumers. The only thing wrong with dyeing pearls is denying it is done and not disclosing it to buyers.

Dyed pearls are not fakes, but they are normally considered less valuable than those of natural color. There is an especially large price difference between true black pearls and those that aren't, so you need to know how to protect yourself from being charged a black pearl price for a dyed pearl. Even if the price is fair, you may just want to avoid buying a dyed black pearl. You can reduce your chances of being misled with the following tests:

Price Test

Is the price unusually low compared to true black pearls of the same size, shape, and overall quality? An average-quality, round, 8-mm Tahitian black pearl can retail for between $300 to $500. A round, 8-mm dyed black pearl may retail for about $50 to $100. Higher qualities will cost more. (Remember to compare pearls of the same size and shape. These factors have a major effect on the price. For example, if we just decreased the size of the dyed black pearl to 6 mm, it could retail for about $15.)

True black pearls are typically expensive, so if the price is low and you are not in Tahiti, assume the pearl is dyed unless otherwise told. (It's illegal to import or sell dyed black pearls in Tahiti.) If the store claims the color is natural, ask if they will write this on the receipt.

Size Test

Is the size less than 9 mm? If so and you are not in Tahiti, assume that it is an Akoya dyed pearl or "blue pearl" unless the store is willing to write on the receipt that it is naturally colored and from the black lip oyster. There are true black pearls less than 9 mm, but it is usually not cost effective to intentionally produce them when farmers can get far more by cultivating larger pearls. Keep in mind, too, that black pearls below 9 mm may be small due to thin nacre.

Akoya oysters, on the other hand, can produce a wide range of pearls below 9 mm ; but rarely do they grow round pearls above 10 mm. Larger Japanese baroque pearls may be available. A photo of some Japanese "blue pearls" ranging from 11.5 to 14 mm can be seen in the fall 1990 issue of *Gems & Gemology* (p. 225).

Once in a while, large round pearls from South Sea oysters are dyed or are "blue pearls." Therefore large size is never proof that a pearl is a true black pearl. It is, however, a positive sign. When buying black pearls, it's always advisable to ask salespeople to specify on the receipt that the pearls are of natural color and from the black lip oyster. When spending large sums of money, also have them tested by an independent gem lab.

Color Test

Are the pearls so dark they are almost black? Do all the pearls in the piece look the exact same color? Is the color perfectly even in all the pearls? These are indications the pearls might be dyed (color photo 10d. It's not easy to find true black pearls that are really black. More often than not they are grayish. It's also not easy to find several black pearls the exact same even color.

If you are interested in black pearls, look at a lot of them. Then look at dyed pearls and compare. Gradually, you will get a sense of what the body colors and overtones of black pearls look like. People that work with black pearls on a regular basis can usually spot dyed pearls instantly. But even experts can be fooled. So when making a major purchase, have your black pearls tested by an independent gem lab.

Shape Test

Are the pearls perfectly round? This is a sign they might be dyed, especially if the price is reasonable. Do they have ring-like formations encircling them? This is a characteristic of Tahitian black pearls. Perfectly round black pearls are rare, which is one reason they are so expensive. Tahitian black pearls often have distinctive shapes and slightly uneven surfaces (figs. 10.2 & 10.3).

Drill-hole Test

If it is possible to look into the drill hole with a loupe, does the nacre inside look white and the nucleus look dark? This is a sign the pearl has been colored by irradiation or the nucleus has been dyed. Is there dye concentrated around the drill hole? This indicates it is dyed.

Infrared Photo Test

If you have a camera, you can photograph the pearls with color infrared film (Kodak, Ektachrome Infrared Film, IE 135-20). Naturally colored pearls tend to look blue, whereas pearls colored with silver salts generally look yellow (or range from greenish blue to yellow green). (Komatsu and Akamatsu, *Gems & Gemology*, Spring 1978). You can use the leftover film to take some interesting aerial photographs. This film is used for topographical analysis.

The following methods require special equipment, but you might be interested in tests that labs may conduct:

UV Fluorescence Test

The pearls are examined under long-wave UV radiation. Natural-color black pearls will generally have a fluorescence ranging from a bright red (pearls from Baja California) to a dull reddish brown (Tahitian pearls). Dyed pearls tend to show no reaction or else fluoresce a dull green. (See page 143 of the 1989 issue of *Gems & Gemology*, part of a good article on the Polynesian black pearl by Marisa Goebel and Dona Dirlam.)

High Magnification

The pearls are viewed under 100+-power magnification through crossed polaroid lenses. Traces of the chemical coloring can be seen. (Hisada and Komatsu, *Pearls of the World*, pp. 92-93).

X-radiograph Test

An x-ray photo called an **x-radiograph** is taken of the pearls. If the pearls are dyed with silver salts, a pale ring between the nacre and the shell bead nucleus can often be seen. Plus there is less of a contrast between the bead and the nacre.

X-ray Fluorescence Test The pearls are exposed to x-rays. Then the emitted wavelengths are measured with an instrument called a spectrometer to detect trace elements such as silver on the surface of the pearl.

As you can see, there is a wide variety of tests for identifying black pearls. Use a combination of the simple tests to help you spot obvious cases of dye. But when it comes to making a major purchase, get help from professionals.

Chapter 10 Quiz

Select the Correct Answer

1. The most valued black pearls have

a. no overtones
b. green overtones
c. silver overtones
d. pink overtones

2. Which of the following is not used to darken the color of pearls?

a. Irradiation
b. Silver salt treatment
c. Heat treatment
d. Colored dyes

3. The size of most natural-color black pearls is usually:

a. less than 9 mm.
b. between 9 and 12 mm
c. between 11 and 15 mm
d. greater than 11.5 mm

4. A dyed-black pearl may have originally been:

a. an off-color Akoya pearl.
b. a light-color pearl from a black-lip oyster.
c. an off-color pearl from an Australian silver-lip oyster.
d. any of the above.

5. Which of the following shapes is the least expensive for a black pearl?

a. round
b. pear-shape
c. circled
d. oval

6. Today most natural-color black pearls are cultivated in:

a. Japan
b. Baja California
c. French Polynesia (Tahiti)
d. Australia

7. The term "black pearl" is used by jewelry salespeople to refer to:

a. natural-color black pearls from the black-lip oyster
b. "blue pearls"
c. dyed black pearls
d. all of the above

True or False?

8. Most black pearls are very round.

9. Gray pearls are not considered to be black pearls.

10. Some cultured black pearls have an inadequate nacre coating.

11. If a pearl is black and over 11 mm in size, its color is natural.

12. Ring-like formation are often seen on Tahitian black pearls.

13. The most reliable way of determining if the color of a black pearl is natural is to have it x-rayed by a gem lab.

14. The color of "blue pearls" is stable.

15. There is no standard for determining how dark a pearl must be to be called black.

Answers:

1. b

2. c

3. b

4. d   But if it's less than 8.5 mm, it was probably an off-color Akoya pearl.

5. c

6. c

7. d   Even though this chapter uses the term "black pearl" to refer to natural-color pearls from the black-lip oyster, you should be aware that some people in the trade also use it to refer to any dark colored pearl, even "blue pearls" and dyed pearls. Therefore, always ask salespeople to specify what they mean by "black pearl."

8. F

9. F

10. T

11. F   Large pearls from the black-lip and silver-lip oysters are also dyed.

12. T

13. T

14. F   Due to their organic pigmentation, "blue pearls" can lose color or decay if holes are drilled through them. (See page 22 of *Pearls* by Shohei Shirai and the other references cited in the first section of this chapter.)

15. T

11

Freshwater Pearls

Bob is in Hong Kong and he's looking at some strands of little pearls that resemble rice. They're white, they glisten, and they are just $5. Since the price is so low, Bob thinks they might be fake. Is he probably right?

No, he's probably wrong. Even though there are imitation pearls like this, it's more likely that they are cultured Chinese freshwater pearls (also called sweetwater pearls). These "Rice-Krispie-like" pearls are usually inexpensive because as many as 50 of them may be found in one mussel, they don't take long to grow (less than 12 months), they can be harvested two or three times from the same mussel unlike Akoya pearls, and Chinese labor costs are low.

The term "Chinese rice pearl" often has negative connotations because so many cheap, poor-quality ones have been produced. There are three main reasons for this low quality: Chinese pearl cultivators tend to be less skilled than those in Japan; Chinese mussels are often overcrowded in the lakes and ponds and thereby deprived of essential nutrients; and the type of mussel often used by the Chinese, the kurasu mussel, tends to produce lower-quality, wrinkled pearls. The Chinese also produce some high-quality pearls. The best ones come from the sankaku or triangle-shaped mussel, which has a longer cultivation period than the kurasu mussel.

The quality of Chinese freshwater pearls has been steadily improving since 1991, thanks to better cultivation techniques and a more widespread use of the sankaku mussel. At the end of 1992, semi-round Chinese freshwater pearls made their appearance on the market and now offer an attractive, lower priced alternative to the round Akoya pearls.

the Japanese, at Lake Biwa, are credited with being the first to succeed in cultivating freshwater pearls on a commercial basis, although freshwater pearls in the shape of Buddha had been cultured in China as far back as the thirteenth century. The technical roots of cultivating freshwater pearls are attributed to Masayo Fujita, the "father of freshwater pearl cultivation"

(p. 136, *Pearls of the World*, article by Hidemi Takashima, a chief engineer at the Nippon Institute for Scientific Research on Pearls).

The first harvest of Biwa pearls was in August 1925 and they had a shell bead nucleus like Akoya oysters. By the 1930's they were being sold overseas. Some merchants from India would buy these Lake Biwa pearls from Fujita and then resell them to the Middle East as highly valuable Persian pearls for huge sums of money. One day, it was accidentally discovered that a shell bead is not necessary for the cultivation of a freshwater pearl. All that is needed is the insertion of a piece of mantle (a membranous tissue that secretes nacre and lines the inner shell surface of mollusks). This is a lot less trouble than inserting both a bead and mantle tissue. Also, it was noticed that after the first harvest, mussels can spontaneously grow pearls a second and third time. What this now means is that cultured freshwater pearls usually have more pearl nacre than cultured Akoya pearls because most do not have a shell bead nucleus.

China and Japan are not the only places where freshwater pearls are found. There are many historical accounts about the natural freshwater pearls of Europe and North America. These pearls are still being sold, but in decreasing quantities. Overfishing, flooding, and pollution has either dwindled or, in some areas, eliminated the supply of these natural pearls.

The cultured freshwater pearl market in the United States, however, is gradually increasing. They are now being cultivated in Tennessee. This area is also known for being the primary source of the shell beads in Akoya pearls. Other places in the US, too, are being considered as cultivation sites. No matter where freshwater pearls may be cultured, their overall value is determined by specific quality characteristics. These are outlined in the next section.

Judging Quality

The grading of freshwater pearls is more variable than that of saltwater pearls. Nevertheless, there is agreement about certain value factors. Freshwater pearls are generally valued according to the following criteria:

Luster

The higher and more even the luster, the greater the value. Low-quality freshwater pearls may seem lustrous to a layperson because often part of their surface is very shiny. However, if some areas of the pearls look milky, chalky, and dull, they are considered to have a low luster. In high-quality freshwater pearls, there is an evenly distributed luster and a high contrast between the light and dark areas of the pearls.

When judging freshwater pearls for luster, examine them on a white background under a bare direct light and be sure to roll them so you can see their entire surface area. If possible, compare strands of different qualities. It's important that your eye become sensitive to luster variations because luster is one of the most important determinants of value in pearls of all types.

Smoothness

The smoother the pearl, the more valuable it is. Even though bumpy, wrinkled surfaces can lower the value of freshwater pearls, the bumps and wrinkles are not considered flaws. Consequently, this chapter treats smoothness as a separate category from blemish.

Figures 11.1 and 11.2 can help you understand how the luster and smoothness of freshwater pearls can affect their value. Both strands are Chinese rice pearls. The lower one retails for $16 in a 32" strand (the pearls average 4 to 5 mm--3/8 inch in length). The upper one with larger pearls could retail for about $2. The reason for this price difference is that the lower strand is a lot smoother and has a much better luster than the $2 strand.

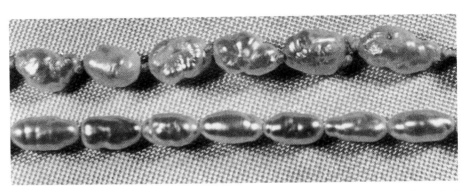

Fig. 11.1 Upper strand--poor quality "rice" pearls, lower strand--good quality "rice" pearls. Compare their smoothness and the evenness of their luster. (3X)

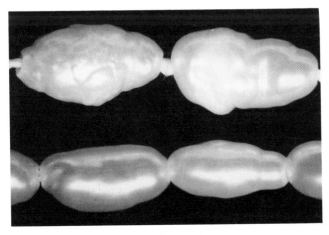

Fig. 11.2 Enlarged view of same strands (7X mag.)

The price difference becomes more noticeable when several strands are twisted to form one necklace. For example, a ten-strand twist of the higher quality pearls would retail for maybe $160 plus the cost of the clasp. Whereas the lower-quality one might be just $20.

Size/Weight

Size is a very important price factor for freshwater pearls. One of the main reasons the high-quality strand of rice pearls in figure 11.1 retails for only $16 is because the pearls are so small. For the most part, the largest cultured freshwater pearls have come from Japan. That is now changing.

Freshwater pearls prices are generally quoted by weight or by the strand. The gram is probably the most common unit of weight used at the retail level, but some dealers quote prices according to carat weight. Suppliers of large quantities of pearls may use the "momme" which equals 3.75 grams or 18.75 carats. The measurements of pearls are often listed along with their weight as an additional description and means of identification. The size of round freshwater pearls may be expressed by their diameter, measured in millimeters.

Shape

Usually the more round a pearl is, the greater its value. Most freshwater pearls are baroque shaped. Since 1992, though, a lot of semi-round (off-round) and ovalish freshwater pearls have become available. Often they are described as *potato, corn*, and *pea shapes*. Some pearl dealers, however, are opposed to the use of these terms because it makes them sound as if they were farmers rather than gem dealers. Ovalish freshwater pearls are sometimes called *rondels* and may sell for about half the price of the semi-round shapes. These pearls can be used to make impressive looking jewelry pieces that sell for moderate prices. Figure 11.4 is an example. A more close-up view of off-round freshwater pearls is provided in figure 11.3. From a distance, the off-round freshwater pearl strand resembles the Akoya pearl strand, even though the difference in shape is obvious in the photo.

Fig. 11.3 Top: Chinese freshwater strand, bottom: Japanese Akoya pearl strand. Off-round freshwater pearls may sell for 1/3 to 1/10 the price of saltwater pearls of similar luster, size, and color.

Fig. 11.4 Freshwater cultured pearl choker and matching bracelet. *Photo courtesy Shogun Trading Co.*

Baroque freshwater pearls can also vary in price depending on their shape. For example, one dealer has found that the cross is the most expensive shape for cultured freshwater pearls that have no shell nucleus. Good symmetry, too, can make a shape more valuable. In addition, thin shapes tend to sell for less than fatter-looking shapes.

Pearl shapes are determined by a variety of factors:

♦ The type of irritant causing the pearl--mantle tissue, shell bead plus mantle tissue, or in the case of natural pearls parasite or shell piece. Round pearls are more easily cultivated with shell beads. Most freshwater pearl mussels are implanted only with mantle tissue.

♦ The shape of the irritant. Pearl shapes tend to conform to that of the irritant. It's relatively easy to cut mantle tissue in a variety of shapes. This is one of the main reasons freshwater pearls come in so many different shapes which make them ideal for creative jewelry designs.

♦ The length of the cultivation period. Generally the longer the pearl is in the mollusk, the more likely it is to have an irregular shape. With Chinese rice pearls, though, too short of a cultivation period may increase their chances of looking wrinkled and unsymmetrical.

♦ The position of the irritant in the mollusk. If the pearl is in a spot where it can be turned as the mollusk moves around, it may have a greater chance of growing smoothly and symmetrically.

♦ The quality of the irritant. For example, baroque shapes are sometimes the result of flaws in the shell bead nuclei.

♦ The type of mollusk used to culture the pearl. As mentioned earlier, in China, the sankaku mussel is more likely to produce a smoother, more round shape than the kurasu mussel.

Flaws

Obvious flaws such as discolorations, pits, cavities, and rough spots can decrease the value of a pearl considerably, especially if the pearl is otherwise of high quality. Normally,

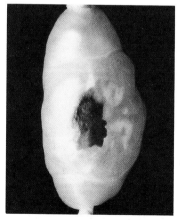

Fig. 11.5 Discoloration & hole on a Chinese "rice" pearl. (9X)

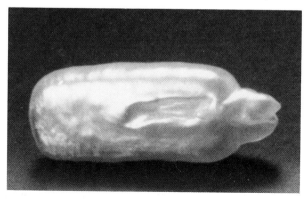

Fig. 11.6 Cavity on an American freshwater pearl. The shell nucleus is about to show through. (3.5X)

though, flaws in freshwater pearls are not very noticeable, due to their baroque shapes. Consequently, flaws tend to have less of an effect on the value of freshwater pearls than on those of saltwater origin. However, if a single freshwater pearl has a large flaw like the one in figure 11.6, this can lower its price significantly.

Color

Freshwater pearls come in a wide variety of body colors--white, pink, orange, yellow, lavender, gray, bronze. Some pearls are even bi-colored. When you ask freshwater pearl dealers what are the most valued body colors, you get a variety of answers. Some of their responses are:

◆ Pink.
◆ White, because that is what's most in demand.
◆ Mauve and metallic.
◆ Colored pearls, due to their rarity, are much more valuable than white pearls.
◆ It doesn't matter what the color is as long as it is not dull and dingy.
◆ Naturally-colored pearls of any color are the most valuable because they are not bleached and processed like white pearls.
◆ Naturally-colored pearls, and the more intense their color, the greater their value. Perhaps true bronze pearls would cost the most because they are so hard to find.
◆ "We price the colors all about the same. Except we add a 5% premium to mauve-colored pearls if they are of high quality because there's a large demand for them in America. We discount our cream-colored freshwater pearls from about 1% to 5%."

What these answers indicate is that the color grading of freshwater pearls is very flexible. Therefore, the best way to know how an individual pearl dealer prices color is to ask.

Most freshwater pearl dealers agree on the following:

◆ The body color does not affect the price of freshwater pearls as much as it does that of saltwater pearls.

◆ The presence of overtone colors such as pink, silver, and blue makes them more valuable. This is because pearls with high luster have overtone colors. On the other hand, a soapy-looking, solid-white color is typical of pearls with a very low luster.

◆ Iridescence (orient) increases the value of pearls. Iridescence and high luster are also interrelated.

Nacre thickness and type of nucleus

Nacre thickness is not as important of a factor in cultured freshwater pearls as it is in saltwater pearls. This is because most freshwater pearls do not have a shell nucleus. When one is present, the nacre tends to be thicker. One of the biggest selling points of freshwater pearls is that they usually have a higher percentage of pearl nacre than their saltwater counterparts.

Cultured freshwater pearls with a shell nucleus often command premium prices. This is because the shell nucleus helps create a pearl which is larger and more regular in shape than one cultured only with mantle tissue.

Place of Origin, Price Factor or Not?

Some members of the pearl industry state that the value of a pearl is based on its quality and size, not on where it comes from. Others feel that the source of a pearl **can** have an impact on its value. Two examples are:

♦ Japanese Biwa pearls tend to be more highly valued than freshwater pearls cultured in other countries.

♦ Saltwater pearls tend to sell for more than freshwater pearls.

We can get a clearer perspective of the gem origin controversy by examining how origin affects the price of other products such as wine. California and France both produce high-quality wines. Yet because France has a longer history of fine wine making, top-quality French wines tend to cost more and enjoy a greater prestige than those from California.

It's not logical that a French wine should be more highly valued than one of equivalent quality from California. Neither is it logical that a gem or garment worn by a famous person should be worth more than one that isn't. Pricing, however, is not always logical. Perceptual and emotional factors also come into play.

When consumers ask about pearl pricing, they want to know how pearls are actually valued, not how they should be valued. In other words, they want to know the reality of the marketplace. Keeping this in mind, let's examine how the origin of freshwater pearls affects their value.

Biwa pearls versus those from other areas

When it comes to cultured freshwater pearls, those from Lake Biwa, Japan have the most prestige. This is because they tend to have a higher, more even luster and smoother surface than many of the pearls cultured in other areas. In addition, the mussels of Lake Biwa have produced larger quantities of high-quality pearls, and they have done so for a longer period of time.

Unfortunately, water pollution has brought the production of Biwa pearls to a halt. Now there are only a couple government experimental farms left. Some pearl dealers still sell Biwa pearls, which they bought before 1990. But for the most part, it's getting hard to find Biwa pearls, and they are starting to become collectors items. The finest strands of Biwa pearls can retail for over $15,000. As they become more scarce, their value could increase.

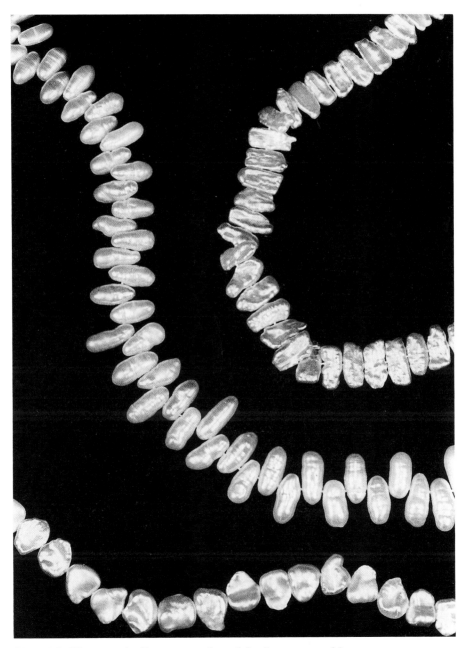

Fig. 11.7 Biwa pearls (Japanese cultured freshwater pearls)

Chinese freshwater pearls are often the lowest priced due to low labor costs. Quality tends to be low, but China has produced a small percentage of high quality pearls. Some of these have been passed off as Biwa pearls. Due to better cultivating techniques, the quality of Chinese pearls has been rapidly improving. This has been particularly evident during the past couple of years. Examine Chinese freshwater pearls with an open mind. You may be pleasantly surprised to find attractive, high-quality pearls at reasonable prices. These prices, however, are rising.

Some distinctive natural and cultured freshwater pearls have been produced in the United States. Compared to Japan and China, however, pearl production has been low. For example, currently, it's hard to find American freshwater pearls in jewelry stores in Los Angeles--a major metropolitan area. Perhaps this will change as pearl production in the US increases.

Freshwater versus saltwater pearls

High-quality saltwater pearls tend to be more highly valued than those that are freshwater. There are some freshwater pearl producers that would disagree. Nevertheless, auction price records and the prices of pearls in jewelry stores indicate that saltwater pearls have commanded the highest prices.

Low prices, though, do not necessarily mean low quality. The $16 strand of Chinese rice pearls in figure 11.1 probably has a better luster, more orient, and a higher percentage of pearl nacre than the majority of cultured saltwater pearls on the market today. Therefore, don't just judge pearls by their price tag. Consider their luster, their color, their uniqueness. If you do, you'll discover that freshwater pearls offer great variety, beauty and value.

Chapter 11 Quiz

Select the correct answer.

1. Most cultured freshwater pearls come from:

a. Japan
b. Korea
c. China
d. USA

2. Most freshwater pearls are:

a. round
b. semi-round
c. oval
d. baroque

3. Which of the following freshwater pearl strands costs the least?

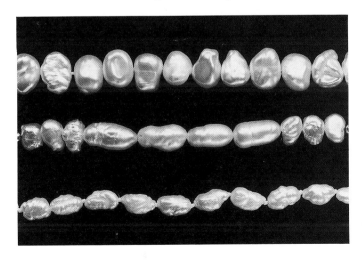

a. The top strand
b. The middle strand
c. The bottom strand

4. What factor affects the price of freshwater pearls the least?

a. luster
b. smoothness
c. size
d. body color

5. What determines the shape of a pearl?

a. The type of nucleus inserted in the mollusk.
b. The position of the nucleus in the mollusk.
c. The length of time the pearl is in the mollusk.
d. All of the above.

6. There is a wide difference of opinion as to what is the best color for a freshwater pearl.

7. The price of freshwater pearls is often quoted according to their weight in grams.

8. A large flaw on a single freshwater pearl can lower its price significantly.

9. Iridescence and overtone colors are desirable characteristics for freshwater pearls.

10.   High-quality freshwater pearls tend to cost more than high-quality saltwater pearls.

Answers:

1. c

2. d

3. c The bottom strand costs less due to its lack of smooth surfaces and smaller size. It also has a much lower luster, which is hard to determine from the photograph. The retail cost of this lower strand is about $2 as compared to $160 for the top strand.

4. d

5. d.

6. T

7. T

8. T

9. T

10. F   Freshwater pearls tend to cost less.

12

Imitation or Not?

Imagine a rosary-bead maker watching a fish being scaled in a basin of water. The water has colorful, pearly reflections which seem to form as the fish scales dissolve. The bead maker then gets the idea to filter the water, recover the pearly substance from it and mix it with a kind of varnish. Later he coats the inside surface of a hollow glass bead with the pearly mixture, fills the bead with wax, and what's the result? The birth of the modern-day imitation pearl.

This occurred in France in the 17th century. Jacquin was the name of the rosary-bead maker. And **essence of orient** (or **pearl essence**) is the name of the pearly mixture he discovered. Today, the finest imitation pearls usually have several coats of essence of orient.

Types of Imitation Pearls

Even though pearl essence is used to make many of the best imitation pearls, such as Majorica pearls. Imitations come in a variety of types. The main ones are:

♦ **Hollow glass beads containing wax**. These pearls, made by the same process as Jacquin's, are most likely to be found in antique jewelry.

♦ **Solid glass beads**. Majorica imitation pearls are an example of this type. They may be covered with as many as forty coats of pearl essence and hand polished between each coat. Imitation glass pearls are also coated with other substances such as synthetic pearl essence, plastic, cellulose, and lacquer.

♦ **Plastic beads**. These may have the same type coatings as the glass type. Plastic imitation pearl necklaces sometimes hang poorly due to their light weight.

♦ **Mother-of-pearl shell beads.** These are coated with the same substances as plastic and glass imitations. A coating made from powdered mother of pearl and synthetic resin may also be used. One company calls such beads **semi-cultured**. This is just a misleading term for imitation. Powdered mother-of-pearl coatings are not new. Centuries ago, American Indians produced imitation pearls by applying such coatings to clay beads and then baking them.

Occasionally, people sell uncoated mother-of-pearl beads as pearls or they describe them as very valuable. In the Pacific Islands, you can buy mother-of-pearl shell bead necklaces from the natives for a couple of dollars. Some of the better ones cost more.

Simulated and **faux pearls** (the French term for fake pearls) are two other terms used to designate imitation pearls. These pearls can be distinguished from natural and cultured pearls with the tests below.

Tests that Require No Equipment Other Than a Magnifier

Tooth Test

Rub the pearls **lightly** along the biting edge of your upper front teeth. If they feel gritty or sandy, it's likely they are cultured or natural pearls. If they feel smooth, they are probably imitations.

There are a few problems with this test. It's not the most sanitary test. It may scratch the pearls, if done improperly. And it doesn't always work. There are some imitation pearls that feel gritty. Also, according to the Fall 1991 issue of *Gems & Gemology* (p. 176), real pearls may feel smooth. A cultured pearl sent to the GIA New York laboratory gave a smooth tooth test reaction because the surface had been polished. Therefore, don't rely solely on the tooth test. If you use it, combine it with the magnification tests listed below.

Surface Magnification Test

Examine the surface of the pearl with a 10-power magnifier such as a loupe. If it looks grainy, like a photo taken at an ISO of 1000 and above, there's a good chance it's an imitation (fig. 12.1). Pearls normally look unusually fine grained, like a photo taken at an ISO of 100 and below. Sometimes, though, dirt or pits on a pearl may make it seem to have a grainy appearance. Occasionally, too, freshwater and South Sea pearls may look a little grainy, but other surface characteristics mentioned in this section can prove they are not imitation.

If you have access to a microscope, also examine the surface at the highest possible magnification. At 50 power and above, a rough, pitted surface like the one in figure 12.2 means it's an imitation. Gas bubbles may also be present.

A surface with tiny, crooked lines giving it a scaly, maze-like appearance is characteristic of cultured and natural pearls (fig. 12.4). These scaly lines are not always evident at first. The surface may look smooth except for the flaws as in figure 12.3. Try using a strong, bare, direct light such as a fiber-optic; and shine it on the pearl from various angles to find the scaly lines. It's curious that pearls, which feel gritty to the teeth, can look so smooth under high magnification; whereas imitations, which feel smooth, tend to look coarse and rough. However, the less smooth an imitation is, the rougher it looks. On pearls, it's the "scaly-line" ridges that cause their gritty feel.

The best way to learn what the surface of pearls and imitations looks like under magnification is to examine many examples of each. When you can recognize how distinctive their surface textures are, you won't need to do any of the other tests to spot an imitation pearl.

Fig. 12.1 Note the grainy surface texture of this large imitation mabe pearl at 10-power magnification.

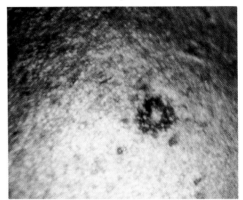

Fig. 12.2 Note how rough and pitted the surface of this imitation pearl looks at 64-power magnification

Fig. 12.3 Note how smooth the surface of this Akoya cultured pearl is at 64-power magnification compared to the imitation in fig. 12.2. Due to the lighting, scaly lines are not visible.

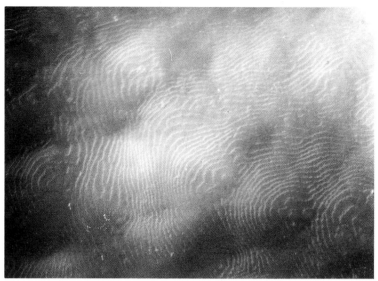

Fig. 12.4 Surface of a cultured black pearl at 64-power magnification. Note the scaly, terraced, maze-like patterns. They prove this is either a cultured or natural pearl. Due to the flattish baroque shape of this pearl, these patterns are visible with the fluorescent microscope light. On a round pearl like the one in figure 12.3, a strong, bare, pin-point light such as a fiberoptic may be necessary.

Drill Hole Test

Examine the drill hole area with a magnifier of 10-power or above. (On some pearls, it may be hard to see into their drill hole.) Cultured pearls tend to show the following characteristics (figs. 12.5 - 12.8):

♦ There is often a clear dividing line between the pearl nacre and shell bead nucleus.
♦ The edges of the drill holes are often sharp and well defined. But when the nacre wears away it can leave the holes looking jagged and rough as in figures 12.7 and 12.8.
♦ The drill holes tend to be like a straight cylinder.
♦ The pearl nacre coating is normally thicker than the coating of imitations.

Imitation pearls tend to show these characteristics (figs 12.9 - 12.12):

♦ There is normally no dark dividing line between the coating and the rest of the pearl. Occasionally, one may see a kind of line, but the other characteristics of the drill hole will look like those of imitations. If you are in doubt, look at the drill hole opening on the other side of the pearl and on other pearls of the strand.

♦ The coating around the edges of the drill holes may have flaked off, making it look ragged or uneven.

♦ The drill holes may be angled outward at the surface of the pearl. Other times the drill holes may round inward at the surface and bow outward inside the pearl.

♦ The coating often looks like a thin coat of shiny paint. The thinness can be seen at the edge of the drill hole or around bare areas which expose the inner bead.

♦ Rounded ridges may have formed around the drill hole (figs. 12.11 & 12.12).

♦ If the bead is made of glass, its glassy luster may be apparent.

Flaw Test

Examine the pearls for flaws. If they appear flawless, this is a sign they are imitation. Also note the types of flaws present. Many of those found on cultured pearls look different from those on imitations. If you examine pearl flaws with a 10-power magnifier whenever possible, it will be easier for you to recognize them. Chapter 6 shows examples of pearl flaws.

Overtone Test

Look for overtone colors in the pearls. Imitations frequently have none, and when they do, the overtones all tend to look the same. It's normal for cultured and natural pearls to have overtones, and these overtones often vary in color within the strand (color photo 12a).

Besides examining the overtones with the naked eye, also look at them with a loupe. The magnification makes the coloring differ-ences between imitations and real pearls even more apparent.

Matching Test

Note the shape, luster, size, and color of the pearls. Imitations often seem perfectly matched, whereas there tend to be variations among the pearls on cultured or natural strands.

Heaviness Test

Bounce the pearls in your hand. If they feel unusually light, they're most likely made of plastic or filled with wax. Solid glass beads may feel heavier or about the same as cultured and natural pearls.

Clasp Test

Is the clasp made of silver, steel, or a gold plated metal. This is a warning sign that the strand may be imitation. But good pearls are occasionally strung with cheap clasps and imitation ones with expensive clasps.

Price Test

Is the price of the pearls unbelievably low? If so, they may be imitation or have hardly any pearl nacre. Jewelers can't stay in business if they sell their pearls below their cost.

Drill Holes of Cultured Pearls

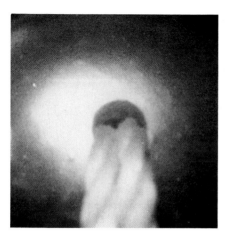

Fig. 12.5 Note the sharp, well-defined edges of the drill hole. The line between the nacre and nucleus is hard to see due to the thickness of the nacre and the small size of the drill hole.

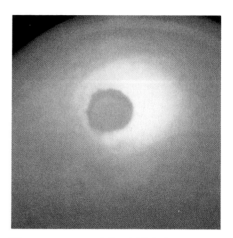

Fig. 12.6 A straight drill hole and the separation line between the core and thin nacre indicate this is a cultured pearl.

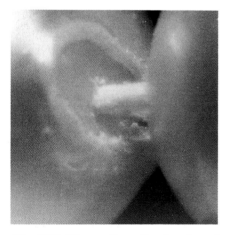

Fig. 12.7 The coating of both cultured and imitation pearls can wear away at the drill hole and look ragged. But pearl nacre has a distinctive appearance and is usually thicker than that of imitations.

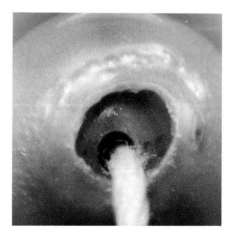

Fig. 12.8 The nacre has separated from the core in this pearl. A separation like this would not be characteristic of an imitation pearl.

Drill Holes of Imitation Pearls

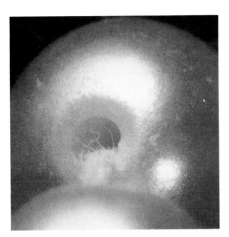

Fig. 12.9 The very thin ragged coating, angled-in drill hole, and lack of dividing line between core and coating indicate this is an imitation.

Fig. 12.10 The distinctive appearance of the coating, lack of dividing line, and the drill-hole which bows outward inside (not visible in photo) mean this is an imitation.

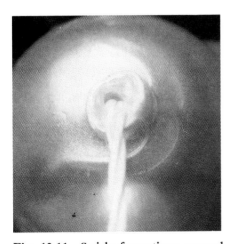

Fig. 12.11 Swirly formations around the drill hole, very thin glossy coating, and lack of dividing line are clues this coated mother-of-pearl shell bead is an imitation.

Fig. 12.12 Another imitation with a mother-of-pearl shell bead nucleus.

Other Tests

X-radiograph Test

An x-ray photo called an **x-radiograph** is taken of the pearls. Imitations are opaque to x-rays making them look solid white on the negative and solid black on the positive print made of it. Cultured and natural pearls are semitransparent to x-rays and usually look grayish. Since imitations pearls can be positively identified with other tests, x-raying them is usually a waste of money. There is, however, a major advantage to the x-ray test. It's quicker to x-ray an entire strand at once than to test each pearl in it individually.

Refractometer Test

The "pearl" is placed on a refractometer (an instrument that measures a gem's **refractive index**--the degree to which light is bent as it passes through the gem). A pearl will generally have a low reading of 1.530 and a high one of 1.685. The numerical difference between these two readings is .155 and is called its **birefringence**. Pearls have an unusually high birefringence compared to other gems. This causes a blinking and pink effect when their refractive index is read through a rotating Polaroid filter. The GIA Pearls Course states that the presence of this "birefringent blink" is proof a pearl is not an imitation.

The refractive index of some imitations can also prove they are not cultured or natural pearls. For example, the Majorica imitation pearls the GIA tested for their Fall 1990 article in *Gems and Gemology* had a refractive index of 1.48, which was a conclusive means of identification.

Distinguishing between imitations and pearls is not hard. Even laypeople can learn how to detect imitations with a loupe, but they do need practice. What's hard is to distinguish cultured pearls from those that are natural. This will be the focus of the next chapter.

Chapter 12 Quiz

Select the correct answer.

1. A strand feels light in weight. There's a good chance it consists of:

a. Cultured pearls with thin nacre
b. Natural pearls
c. Plastic imitation pearls
d. Solid glass imitation pearls

2. Which of the following tests can prove that your pearls are not imitations?

a. The tooth test.
b. The surface magnification test
c. The overtone test
d. All of the above

3. Which is a typical characteristic of the drill holes of imitation pearls.

a. a clear dividing line between the coating and the core of the "pearl."
b. a straight hole with well defined edges
c. a thick coating of lacquer, paint, or pearl essence.
d. none of the above

4. Which of the following is an imitation pearl?

a. A semi-cultured pearl
b. A Majorica pearl
c. A faux pearl
d. b and c
e. a, b, and c

5. Under 10-power magnification the surface of an imitation pearl tends to:

a. look grainy
b. show scaly maze-like patterns
c. appear striped
d. none of the above

6. If a jeweler can't tell that the pearls you are wearing are imitation or not this means:

a. He's a lousy jeweler.
b. He needs to read *The Pearl Buying Guide.*
c. He must have poor eyesight.
d. All of the above
e. None of the above.

7. Which of the two strands below is most likely imitation. Explain your answer.

a. top strand
b. bottom strand

Answers:

1. c

2. b   The results of the tooth and overtone tests are good indications but they don't provide positive proof. Some imitations feel gritty to the teeth and have overtones that vary. Thin-nacre pearls may have no overtones, and polished pearls may give a smooth tooth-test reaction.

3. d   The coating on imitation pearls tends to be very thin, not thick.

4. e   Majorica, faux, and semi-cultured pearls are all imitations.

5. a

6. e   Even pearl specialists can be fooled by imitations, particularly when viewing pearls from a distance. In some cases, they may need to examine the pearls under magnification to determine that they are imitation.

7. a   The top strand is in fact imitation. It would be hard to find natural or cultured pearls that are so round and perfectly matched (some pearl strands, however, are exceptionally well-matched).

     Note the slight irregularities of shape, size, luster, and depth of color in the bottom strand. This is typical of cultured pearls. A natural pearl strand would tend to be even more irregular. Variations among pearls on a strand do not prove they are real. Sometimes imitations are poorly matched.

13

Natural or Cultured?

In 1917, Cartier bought their building in New York with two strands of natural pearls valued at a million dollars. In 1957, the pearls were sold at auction for $157,000. Perhaps one of the main reasons for this drop in price, was the introduction of the cultured pearl, which decreased the demand for natural pearls.

Prices of natural pearls have risen considerably since 1957, but they still don't match those of the early 1900's. Nevertheless, natural pearls are still worth a lot more than cultured pearls. Therefore, it's important to be able to distinguish between them. X-ray tests are generally required to prove a pearl is natural, but they are costly. Other tests can help you determine a pearl is cultured and thereby save you the expense of an x-ray. These tests are listed below. Keep in mind that almost all the pearls produced today are cultured. You are most likely to find natural pearls in antique pieces. (Whole pearls were not cultured before the 1900's.) However, the natural pearls in antique jewelry may have been replaced with cultured ones.

Tests a Layperson Can Do

Drill Hole Test   Look inside the drill hole with a 10-power magnifier. If you can see a dark dividing line separating the nacre from a pearl bead nucleus, the pearl is cultured. Natural pearls may show a series of growth lines, which get more yellow or brown towards the center of the pearl. A black deposit at the center of a white pearl can be a sure sign the pearl is natural. (From *Gem Testing* by B W Anderson, page 219.)

Also note the size of the drill hole. The drill holes of natural pearls are rarely larger than .04 mm (.016 inch). Those of cultured pearls tend to measure .06 mm (.024 inch). (From *Pearls* by Jean Taburiaux, page 193.)

Shape Test   Do the pearls look perfectly round? If so, then it's likely they are cultured. Natural pearls tend to have at least slightly irregular shapes, even though a few are round. This test is only an indication. It is not proof.

Blink Test   Hold the strand near the front edge of a strong desk lamp. The light should shine through the pearls but not in your eyes. Rotate the strand. If the pearls blink from light to dark as they are turned, this indicates they are cultured and have a thin coating of nacre (imitation pearls with mother-of-pearl shell-bead centers may also blink). The dark areas result when mother of pearl layers on the shell bead block the light. Figure 13.1 shows light and dark views of shell beads with transmitted light. Thin-nacre cultured pearls may show only one view when rotated. In other words, they don't necessarily blink.

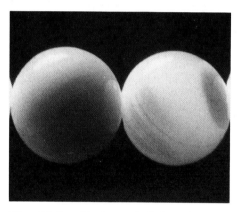

Fig. 13.1   Dark and light views of mother-of-pearl shell beads

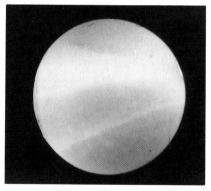

Fig. 13.2 Stripes in a thin-nacre cultured pearl viewed with transmitted light

Stripe Test   As you rotate the pearls with strong light shining through them, look for curved lines and stripes (fig. 13.2). These are the layers of the shell beads. If they are visible, the nacre is very thin and the pearls are cultured. Not all shell bead nuclei show stripes, though. This can be seen in figure 13.3. Keep in mind that imitation pearls with shell-bead centers can also display this banded effect. Natural pearls, however, will not look striped.

Color Test   Examine the color. Cultured pearls often have a faint greenish tint, unlike natural pearls. Some people say the color of cultured pearls tends to be less even than that of natural pearls. Color can only suggest a pearl might be cultured. It is not proof.

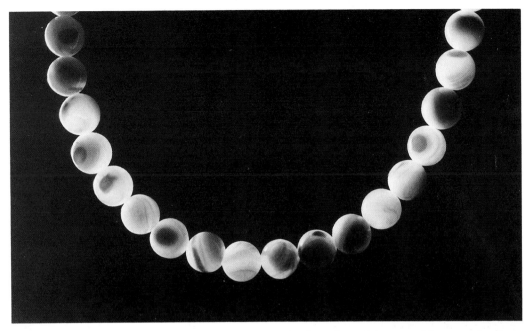

Fig. 13.3 Mother-of-pearl shell beads (the core of cultured pearls) seen with transmitted light

Other Tests

X-radiograph Test

This is the most reliable way to distinguish between natural and cultured pearls. On an x-radiograph negative, cultured pearls usually show a clear separation between core and nacre. Plus, their core normally looks lighter than the nacre coating. X-rayed natural pearls tend to either look the same tone throughout or get darker in their center. A mantle tissue nucleus will look like a very dark, irregular-shaped void.

The disadvantage of x-ray tests is that it can cost between $100 and $300 to have them done, and there are few gem labs that have the required equipment.

X-ray Fluorescence Test

This test is used in combination with an x-radiograph to provide the added information of whether the pearl is freshwater or saltwater. Natural saltwater pearls rarely fluoresce to x-rays, whereas natural freshwater pearls have a fairly strong x-ray fluorescence, usually moderate to strong yellowish white. (Cultured saltwater pearls with a freshwater shell-bead nucleus fluoresce moderately strong to very weak, depending on nacre thickness.)

Non-nucleus cultured Biwa pearls have a distinct fluorescent color and a longer phosphorescence (after glow) than cultured saltwater pearls, which show a greenish yellow fluorescence. Cultured pearls dyed with silver salts show usually show no fluorescence.

Specific Gravity Test   The pearls are placed in a liquid that has a specific gravity of 2.71 (purchased at gem instrument stores and tested with a piece of pure calcite). The majority of natural pearls will float and others will sink slowly. Most cultured pearls with shell nuclei will sink quickly since they tend to be heavier than natural pearls. The biggest problem with this test is that the heavy liquid may damage the pearls, especially if the pearls are left in it too long.

UV Fluorescence Test   The pearls are placed under long-wave ultraviolet light and compared to known samples of cultured and natural pearls. In his book *Gemstones* (p. 448), G F Herbert Smith mentions how cultured pearls can display a peculiar greenish fluorescence which differs markedly from the sky-blue effect of many natural pearls. He points out that this is not an infallible test because natural pearls can also have a greenish fluorescence, particularly if they are from waters adjacent to those of cultured pearls. Consequently, gem labs with x-ray equipment do not use this test. However, this test may help those without x-ray machines. Seeing a unique sky-blue fluorescence under LW UV light instead of a greenish-yellow glow may serve as an additional incentive to pay for an x-ray to test for natural origin. (This test is also mentioned in Webster's *Gems* on page 539.)

If the pearls are of good quality and preliminary tests suggest they may be natural, then it's advisable to have them x-rayed. Appraisers and jewelers can send them to the appropriate labs for you. Some of the gem labs that have the facilities to do x-ray tests are listed below. Jewelers in your area may know of others.

Asian Institute of Gemological Sciences
12/1 Surasak Road
Bangkok, 10500 Thailand
662 237-3600-3

Gem Testing Laboratory of Great Britain
27 Greville Street (Saffron Hill Entrance)
London EC1N8SU
Tel. (071) 405-3351

GIA Gem Trade Laboratory, Inc.
1630 Stewart Street
Santa Monica, CA 90404
Tel. (310) 828-3148
        or
580 Fifth Ave.
New York, NY 10036
Tel. (212) 221-5858

Gubelin Gemmological Laboratory
Maihofstrasse 102
CH-6000 Lucerne 9   Switzerland
Tel. 041/26 17 17

The Laboratory
2 Place de la Bourse
75002 Paris

Swiss Gemmological Institute
Lowenstrasse 17
CH-8001 Zurich
Tel. 01-211-24-71

Chapter 13 Quiz

Select the correct answer:

1. As you rotate a strand of "pearls" under a light, they blink and/or show faint stripes. This indicates the "pearls" are:

a. imitation
b. cultured
c. natural
d. imitation or cultured

2. You are examining a "pearl." Its drill hole looks ragged and some of the coating has peeled off around it. This means the "pearl" is:

a. imitation.
b. cultured.
c. either imitation or cultured.
d. either cultured or natural.

3. Which of the following can help a gemologist distinguish between natural and cultured pearls?

a. An X-ray test
b. A refractometer test
c. A hardness test
d. All of the above

4. Natural pearls:

a. tend to be very round
b. tend to have greenish overtones
c. tend to have smaller drill holes than cultured pearls and imitations.
d. None of the above.

5. An appraiser tells you your pearls must be sent to another lab for an x-ray in order to determine if they are natural. The appraiser:

a. is not very competent.
b. has a poorly equipped lab.
c. is trying to make extra money on unnecessary lab tests.
d. is correct, and this does not mean that he/she is a poor appraiser.

True or False?

6. If an antique pearl piece was made before 1900, the pearls in it are natural.

7. Most cultured pearls tend to be slightly heavier than natural pearls.

8. Natural pearls tend to have irregular shapes.

9. If a pearl does not blink to show stripes when it is rotated under an overhead light, then it is not cultured.

10. The nacre of cultured pearls has a different chemical composition than that of natural pearls.

Answers:

1. d   Imitation pearls with shell cores and translucent coatings can show stripes like those of thin-nacre cultured pearls.

2. c.   The coating can peel off of both imitation and cultured pearls leaving their core exposed.

3. a

4. c

5. d

6. F   When natural pearls fall out of antique pieces, they are often replaced with cultured pearls or imitations.

7. T

8. T

9. F   Cultured pearls with thick nacre or with no shell nucleus normally don't blink or show stripes. Not all cultured pearls with thin nacre display the blinking or striped effect.

10. F

14

Choosing the Clasp

Mrs. Kirk was proud of the beautiful pearl necklace her daughter had given her, but she hardly ever wore it. She had arthritis, and that made it hard for her to fasten and undo the clasp. Since she lived by herself, nobody was around to help her put on the necklace, so it was easier to leave it in her jewelry box.

Mrs. Kirk is not alone. Complicated or hard-to-fasten clasps keep a lot of people from wearing some of their jewelry pieces. This could be prevented with a bit of forethought. When choosing a clasp, consider:

♦ How secure is it?
♦ How easy is it to open?
♦ How versatile is it?
♦ How much does it cost?

Determine what is most important to you about the clasp because normally, some compromises will have to be made. For example, to get a clasp that is easy to open, you may have to accept less security.

Fig. 14.1 Fish-hook clasp

Fig. 14.2 Push clasp

Fig. 14.3 Screw clasp (mystery clasp)

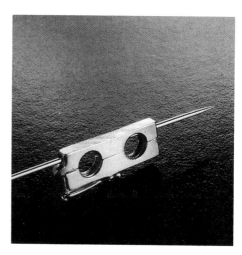

Fig. 14.4 Pin pearl adaptor

Listed below are three basic pearl clasps along with their advantages and disadvantages.

◆ **Fish-hook clasp** (fig 14.1): This is a popular clasp because it's inexpensive and secure. It may be silver, gold, or gold-plated. The main drawback of the fish-hook clasp is that it can be hard to undo, especially for someone with arthritis.

◆ **Push clasp** (fig. 14.2): The main advantage of this clasp, is that it is fairly easy to open, even with one hand when it's used on a bracelet. It's also relatively inexpensive. Unfortunately, it is not as secure as some of the other clasps.

◆ **The screw clasp** (fig. 14.3): This clasp can add versatility when it is inserted in pearls to form a **hidden or mystery clasp**. For example, a long strand of pearls with three mystery clasps can be unscrewed and turned into a bracelet and two smaller necklaces.

Mystery clasps are fairly easy to open and close and are secure, provided they are screwed in all the way and are not stripped out. They tend to cost a little more than the fish-hook and push clasps.

Sometimes the string breaks on necklaces with mystery clasps. This can happen when people unscrew the clasp incorrectly or when they can't find the clasp and try to unscrew the necklace in a spot where there is no clasp. This problem can be avoided by having the jeweler show you how to find and open the clasp. When undoing it, be sure to grasp at least two pearls on either side of the clasp. Turn them together as a unit. Don't twist the string.

There are a wide variety of clasps besides these three basic ones. Some are both decorative and versatile (figs. 14.5 & 14.6).

Fig. 14.5 A hinged clasp, trademarked **Applaudere** by A & Z Pearls Inc. Note how each end of the strand is attached to a clasp. The pair of clasps can be fastened over any of the pearls on the necklace allowing a variety of styles from a single strand of pearls. See Chapter 15 for examples.

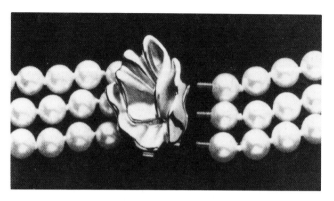

Fig. 14.6 A clasp that can be worn to the side, front or back with one to three strands. It forms part of a pearl linking system which allows a rope-length strand to also be worn as a three strand choker or an opera length necklace. This system is trade-marked **Multipearls** by Mastoloni Cultured Pearls. Photo courtesy Frank Mastoloni & Sons, Inc.

Many clasps are jewelry pieces by themselves and are best worn to the side or in the front. Figure 14.5 is an example of this.

Sometimes accessories are used to accent pearls with plain clasps. With the **pin pearl adaptor** (see figure 4.4), a pin can be attached to two strands to look like a decorative clasp or it can be worn as a pearl shortener (see fig. 15.7 in the next chapter). The pin pearl adaptor slides on to any pin and then can be closed over two strands of pearls.

One of the most popular pearl accessories is the **pearl enhancer**. It is a pendant which can be attached to a strand of pearls, as well to as a gold chain or bead necklace. The top of the pearl enhancer has a hinged clasp which closes over the necklace between two pearls (see fig. 15.14 in the next chapter).

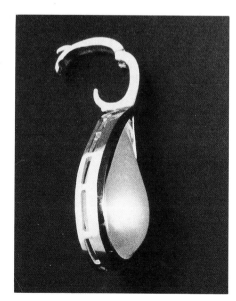

Fig. 14.7 Pearl enhancer

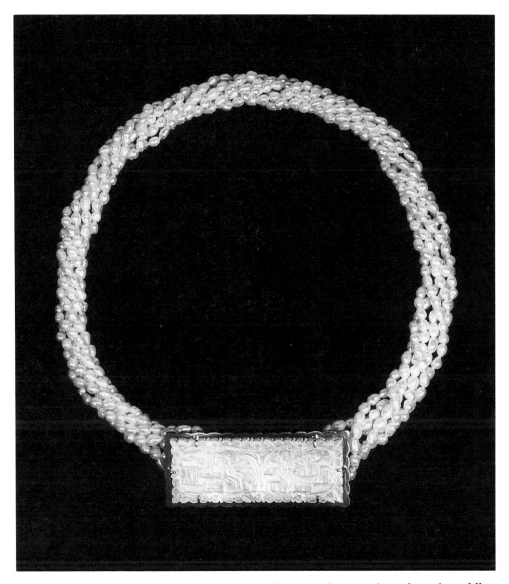

Fig. 14.8 Freshwater pearl necklace clasped with an antique mother-of-pearl gambling chip. The piece portrays a scene from Chinese life and was probably carved during the 19th century.

There are many other types and styles of clasps besides the ones pictured in this chapter. You can see them on display in jewelry stores. No matter what type you choose do not take a necklace or bracelet home without first having the salesperson show you how to fasten and unfasten the clasp. Then try doing it at least two times by yourself. Some clasps are like puzzles, and if you try to figure them out on your own, you could damage the clasp and/or the pearls.

If your budget is limited, put your money into the pearls first, rather than into a fancy clasp. You can always upgrade the clasp later on. When buying a pearl necklace, your first priority should be the pearls.

15

Versatile Ways to Wear a Strand of Pearls

There are no other gems that offer more versatility than pearls. Queen Elizabeth I of England made the most of this feature. She wore yards of them as necklaces hanging down as far her knees. She had them threaded in her wigs, embroidered in her clothing, and set in her crown and other regal jewelry. You can also enjoy the versatility of pearls. The styles listed below and shown in figures 15.1 - 15.15 can be made with just one opera-length necklace (about 28 to 34 inches) and a pair of hinged clasps like the Applaudere, pictured in figure 14.5 of the previous chapter.

♦ A single strand of adjustable lengths with the clasp in the back (fig. 15.1)
♦ A double strand on one side and single on the other (fig. 15.2)
♦ A double strand choker or princess necklace (fig. 15.3)
♦ A single strand clasped to form one "chain" hanging in the front. (fig. 15.4). An opera-length strand can be worn as a belt in the same manner.
♦ A single strand tied or knotted in front to form two "chains" hanging in the front (fig. 15.5)
♦ Double strand in back and triple strand in the front (fig. 15.6)
♦ A single strand looped in the front with a pearl shortener (fig. 15.7)
♦ Double strand in front and single strand in back (fig. 15.8)
♦ Double strand looped together in front (fig. 15.9)
♦ Single strand with a clasp to the side or in the center (fig. 15.10)
♦ Single strand knotted in the front (fig. 15.11). Dresses with low V-backs can be accented with a rope-length strand tied like this in the back.

Fig. 15.1

Fig. 15.2

Fig. 15.3

Fig. 15.4

Fig. 15.5

Fig. 15.6

Fig. 15.7

Fig. 15.8

Fig. 15.9

Fig. 15.10

Fig. 15.11

Fig. 15.12

Fig. 15.13

Fig. 15.14

Fig. 15.15

Fig. 15.16 Photo courtesy of the Cultured Pearl Associations of America & Japan

Fig.15.17 Photo courtesy Cultured Pearl Associations of America & Japan

Fig. 15.18 Photo courtesy Cultured Pearl Associations of America & Japan

- Double strand twisted and clasped in the back (fig. 15.12)
- Double strand with a loop hanging in the front like a pendant (fig. 15.13)
- Double or single strand with a pearl enhancer (detachable pendant) (fig. 15.14)
- Multi-strand bracelet (fig. 15.15)
- Wrapped in the hair around a chignon or ponytail (fig. 15.16)
- Attached to the side with a pin and hanging asymmetrically
- Pinned across a V-back dress or sweater

Other options are possible with longer or multi-piece necklaces. For example:

- Attached to the shoulders of a dress as in figure 15.17
- Looped through button-holes or openings in clothing as in figure 15.18
- Wrapped around a hat

These are only some of the ways pearls can be worn. Use your imagination and you'll discover many more.

16

Caring for Your Pearls

Which of the following is hardest and which is softest?

- ♦ A pearl
- ♦ An opal
- ♦ Pure gold
- ♦ A tooth

The hardest is the opal. It has a hardness of 5 1/2 - 6 1/2 on the Moh's scale, which rates the relative hardness of materials from 1 to 10. (The 10 rating of a diamond is the highest, but a diamond is over 1000 times harder than an opal.) **Hardness** is a material's resistance to scratching and abrasions.

The softest of the four materials above is pure gold, which has a hardness of 2 - 2 1/2. When alloyed with other metals, the hardness of gold increases, but it is still a relatively soft metal.

Tooth enamel has a hardness of 5, and a pearl has a range of 2 1/2 - 4. In other words, a pearl is a relatively soft material.

Knowing how soft a pearl is can help us understand why pearls should not be tossed on top of or next to other gems in a jewelry box. Knowing that a tooth is harder than a pearl helps us understand why the "tooth test" for identifying imitations should only be done very lightly or else avoided. The basic concept of hardness is that a harder material will scratch one that is softer.

Besides being soft, pearls are easily damaged by chemicals or eaten away by acids such as vinegar and lemon juice. Heat can turn pearls brown or dry them out and make them crack.

One advantage of pearls is they are fairly tough considering their softness. In his book *Pearls*, Alexander Farn relates how jewelers and pearl merchants of old would separate imitation pearls from real ones by having footmen stomp on them. Those that were crushed were imitation. The natural pearls normally would resist such blows. Cultured pearls, especially those with thin nacre, are not this durable. Therefore, it's best to avoid dropping or crushing them.

Cleaning Your Pearls

The softness of pearls and their low resistance to heat and chemicals mean that special precautions must be taken when cleaning them. Keep in mind the following guidelines:

♦ Do not use commercial jewelry cleaners on pearls unless the labels say they are safe for pearls. Many of them contain ammonia, which will cause deterioration.

♦ Never clean pearls in an ultrasonic cleaner. It can damage the pearls and wash out the color if the pearls have been dyed.

♦ Never steam-clean pearls. Heat can harm them.

♦ Never use detergents, bleaches, powdered cleansers, baking soda, or ammonia-based cleaners on pearls.

♦ Do not use toothbrushes, scouring pads, or abrasive materials to clean pearls. They can scratch their surface. If there's a lump of dirt that can't be rubbed off with a soft cloth, try using your fingernails. They have a hardness of only 2 1/2 or less.

Cleaning pearls is not complicated. After you wear them, just wipe them off with a soft cloth or chamois which can be dry or damp. This will prevent the dirt from accumulating and keep perspiration, which is slightly acidic, from eating away at the pearl nacre.

If the pearls have not been kept clean and are very dirty, they can be cleaned by your jeweler or they can be washed in water and a mild soap such as Ivory or Lux liquid (some liquid soaps, such as Dawn, can damage pearls) and cleaned with a soft cloth. Pay attention to the areas around the drill holes where dirt may tend to collect. After washing them, lay the pearls flat in a moist kitchen towel to dry. After the towel is dry, they should be dry. Do not wear pearls when their string is wet. Wet strings stretch and attract dirt which is hard to remove. Likewise do not hang pearls to dry.

Storing Your Pearls

Pearls are composed of about 2 to 4% water along with calcium carbonate and an organic binder called conchiolin. If the pearls become dehydrated, they can get brittle and crack. Consequently, they should not be kept near heaters or in places that get strong sunlight, such as on a window sill. Safe deposit boxes can be unusually dry, so if you ever store pearls there, try to take them out occasionally and expose them to humidity or moisture. Sealed plastic bags are not the best place for pearls. They can keep them from breathing and getting moisture.

Since pearls are soft, they should be kept in something that will protect them from scratches. Jewelry pouches or cloth bags are ideal. Pearls can also be wrapped in soft material and kept wherever convenient. Jewelry boxes may be handy, but they are also the first place burglars look.

Having Your Pearls Strung

Pearl necklaces can stretch with time and the string can get dirty and weak. Thus, they should be restrung periodically--about once a year, but that depends on how often they are worn. Fine pearls should be strung with silk and with knots tied between each pearl. This prevents them from rubbing against each other and from scattering if the string should break.

Occasionally pearls are strung with gold beads. According to a Los Angeles pearl stringer, gold turns pearls ivory-colored and coral black, and this is a permanent discoloration. Therefore, it's not advisable to string expensive pearls with gold beads.

Miscellaneous Tips

♦ Take your pearls off when applying cosmetics, hair sprays, and perfume. These beauty aids are made of chemicals and acids which can harm your pearls.

♦ Take your pearls off when showering or swimming. It's not good to get the string wet, plus the chlorine or soap can damage the pearls. Pearl rings should be taken off when washing your hands or the dishes. Put the ring in a protective container or safe spot where it won't accidentally fall in the drain or get lost.

♦ When selecting pearl jewelry, check to see if the pearl is mounted securely. Preferably, the pearl will have been drilled and glued to a post on the mounting, especially if it is a ring. Otherwise, the pearl may come loose. If the pearl is flawless, a drill hole could lower it's value. In such a case, it would be safer to set the undrilled pearl in a pin, pendant or earring than in a ring.

♦ When taking off a pearl ring, grasp the shank or metal part rather than the pearl. This will prevent the pearl from loosening and coming into contact with skin oil on your hand.

♦ Avoid wearing pearls with rough fabrics such as Shetland wool. They can scratch the pearls.

♦ About every six months, have a jewelry professional verify that the pearls on your jewelry are securely mounted or that the string is still good. Many jewelers will do this free of charge, and they'll be happy to answer your questions regarding the care of your jewelry.

Chapter 16 Quiz

True or False?

1. The best way to clean pearls is to put them in an ultrasonic cleaner.

2. You should take your pearls off when you shower or go swimming.

3. Decorative gold beads strung between pearls never damage or discolor the pearls.

4. The pearl is an ideal gem for an every-day wedding ring.

5. You should put on make-up and perfume before you put on your pearls.

6. Pearls should **not** be worn when their string is wet.

7. It doesn't matter if hair spray gets on your pearls because the lacquer makes them more lustrous and serves as a protective coating.

8. After wearing pearls, it's a good idea to wipe them off with a chamois.

Answers:

1. F   Pearls should never be placed in ultrasonic cleaners.

2. T

3. F

4. F

5. T

6. T

7. F

8. T

17

Finding a Good Buy

Charlene is in a jewelry store. She's telling Scott, the owner, that she wants a nice pearl necklace but she's on a very limited budget. Although she's looked elsewhere, she hasn't found a strand she likes at a good price.

Scott first shows her a strand of Japanese saltwater pearls. He points out that the pearls are round and well matched, but their pearl coating is very thin. Consequently the strand is not a good choice for long-term, every-day wear. He adds that the round white saltwater pearls in her price range tend to have a thin coating, no matter where they're sold. Charlene wonders why no other jewelers ever mentioned this to her.

Scott then shows her some strands of freshwater pearls and asks her to compare them to the first strand. They're a lot more lustrous. Then he helps Charlene pick out an affordable strand that looks good on her. Charlene is impressed with Scott's selection of pearls and his straightforward approach. She plans on coming back to him for the rest of her jewelry needs, including a strand of good saltwater pearls when she has more to spend.

Jeff wants to buy his wife some pearls for their 30th anniversary, since this is the traditional gift. He and his wife have been happily married for many years, so he wants the pearls to be of unusually fine quality. Jeff has read *The Pearl Buying Guide* and is aware that pearls have many subtle quality differences. He realizes he will need some expert help.

As he shops, he discovers that he knows more than a lot of the salespeople. Eventually, Jeff finds somebody who is really knowledgeable about pearls--Sandy, a college student who works part-time to pay her way through school. Sandy has always had a keen interest in gems, especially pearls, and she takes advantage of every opportunity to learn as much as possible about them.

Jeff already knows that he wants either pink or white saltwater pearls in the 7 to 8 millimeter range. Sandy brings out a variety of strands and points out the fine nuances of luster, color, and surface markings. Then she helps him choose two strands, which they will have strung with three mystery clasps. That way his wife can wear the pearls in different necklace lengths and as a bracelet. This is a quick and easy sale for Sandy, and it's a pleasant experience for Jeff. He's gotten efficient, professional help and exactly the kind of pearls he was looking for.

Erica is in a Tahitian jewelry store looking through a bowl of black pearls. Before coming to Tahiti on holiday, she read *The Pearl Buying Guide*. The salesman in the store tells her that she can have any of the pearls in the bowl for the equivalent of $120. Erica first picks out the ones with the best luster. Then she eliminates those that are either too light or have no overtone colors. Finally, she ends up with a fairly large, tear-drop-shaped, dark-gray pearl with some greenish and purplish highlights. One side of the pearl, however, is badly flawed. But Erica plans to wear it as a pendant, so the flaws won't show.

On the flight back home, she sketches a design for the pendant and then later has her jeweler make it. He tells her he could never find a black pearl as attractive as hers for such a low price. When the pendant is finished, Erica tries it on. She's very pleased with how it looks. But she's even more pleased that she owns a unique piece which she has helped create.

Shopping for pearls turned out to be a positive experience for Erica, Jeff, and Charlene. This was largely because they took the time to learn about pearls beforehand and/or they dealt with a competent salesperson. Listed below are some guidelines that helped them and can help you when you shop for pearls.

♦ **Look for luster.** This was the first quality factor that Erica focused her attention on because it's the most important one. To understand why, just compare dull milky pearls to some highly lustrous ones. Chapter 4 gives you tips on judging luster.

♦ **When judging prices, try to compare pearls of the same type, shape, size, color, luster, and blemish quality.** All of these factors affect the cost of pearls. Due to the complexity of pearl pricing, it's easier for consumers to compare pearls that are alike or at least similar.

♦ **Look at a variety of qualities** so you'll have a basis for comparison.

♦ **Remember that there is no standardized system for grading pearls.** As a consequence, grades such as "A" have no meaning other than what the seller assigns to them. In some cases, an "A" grade may be the lowest quality a store stocks. The lack of standardization does not mean there's no point in grading pearls. It's just an added reason why you need to know how to judge pearl quality yourself.

♦ **Be willing to compromise.** Both Charlene and Erica had to settle for something other than what they might have preferred in order to stay within their budget. Charlene got freshwater instead of saltwater pearls. Erica's pearl was badly flawed on one side. Even people with unlimited budgets have to compromise sometimes on the size, shape, color, or quality due to lack of availability. A pearl doesn't have to be perfect for you to enjoy it.

♦ **Beware of sales ads that seem too good to be true.** The advertised pearls might be of unacceptable quality, especially in terms of nacre thickness. Or they might be stolen or misrepresented. Jewelers are in business to make money, not to lose it.

♦ **If possible, establish a relationship with a jeweler** you can trust and who looks after your interests. He can help you find buys you wouldn't find on your own.

♦ **Place the pearls against your hand and answer the following questions.** A negative answer suggests the pearls are a poor choice.

    a. Do the pearls have bright, sharp light reflections?

    b. Do the pearls have overtone colors? (This is a characteristic of pearls with good luster.)

    c. Does the color of the pearls look good next to your skin?

The above guidelines in essence suggest that you learn how to evaluate pearls. But why is it so important for you to do this? Why should jewelers educate you about pearl quality? Is it just to help you compare prices?

No. Learning more about pearls will help you make a choice you can enjoy for a lifetime and will help you appreciate the unique qualities of the pearls you choose. How can you appreciate something you don't understand?

As you learn to compare luster differences among pearls, you will see how pearl brilliance differs from that of other gems. The brilliance of faceted gems normally appears best in their face-up position. No matter how you hold or wear good pearls, they glow. Even away from light they glow. And this glow has an intensity and depth unmatched by any other shiny round object.

As you learn to compare the color nuances of pearls, you'll see that good pearls are not just white. They have a variety of underlying colors which add to their beauty. And they come in a wide spectrum of body colors. Some people say that pearls make them look washed out. These people change their mind when they see black pearls and when they try on lighter pearls that enhance their body coloring.

As you are introduced to the different pearl shapes, you'll see how pearls offer creative design possibilities unlike any other gem. Even a basic strand of round pearls can be worn in creative, versatile ways.

Pearls can be worn anywhere, at any time, with anything. And even though pearls offer all these positive features, you don't have to be rich to own fine-quality pearls. If you are willing to compromise on the type of pearls you choose, you should be able to find good ones to fit almost any budget.

But to spot good pearls, you need to know how to judge their quality. So look at pearls whenever possible. Take time to analyze them. Ask jewelers to explain their quality differences. Gradually, you'll learn to recognize good value, and you'll see that the pearl is a remarkable gem which has no peer.

Appendix

Chemical, Physical, & Optical Characteristics of Pearls

(The information below is mainly based on the following three sources:

Gems by Robert Webster
GIA Gem Reference Guide
GIA Colored Stones Course, Chapters 13 & 14 (1980 version)

Chemical composition:	$CaCO_3$ (most of it aragonite, the rest calcite) 82 to 92 %
	H_2O 2 to 4%
	Conchiolin 4 to 14%
	Other about 0.4%
Mohs' hardness:	2 1/2 to 4
Specific gravity:	White natural saltwater pearls: 2.66 - 2.76 except for some Australian pearls whose density may be as high as 2.78
	Black natural saltwater pearls (Gulf of California): 2.61 - 2.69
	Natural freshwater pearls: 2.66 - 2.78
	Japanese Akoya cultured pearls: 2.72 - 2.78 or more
	Mantle-tissue nucleated cultured pearls: 2.67 - 2.70
Toughness:	Usually good, but variable. Old, dehydrated, or excessively bleached pearls are not as tough.
Cleavage:	None
Fracture:	Uneven
Streak:	White
Crystal character:	An aggregate composed mostly of tiny orthorhombic (pseudo-hexagonal) aragonite crystals and sometimes hexagonal calcite crystals. Conchiolin, an organic binding material, is noncrystalline.
Optic Character:	AGG, if not opaque (also listed as doubly refractive)
Refractive Index:	1.530 - 1.685

Birefringence:	.155
Dispersion:	None
Luster:	Dull to almost metallic. Fractures may look pearly to dull.
Phenomena:	Orient. Varies from almost none to very noticeable.
Pleochroism:	None
Chelsea-filter reaction:	None
Absorption spectra:	Varies greatly, not diagnostic
Ultraviolet fluorescence:	None to strong light blue, yellow, green, or pink under both LW and SW. Natural color black pearls - weak to moderate red to orangy red under LW.
Reaction to heat:	Pearls can burn, split, crack, or turn brown in excessive heat such as an open flame. Prolonged heat may cause dehydration, which may cause the nacre to crack.
Reaction to chemicals:	Attacked by all acids. Lotions, cosmetics, perspiration, and perfumes can also damage the nacre.
Stability to light:	Stable except for some dyed pearls.
Effect of irradiation:	Darkens color
Transparency to x-rays:	Semitransparent
X-ray fluorescence:	Natural saltwater pearls--inert except for a few white Australian pearls, which fluoresce faintly, cultured saltwater pearls-- moderately strong to very weak greenish yellow depending on nacre thickness, freshwater pearls--moderate to strong yellowish white.
X-radiograph:	Cultured pearls usually show a clear separation between core and nacre, and their core normally looks lighter than the nacre coating. A mantle tissue nucleus will look like a very dark, irregularly shaped void. Natural pearls show a more or less concentric structure, and they tend to look the same tone throughout or get darker in the center.

Bibliography

Books and Booklets

Ahrens, Joan & Malloy, Ruth. *Hong Kong Gems & Jewelry.* Hong Kong: Delta Dragon, 1986.

Anderson, B. W. *Gem Testing.* Verplanck, NY: Emerson Books, 1985.

Arem, Joel. *Gems & Jewelry.* New York: Bantam, 1986.

Australian Gem Industry Assn. *Australian Opals & Gemstones.* Sydney: Australian Gem Industry Assn, 1987.

Avery, James. *The Right Jewelry for You.* Austin, Texas: Eakin Press, 1988.

Ball, Sydney H. *Roman Book on Precious Stones.* Los Angeles: G.I.A., 1950.

Bauer, Jaroslav & Bouska, Vladimir. *Pierres Precieuses et Pierres Fines.* Paris: Bordas, 1985.

Bauer, Dr. Max. *Precious Stones.* Rutland, Vermont & Tokyo: Charles E. Tuttle, 1969.

Bingham, Anne. *Buying Jewelry.* New York: McGraw Hill, 1989.

Blakemore, Kenneth. *The Retail Jeweller's Guide.* London: Butterworths, 1988.

Bruton, Eric, *Legendary Gems or Gems that Made History.* Radnor, PA: Chilton 1986.

Ciprani, Curzio & Borelli, Alessandro. *Simon & Schuster's Guide to Gems and Precious Stones.* New York: Simon and Schuster, 1986.

Dickenson, Joan Younger. *The Book of Pearls.* New York: Crown Publisher's, 1968.

Farn, Alexander E. *Pearls: Natural, Cultured and Imitation.* London: Butterworths, 1986.

Farrington, Oliver Cummings. *Gems and Gem Minerals.* Chicago: A. W. Mumford, 1903.

Federman, David & Hammid, Tino. *Consumer Guide to Colored Gemstones.* Shawnee Mission, KS: Modern Jeweler, 1989.

Field, Leslie. *The Queen's Jewels.* New York: Abrams, 1987.

Fisher, P. J. *The Science of Gems.* New York: Charles Scribner's Sons, 1966.

Freeman, Michael. *Light.* New York: Amphoto, 1988.

Gemological Institute of America. *Gem Reference Guide.* Santa Monica, CA: GIA, 1988.
Gemological Institute of America. *The GIA Jeweler's Manual.* Santa Monica, CA: GIA, 1989.
Gemological Institute of America. *Proceedings of the International Gemological Symposium* 1991. Santa Monica, CA: GIA, 1992.

Goldemberg, Rose Leiman. *All About Jewelry*. New York: Arbor House, 1983.

Greenbaum, Walter W. *The Gemstone Identifier*. New York: Prentice Hall Press, 1988.

Idaka, Kimiko. *Pearls of the World*. Tokyo: Shinsoshoku Co., 1985.

Jackson, Carole. *Color Me Beautiful*. New York: Ballantine, 1985.

Japan Pearl Exporters' Association. *Cultured Pearls*. Japan Pearl Exporters' Association.

Jewelers of America. *The Gemstone Enhancement Manual*. New York: Jewelers of America, 1990.

King, Dawn. *Did Your Jeweler Tell You?* Oasis, Nevada: King Enterprises, 1990.

Kunz, George Frederick. *The Curious Lore of Precious Stones*. New York: Bell, 1989.

Kunz, George & Stephenson, Charles. *The Book of the Pearl*. New York: Century Co., 1908.

Liddicoat, Richard T. *Handbook of Gem Identification*. Santa Monica, CA: GIA, 1981.

Lintilhac, Jean-Paul. *Black Pearls of Tahiti*. Papeete, Tahiti: Royal Tahitian Pearl Book, 1985.

MacFall, Russell P. *Gem Hunter's Guide*. New York: Thomas Y. Crowell, 1963

Matlins, Antoinette L. & Bonanno, A. *Jewelry & Gems the Buying Guide*. South Woodstock, VT: Gemstone Press, 1987.

Marcum, David. *Fine Gems and Jewelry*. Homewood, IL: Dow Jones-Irwin, 1986.

Miguel, Jorge. *Jewelry, How to Create Your Image*. Dallas: Taylor Publishing, 1986.

Miller, Anna M. *Gems and Jewelry Appraising*. New York: Van Nostrand Reinhold Company, 1988.

Muller, Andy. *Pearls*. Kobe: Golay Buchel Japan, 1990.

Nadelhoffer, Hans. *Cartier Jewels Extraordinary. New York: Harry Abrams, 1984.*

Nassau, Kurt. Gemstone Enhancement. London: Butterworths, 1984.

O'Donoghue, Michael. *Identifying Man-made Gems*. London: N.A.G. Press, 1983.

Preston, William S. *Guides for the Jewelry Industry*. New York: Jewelers Vigilance Committee, Inc., 1986.

Rosenthal, Leonard. *The Pearl and I*. New York: Vantage Press, 1955.
Rosenthal, Leonard. *The Pearl Hunter*. New York: Henry Schuman, 1952.

Salomon, Paule. *The Magic of the Black Pearl*. Papeete, Tahiti: Tahiti Perles, 1986.

Schumann, Walter. *Gemstones of the World*. New York: Sterling, 1977.

Shirai, Shohei. *Pearls*. Okinawa, Marine Planning Co. Ltd., 1981.

Smith, G.F. Herbert. *Gemstones*. London: Pitman, 1949.

Taburiaux, Jean. *Pearls: Their origin, treatment & identification*. Radnor, PA: Chilton, 1985.

Webster, Robert. *Gemmologists' Compendium*. New York: Van Nostrand Reinhold, 1979.
Webster, Robert. *Gems*. London: Butterworths, 1983.
Webster, Robert. *Practical Gemmology*. Ipswich, Suffolk: N. A. G. Press, 1976.

Zucker, Benjamin. *Gems & Jewels*. New York: Thames & Hudson, 1984.

Articles

Austin, Gordon T. "Tennessee is the Pearl of U.S. Gem Production." *Colored Stone*. May/June, pp. 29-30, 1991.

Austin, Richard. "Pearls and the Jewelry Maker." *Gems and Minerals*. January, pp. 46-48. 1980.

Berrenblatt, Alena Joy. "Everything Plus Pearls." *National Jeweler*. October 16, pp. 32-44, 1991.

Brown, Grahame. "The Genesis of a Pearl--An unlikely fairy-tale." *Wahrongai News*. December, 1990.

Crowningshield, Robert. "Cultured Pearl, Accidentally Tissue-Nucleated. *Gems & Gemology*. Fall p. 175, 1991.
Crowningshield, Robert. "Green-dyed Natural Pearls." *Gems & Gemology*. Fall p. 175, 1991.
Crowningshield, Robert. "Remarkable Cultured Pearl." *Gems & Gemology*. Fall p. 176, 1991.
Crowningshield, Robert. "Two different Mabe Pearls." *Gems & Gemology*. Fall p. 177, 1991.
Crowningshield, Robert. "Rare Assembled Cultured Blister Pearls." *Gems & Gemology*. Summer p. 111, 1991.
Crowningshield, Robert. "Pearls: from Baja California." *Gems & Gemology*. Spring, p. 42, 1991.
Crowningshield, Robert. "Dyed Black Cultured, Origin of Color." *Gems & Gemology*. Winter, pp. 296-7, 1990.
Crowningshield, Robert. "Uncommon Cultured." *Gems & Gemology*. Winter, p. 297, 1990.
Crowningshield, Robert. "Gray Baroque Cultured." *Gems & Gemology*. Fall, p. 224, 1990.
Crowningshield, Robert. "Well-Worked Pearl." *Gems & Gemology*. Summer, pp. 155-6, 1990.
Crowningshield, Robert. "Irradiated." *Gems & Gemology*. Winter, p. 244, 1988.
Crowningshield, Robert. "Pear-shaped, Saltwater." *Gems & Gemology*. Winter, p. 245, 1988.
Crowningshield, Robert. "Imitation." *Gems & Gemology*. Summer, p. 114, 1988.
Crowningshield, Robert. "A Rare Cultured Pearl." *Gems & Gemology*. Summer, p. 114-5, 1988.
Crowningshield, Robert. "Early 'Japanese Pearls'." *Gems & Gemology*. Spring, p. 49-50, 1988.
Crowningshield, Robert. "Eroded Natural Pearls." *Gems & Gemology*. Winter, pp. 238-9, 1986.
Crowningshield, Robert. "Pearls with Unusual Drilling Features." *Gems & Gemology*. Spring, pp. 50-51, 1986.
Crowningshield, Robert. "Imitation Pearls." *Gems & Gemology*. Summer, p. 111-2, 1985.
Crowningshield, Robert. "Pearl Simulants, Shell Hinges." *Gems & Gemology*. Spring, p. 45, 1985.
Crowningshield, Robert. "Dyed Cultured Pearls." *Gems & Gemology*. Spring, p. 229, 1984.
Crowningshield, Robert. "Accidental, or "Keshi," Pearls?." *Gems & Gemology*. Fall, pp. 169-170, 1984.
Crowningshield, Robert. "Cultured Pearl Mystery." *Gems & Gemology*. Fall, p. 170, 1984.
Crowningshield, Robert. "Imitation 'Rice Grain' Biwa Cultured Pearls." *Gems & Gemology*. Fall, p. 170, 1984.
Crowningshield, Robert. "More Imitation Pearls." *Gems & Gemology*. Fall, p. 170-171, 1984.

DelRe, Nicholas. "Natural- and Treated-Color Black Cultured Pearls in the Same Necklace. *Gems & Gemology*. Fall, p. 175, 1991.

DelRe, Nicholas. "A 'Teething' Problem." *Gems & Gemology*. Fall, pp. 175-76, 1991.

Depasque, Lorraine. "Prime Time for Pearls." *Modern Jeweler*." November, pp. 44-60, 1988.

DiNoto, Andrea. "No wonder the ancients believed that pearls grow in the brains of dragons." *Connoisseur*, August, pp. 76-87, 1983.

Dirlam, Dona, Miswiorowski, Elise & Thomas, Sally. "Pearl Fashion Through the Ages." *Gems & Gemology*, Summer, pp. 63-78, 1985.

Edelstein, Cindy. "Opposites Attract." *Jewelers' Circular Keystone*. October, pp. 77-100, 1990.
Edelstein, Cindy. "Pearl Classics are Back." *Jewelers' Circular Keystone*. April, pp. 53-57, 1990.
Edelstein, Cindy. "Pearls: The Must Accent for '89." *Jewelers' Circular Keystone*. April, pp. 44-64, 1989.
Edelstein, Cindy. "Pearls: Ride the Fashion Wave." *Jewelers' Circular Keystone*. October, pp. 34-58, 1988.

Federman, David. "The ABC's of Pearl Beauty." *Modern Jeweler*. September, 1989.
Federman, David. "Exotic Pearls, The New Fancy for Fancies." *Modern Jeweler*. September, pp. 43-47, 1991.
Federman, David. "Biotechnology: A New Dawn for Pearl Farming." *Modern Jeweler*. September, pp. 40-48, 1990.

Fritsch, Emmanuel & Misiorowski, Elise. "The History and Gemology of Queen Conch 'Pearls'." *Gems & Gemology*. Winter, 208-221, 1987.

Fryer, C. W. "First American Freshwater Cultured Pearls from Tennessee." *Gems & Gemology*. Winter, pp. 229-30, 1984.

Gemmological Association of Great Britain. "Defining the Thickness of Nacre on Cultured Pearls." *Gem and Jewelry News*. December, p. 7, 1991.

George, C. Denis. "The Black Pearls: History & Development." *Lapidary Journal*, April, 136-147, 1971.

Goebel, Marisa & Dirlam, Dona. "Polynesian Black Pearls." *Gems & Gemology*. Fall, p. 130, 1989.

Hanano, June, Wildman, M. & Yurkiewicz, P. "Majorica Imitation Pearls." *Gems & Gemology*. Fall, pp. 178-88, 1990.

Hargett, David. "Gray Cultured Pearls." *Gems & Gemology*. Spring, p. 97, 1990.
Hargett, David. "Chipped." *Gems & Gemology*. Fall, pp. 173-4, 1989.
Hargett, David. "Pinked." *Gems & Gemology*. Fall, p. 174, 1989.
Hargett, David. "Black Cultured Pearls." *Gems & Gemology*. Fall, p. 166, 1987.
Hargett, David. "A Cultured Pearl Puzzle." *Gems & Gemology*. Summer, p. 104, 1987.

Hiss, Deborah. "Pearl: The Organic Jewel." *Jewelers Circular Keystone.*" October, pp. 61-65, 1988.

Hurwit, Karin. "Treated' Mabe Pearls." *Gems & Gemology*. Fall, p. 177, 1991.
Hurwit, Karin. "Cultured 'Demi-Pearl'." *Gems & Gemology*. Summer, pp. 110-11, 1991.
Hurwit, Karin. "Cultured Calcareous Concretions." *Gems & Gemology*. Summer, p. 153, 1990.
Hurwit, Karin. "Pearls: Cultured with Colored Bead Nuclei." *Gems & Gemology*. Fall, pp. 222-223, 1990.
Hurwit, Karin. "Cultured Pearl, Treated Black." *Gems & Gemology*. Winter, p. 240, 1989.
Hurwit, Karin. "Demi-pearl." *Gems & Gemology*. Fall, p. 174, 1989.
Hurwit, Karin. "A 'Fossilized Pearl' from Utah." *Gems & Gemology*. Fall, p. 174, 1989.
Hurwit, Karin. "Natural Pearl & Diamond Tiara." *Gems & Gemology*. Spring, p. 50, 1988.
Hurwit, Karin. "Cultured Black Pearl." *Gems & Gemology*. Winter, pp. 234-5, 1987.
Hurwit, Karin. "Pearls: An unusual clam 'pearl'." *Gems & Gemology*. Spring, pp. 45 & 46, 1987.
Hurwit, Karin. "Imitation Pearls, 'Coque de Pearl'." *Gems & Gemology*. Winter, p. 239, 1986.
Hurwit, Karin. "Freshwater Cultured Pearls from China." *Gems & Gemology*. Summer, p. 111, 1985.
Hurwit, Karin. "Abalone Pearl." *Gems & Gemology*. Fall, p. 169, 1984.
Hurwit, Karin. "Dyed Cultured Pearls." *Gems & Gemology*. Winter, p. 229, 1984.

Kane, Robert. "Freshwater Natural." *Gems & Gemology*. Fall, pp. 223-224, 1990.
Kane, Robert. "South Seas Cultured Pearl." *Gems & Gemology*. Fall, pp. 172, 1988.
Kane, Robert. "Damaged Mabe." *Gems & Gemology*. Spring, p. 45, 1985.
Kane, Robert. "Natural Seed Pearls and Glass Imitations." *Gems & Gemology*. Fall, p. 171, 1984.

Koivula, John and Kammerling, R. "Pearls: Two remarkable natural freshwater pearls from Texas." *Gems & Gemology*. Summer p. 115, 1989.

Montgomery, George E. "Pearls--/gems from the sea." *Gems and Minerals.* January, p. 79-80, 1980.

Moses, Thomas. "Freshwater 'Rosebud' Pearls." *Gems & Gemology.* Summer, p. 111, 1991.
Moses, Thomas. "Assembled Pearl." *Gems & Gemology.* Winter, p. 240, 1989.

Porter, Bruce. "The Black Pearl Connection." *Connoisseur."* April, pp. 120-126, 1991.

Reilley, Barbara. "American Pearls: Prospects & Problems." *Jewelers' Circular Keystone."* August, 95-102, 1990.
Reilley, Barbara. "Pearl Sales: Lustrous Outlook for the '90s." *Jewelers' Circular Keystone."* April, 58-62, 1990.

Schupak, Hedda. "Pearl the Versatile Jewel." *Jewelers' Circular Keystone.* October, pp. 84-96, 1991.

Schuster, William. "US Cultured Pearls." *Jewelers' Circular Keystone."* January, pp.182-186, 1988.

Smith, Jane Victoria. ""Pearl Jewelry: New Demand for Quality." *Jewelers' Circular Keystone."* October, pp. 59-70, 1987.

Sweaney, James & Latendresse, John R. "Freshwater Pearls of North America." *Gems & Gemology.* Fall, pp. 125-45. 1984.

Walowitz, Hedda. "Treasures from the Deep Sea." *Jewelers' Circular Keystone.* October, pp. 86-88, 1988

Ward, Fred. "The Pearl." *National Geographic."* August, pp.193-222, 1985.

Welch, Clayton. "Pearls and Their Apparent Colors." *Gems & Gemology.* Spring, p. 46, 1987.

Weldon, Robert. "Pearls." *Jewelers' Circular Keystone.* September, Part II, p.174, 1991.

Periodicals

Colored Stone. Devon, PA: *Lapidary Journal* Inc.

GAA Market Monitor Precious Gem Appraisal/Buying Guide. Pittsburgh, PA: GAA.

Gems and Gemology. Santa Monica, CA: Gemological Institute of America.

The Guide. Chicago: Gemworld International, Inc.

Lapidary Journal. Devon, PA: *Lapidary Journal* Inc.

Jewelers Circular Keystone. Radnor, PA: Chilton Publishing Co.

Modern Jeweler. Lincolnshire, IL: Vance Publishing Inc.

National Jeweler. New York: Gralla Publications.

Pearl World. The International Pearling Journal. Haggis House, Inc., Phoenix, AZ., April to November 1993.

Palmieri's Auction/FMV Monitor. Pittsburgh, PA: GAA

Rock & Gem. Ventura, CA: Miller Magazines, Inc.

Miscellaneous: Courses, leaflets etc..

A & Z Pearls Price List. Los Angeles, CA

"Cultured Pearls." The American Gem Society.

Gemological Institute of America Gem Identification Course. Santa Monica, CA.

Gemological Institute of America Colored Stones Course. 1980 & 1989 editions.

Gemological Institute of America Pearls Course.

"Grading and Information Guide." Midwest Gem Lab. Brookfield, Wi.

"Hints to select your cultured pearls." Rio Pearl. Hong Kong.

"I am a pearl." Mastoloni Pearls. New York, NY.

"Mastering Cultured Pearls." Adachi America Corporation. Los Angeles, CA.

"Pearl: Miracle of the Sea." American Gem Society.

"Pearls of Japan." Japan Pearl Exporters' Association."

"Perle Noire: Quality comes first." Tahiti perles S C. Tahiti.

"Quality Cultured Pearls Price List." Adachi America. Los Angeles, CA.

"A Selling Guide for Retailers." Japan Pearl Exporters' Association.

"A Shopper's Guide to Cultured Pearls." J. C. Penney.

Shogun Trading Co. Price List. New York, NY.

Tara & Sons Inc. Price List. New York, NY

"Treasures from the Sea." Shogun Cultured Pearls. New York, NY.

"What you should know about cultured pearls." Jewelers' of America.

Index

Order Form

To: International Jewelry Publications
P.O. Box 13384
Los Angeles, CA 90013-0384 USA

Please send me:

___ copies of **THE PEARL BUYING GUIDE**
Within California $21.60 each (includes sales tax)   _____
All other destinations $19.95 US each   _____

___ copies of **THE RUBY & SAPPHIRE BUYING GUIDE.**
Within California $21.60 each (includes sales tax)   _____
All other destinations $19.95 US each   _____

___ copies of **THE GOLD JEWELRY BUYING GUIDE.**
Within California $21.60 each (includes sales tax)   _____
All other destinations $19.95 US each   _____

___ copies of **THE DIAMOND RING BUYING GUIDE**
Within California $14.02 each (includes sales tax)   _____
All other destinations $12.95 US each   _____

Postage & Handling for Books

USA: first book $1.50, each additional copy $.75
Canada & foreign - surface mail: first book $2.50, ea. addl. $1.50   _____
Canada & Mexico - airmail: first book $3.75, ea. addl. $2.50   _____
All other foreign destinations - airmail: first book $9.00, ea. addl. $5.00   _____

___ copies of **DIAMONDS: FASCINATING FACTS.**
Within California $4.28 each (includes sales tax)   _____
All other destinations $3.95 US each   _____

Postage for Diamonds: Fascinating Facts
USA: $0.55 per booklet   _____
Canada & Mexico - airmail: $0.80 per booklet   _____
All other foreign destinations - airmail: $1.25 per booklet   _____

Total Amount Enclosed   _____
(Check or money order in USA funds)

Ship to:

Name_____

Address_____

City_____ State or Province_____

Postal or Zip Code_____ Country _____

The Diamond Ring Buying Guide:
How to Spot Value & Avoid Ripoffs

A comprehensive guide to evaluating, selecting, pricing, and caring for diamond jewelry.

Find out:

- ♦ How to judge diamond quality
- ♦ How to detect diamond imitations
- ♦ How to choose between platinum, white gold, and yellow gold
- ♦ How to select a ring style that's both practical and flattering
- ♦ How to compare prices of diamond jewelry

"Filled with useful information, drawings, pictures, and short quizzes. . . presents helpful suggestions on detecting diamond imitations, in addition to well-though-out discussions of diamond cutting, and how the various factors can influence value . . . a very readable way for the first-time diamond buyer to get acquainted with the often intimidating subject of purchasing a diamond."
Stephen C. Hofer, President, Colored Diamond Laboratory Services, *Jewelers' Circular Keystone*

"Will definitely help consumers . . . Written in a popular style with lots of personalized examples, the book should be easy reading for the young people who are thinking about their first diamond purchases."
Lapidary Journal

"Highly informative . . . *The Diamond Ring Buying Guide* is a useful book for the first-time diamond buyer, the gemologist, who needs a good review on diamonds, and the retailer seeking more information to give to customers."
GIA's Gems and Gemology

AVAILABLE AT bookstores, jewelry supply stores, the GIA, and through the *Lapidary Journal* & Jeweler's Book Clubs or by mail: See reverse side for order form.

151 pages, 85 black and white photos, 7" by 9", $12.95 US.

Diamonds: Fascinating Facts

An informative booklet with entertaining facts, poems, and statistics about diamonds.

A novel and appropriate greeting card to include with a diamond gift. It comes with a 6" x 9" white envelope. The inside front cover is designed to allow for a personal message.

Full-color, 16-page, self-cover booklet with six 5" x 7 1/2" photos, $3.95 US.

The Ruby & Sapphire Buying Guide:

Shows you:
- ♦ How to choose a good-quality stone
- ♦ How to tell a fake from a real ruby or sapphire
- ♦ How to compare prices and save money
- ♦ How to buy gems abroad

"Solid, informative and comprehensive . . . dissects each aspect of ruby and sapphire value in detail and quizzes the reader on key points at the end of each chapter. . . a wealth of grading information . . . *The Ruby & Sapphire Buying Guide* is a definite thumbs-up for both the unskilled and semiskilled buyer and seller. There is something here for everyone."
   C. R. Beesley, President, American Gemological Laboratories. *Jewelers' Circular Keystone*

"Highly recommended . . . includes a great deal of gemmological as well as commercial information; text photographs are clear and cover many situations for appraisal which have rarely been put forward in gemmology texts before. . . . useful to the gemmology student as well as to the dealer or purchaser of jewelry."
   The Journal of Gemmology, a publication of the British Gemmological Association

204 pages, 40 color and 85 black/white photos, 7" by 9", $19.95 US.

The Gold Jewelry Buying Guide

A how-to manual on judging jewelry craftsmanship and testing gold, plus practical information on gold chains, Black Hills gold, gold-coin jewelry, and nugget jewelry.

"Concise, thorough, and completely readable for the jewelry neophyte. In chapters such as Manufacturing Methods, Gold Terms & Notation, and Judging the Setting, Newman allows consumers confidence and facility in judgements of quality. Professionals in need of quick reference on jewelry evaluation elements may also profit from the completeness and clarity of this book's organization."
   Cornerstone, Journal of the Accredited Gemologists Association

"Provides easily understood details on how to judge the quality of gold jewelry...Newman breaks down points such as determining karat value and which chains are more likely to break. She explains tests for jewelry sturdiness and authenticity in layman's terms...a handy guide."
   Chicago Sun Times

"A gold mine of info...a regular everything-you-always-wanted-to-know primer on Midas favorite subject."
   Asbury Park Press

172 pages, 7" X 9", 35 color and 96 black & white photos, $19.95 US

AVAILABLE AT bookstores, jewelry supply stores, the GIA and *the Lapidary Journal &* Jeweler's Book Clubs, or by mail: See reverse side for order form.

Order Form

To: International Jewelry Publications
P.O. Box 13384
Los Angeles, CA 90013-0384 USA

Please send me:

____ copies of **THE PEARL BUYING GUIDE**
Within California $21.60 each (includes sales tax)
All other destinations $19.95 US each

____ copies of **THE RUBY & SAPPHIRE BUYING GUIDE.**
Within California $21.60 each (includes sales tax)
All other destinations $19.95 US each

____ copies of **THE GOLD JEWELRY BUYING GUIDE.**
Within California $21.60 each (includes sales tax)
All other destinations $19.95 US each

____ copies of **THE DIAMOND RING BUYING GUIDE**
Within California $14.02 each (includes sales tax)
All other destinations $12.95 US each

Postage & Handling for Books

USA: first book $1.50, each additional copy $.75
Canada & foreign - surface mail: first book $2.50, ea. addl. $1.50
Canada & Mexico - airmail: first book $3.75, ea. addl. $2.50
All other foreign destinations - airmail: first book $9.00, ea. addl. $5.00

____ copies of **DIAMONDS: FASCINATING FACTS.**
Within California $4.28 each (includes sales tax)
All other destinations $3.95 US each

Postage for Diamonds: Fascinating Facts
USA: $0.55 per booklet
Canada & Mexico - airmail: $0.80 per booklet
All other foreign destinations - airmail: $1.25 per booklet

Total Amount Enclosed
(Check or money order in USA funds)

Ship to: 471016

Name_____

Address_____

City_____ State or Province_____
Postal or Zip Code_____ Country _____

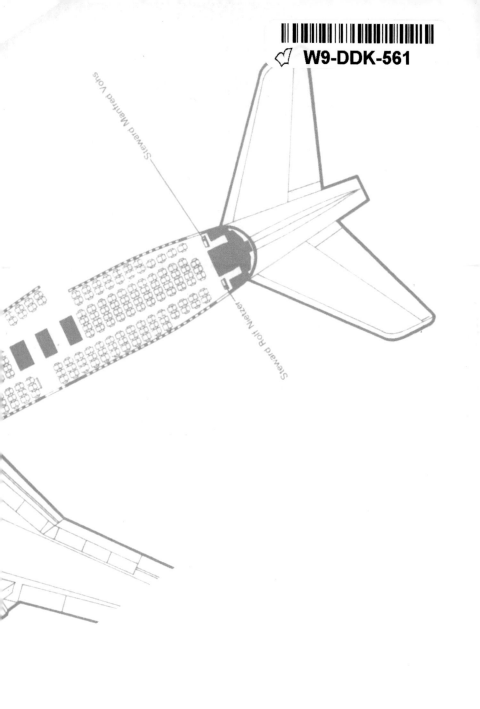

Steward Manfred Vohs

Steward Rolf Netzer

PLATFORM

PRESS
DOYLESTOWN
PENNSYLVANIA

Fasten Your FINANCIAL SEATBELT

What Surviving an Airline Crash Taught Me About RETIREMENT PLANNING

THOMAS C. SCOTT
CFP®, CFS

Thomas C. Scott
www.FinancialSeatbelt.com
Tom.Scott@FinancialSeatbelt.com

Published in the United States by
Platform Press
The nonfiction imprint of
Winans Kuenstler Publishing, LLC
47 West Oakland Avenue
Doylestown, Pennsylvania 18901
www.wkpublishing.com

Platform Press and colophon are registered trademarks

ISBN: 978-0-9824117-1-1

Library of Congress Control Number: 2009927376

First Edition

Dedicated to those investment professionals who share a passion for educating clients about how money works, how wealth is created and preserved, and how to make responsible financial decisions.

"The saving man becomes
the free man."
　　　　—Chinese Proverb

Preface

Mountains of books have been published about how to achieve financial goals, but little attention is paid to what happens when you reach them. *Fasten Your Financial Seatbelt* is the distillation of twenty-five years' experience helping people define their goals, reach them, and—the hardest task of all—stay there.

I've been intrigued by the role money plays in our lives since I was a young man, working with my father in his elevator maintenance business, watching him achieve real financial success through hard work and integrity. I also watched with dismay as he then squandered it all, trying to grow richer quicker by investing in risky ventures and questionable schemes. It was both heartbreaking and instructive.

My father passed on to me a conscientious attitude about hard work and high standards. But my relationship

with money couldn't have been more different. My mother called me her "little old man." I was the pink-cheeked seven-year-old the tellers cooed over when she took me to the savings and loan–at my insistence–and hoisted me up so I could see into the teller cage and hand over my well-thumbed savings passbook. The teller would stamp the number of pennies of interest my little balance had earned since the last time I was in. I loved looking at the account balance column and its long string of ever-increasing entries.

From an early age I grasped the relationship between caring for my money and increasing my personal freedom. My relationship with money allowed me to pay for my own flying lessons from the age of twelve and later to buy my own sailplane. Instead of hoping and agonizing over a big bet on a risky venture like my father did, I let my money grow slowly and steadily and spent entire worry-free days—eight hours at a stretch—soaring alone in my sailplane on the thermals of the southern California deserts.

Money, an old proverb reminds us, is a good servant but a bad master. The desire for more and the fear of losing it enslaves us, becoming the root of much misery and evil behavior. It doesn't have to be that way. Wealth, and the freedom it grants, should serve your goals, not the other way around. Money can be the root of happiness, however one chooses to define happiness.

The goal of one of my clients was to be able to retire and travel the world, scuba diving in out-of-the-way places. He kept a modest home in California while he spent his retirement income indulging his passion and seeing the world. Another client accumulated real estate he hopes to sell off one day so he can afford to buy his dream oceanfront estate.

What unifies these two extreme goals is that, like most people, these clients came to me confused by the investment industry hype and clutter about how to get—and stay—where they wanted to be. They were typical of most people who have the means and the desire to reach their personal financial independence day. They've had some success, made some common mistakes, discovered that financial security is not a destination or a state of being but a lifelong journey, and realized they needed a guide to lead them out of the wilderness.

It's been my observation after helping thousands of clients with their financial decisions that human emotion is our worst enemy The instinct that brings us together as a roaring crowd to cheer the home team is the same instinct that causes stock market and real estate bubbles and a host of other flawed financial choices. So often I see people imitating the decisions of others out of fear of being left behind, rather than making choices that are right for them.

Some of this can be laid at the feet of the investment industry which makes its living promoting the latest new-and-improved financial products. Some of it has to do with cultural myths and misconceptions—messages passed down through the generations that grew out of cataclysmic events such as the Great Depression.

Very few people arrive in my office for the first time truly understanding money and how it works or having thought through their goals and their relationship with money. Even those who have thought them through bring with them common misconceptions and a history of miscalculations that cost them wealth and opportunity, delaying and even destroying their financial independence.

I can't guarantee that you'll find all the answers to your questions in these pages. But if you take the time to read on, chances are good that you'll see yourself in some of the stories and examples. These may help you think about and redefine your relationship with money in a way that helps you achieve your goals.

—*Thomas C. Scott, 2009*
Irvine, California

Contents

About the Author

Thomas C. "Tom" Scott is founder and CEO of Scott Wealth Management Group, Inc. in Orange County, California, where he has been an investment and financial planning professional since 1983.

His practice is affiliated with LPL Financial, one of the nation's largest independent brokerage firms, where he is a member of LPL's Chairman's Council, an honor reserved for those advisers ranked in the most successful top two percent of nearly 12,000 investment advisors.

His professional credentials include:

Certified Financial Planner (CFP) from the College for Financial Planning and the University of Southern California.

Certified Fund Specialist (CFS) from the Institute of Business and Finance.

Member, Financial Planners' Association (FPA).

He lives in Irvine, California and is the father of two grown daughters.

Foreword

As this book went to press in 2009, the world's economy appeared to be spinning out of control, and the U.S. economy was in a historic tailspin. Stock prices had fallen to apocalyptic lows, there was widespread deflation, America's auto industry teetered on the precipice of bankruptcy, and unemployment was spreading rapidly. Our government was forced to step in and effectively socialize—bail out—our economic system.

This period has been a disaster, but like any other sort of disaster, such as an airline crash, those who were prepared are more likely to "survive." That's the philosophy behind the concept of fastening your financial seatbelt. The time to prepare for disaster is before there's a disaster. This is true in an airplane, and it's true in your financial life. You hope the worst never happens, but history tells us it will, again and again.

We've been here before and those who bought into the idea of a "new" economy are learning some ancient truths. As Mark Twain observed, history may not repeat itself, but it does rhyme.

We can draw many parallels between recent events and previous periods of wretched excess followed by financial hangovers. In the 1880s, there was a technology bubble precisely like the tech bubble of the period between 1982 and 2000. The principal technological advance back then was the building of a national rail network, but every aspect of life from the 1870s to the early 1890s became more efficient and productive because of the telephone, electricity, artificial light, and industrialized manufacturing.

It all blew up in 1893 when the railroads had become so overbuilt and Wall Street had helped inflate stock prices to such ridiculous levels that the whole house of cards fell in on itself. By the time the "Panic of 1893" had played itself out, many of the largest railroads (like the Internet companies of the 1990s) went bankrupt, more than 15,000 companies went out of business, some 500 banks failed, and unemployment approached 20 percent.

In spite of the lessons learned from 1893, there was another Wall Street cataclysm in 1907 that was so bad the government created a new entity to prevent a future financial collapse. That was the Federal Reserve Bank, founded in 1913.

The Federal Reserve did such a "good" job that it actually helped set the stage for the Crash of 1929 and the Great Depression, in part by making it easier for people to borrow money to buy stocks, and for Wall Street to push prices to ridiculous levels. Some 9,000 banks failed, unemployment reached 25 percent, and it took a world war to pull us out of that hole.

The Crash of 1929 produced the Securities and Exchange Commission, which was supposed to make sure we never had such a disaster again. But we did, in the mid-1970s, and we did again in the late 1980s, and we did again in 2000. Statistically, this time could be the worst ever, but the point I'm making in this book is that, as individuals, we are not automatically condemned to go down with the ship every time the financial world turns upside down.

We are not automatically condemned to go down with the ship every time the financial world turns upside down.

In the same way that loss of life on the *Titanic* could have been limited had the passengers been drilled and there had been enough lifeboats, the message I hope you will take away from this book is that the key to financial security is to expect the unexpected. So by *Fasten Your Financial Seatbelt*, I'm urging a return to some basic principles such as living within your means, making sure you understand how money works and, most importantly, managing your financial expectations and emotions.

Consider this book like the pocket guide on an airliner that tells you where the exits are, and what to do in the event of an accident. Those guides have saved lives, and I hope this one will help save your financial sanity.

PART **ONE**

Money Myths, Misconceptions, and Meaning

Out of the Wreckage

> **❝ Money is like a sixth sense without which you cannot make a complete use of the other five.❞**
>
> —W. Somerset Maugham,
> in *Of Human Bondage*

The book you hold in your hands is in part the manifestation of a rare gift— a second chance at life.

I'd grown up in a household where money was a frequent topic of conversation and consternation. My father had maintained and repaired elevators for a living in the New York City area and was so good at his work that after we moved to southern California—a better climate for my asthma—he went out on his own with a partner. It was the 1960s, during a building boom. The business thrived, affording my siblings and me solid, upper middle-class, childhoods.

Starting at age twelve, I went with my dad on his weekend calls, and from age fourteen on I worked side by side with him during the summer in elevator shafts, up to sixteen hours a day at seventy-five cents an hour. When we weren't performing regular maintenance, we were often responding to emergencies, rescuing terrified people who'd gotten stuck between floors. It was a rare occasion when we were greeted with anything less than gratitude and relief. Elevators, like airplanes, push emotional buttons about intimacy, heights, and vulnerability.

My father could fix anything, and I loved working with him. It made me feel grown-up to come home from a day of crawling around grimy motor rooms and greasy cables and be included in my mother's scolding rant about how filthy we were. I looked up to my dad for his knowledge, skill, and work ethic. We were very different, however, when it came to money.

> **I looked up to my dad for his knowledge, skill, and work ethic. We were very different, however, when it came to money.**

My Money DNA

I seem to have inherited the good financial genes from each branch of the family. My mother's father had been a young banker when the stock market crashed in 1929. He rebounded into a long career in management at the Federal Reserve Bank on Wall Street and he played the stock market, doing well enough to retire early.

He knew his way around money and how to make it grow. On family visits to New York, he'd take me with him to the New York Stock Exchange where I reveled in the frenzy and roar of the crowd. I'd watch him celebrate when he was doing well, or curse and chew his cigar when he was losing. From him I developed an interest in the stock market and a commonsense approach to investing.

My father was Canadian, a World War II–era veteran of the Royal Canadian Air Force. His father had been a successful entrepreneur in the small town of Caledonia, Nova Scotia, owning the local department store, grocery, and barber shop.

We rarely saw my Canadian grandparents, but my father clearly had inherited his father's entrepreneurial urges. As my dad's fortunes improved with the growth of his elevator business, he reimagined himself as a brilliant investor, plunging large sums into one venture after another. But unlike his father, who managed his businesses himself, my father was drawn to other people's get-rich-quick schemes, with inevitable results.

The money conversation in our home vacillated between my father bragging about how rich his newest investment would make us and my mother complaining about how much he'd lost on the last one. Through a string of messy financial disasters, he remained the eternal optimist, the guy who falls off a building and remains hopeful all the way down to the pavement.

I wanted to help my father and gave him some suggestions that were less risky. After he sold his elevator maintenance business, I begged him to do something simple. "Why don't you just buy a McDonald's franchise or something?"

"Yeah, yeah. You're probably right. Soon as this gold mine deal goes through, you'll see. We'll be sitting pretty. I'll buy a whole chain of McDonald's!"

He was hooked on the grand quest for the mother lode. When he could no longer afford the payments on the second and third mortgages he'd taken out on the family house, my parents sold it and moved into a condo. It broke my heart because I knew things could have turned out so differently.

My father assured me, "Soon as this gold mine deal goes through, you'll see. We'll be sitting pretty. I'll buy a whole chain of McDonald's!"

Discovering That Money Earns Money

At a young age, I was a good listener and enjoyed hanging around with adults, so I was susceptible to my father's optimism and desire to achieve financial independence as well as my Wall Street grandfather's sober investment instincts.

In high school I bought my first few shares of stock, choosing companies I knew something about through my father's business. It was expensive and complicated in those days to make small trades, but I managed a make a little profit.

Flying was an early passion and when I was twelve I started taking lessons, and soon earned my license. My ambition became to one day pilot big passenger jets. In the meantime, I bought my own sailplane—a glider. I sometimes packed food, water, and an empty bottle for elimination and spent long hours in the air, riding the Mojave Desert thermals.

When I graduated high school, I ignored my friends' warnings that I was throwing my life away and skipped college. I worked in the elevator business for a couple of years, saving money to buy a house. But in the late 1960s, I got the youthful travel bug and spent some of the money I had saved going to Europe. I liked it so much I got a job in a store on an American military base, learned German, and met a German girl who I later married and brought back to California.

I got my first paying pilot's job, flying for a charter company. But my wife missed her family so we pulled up stakes and moved to Frankfurt where I soon found work with Lufthansa, starting as a cabin crewmember but on the waiting list to be promoted to pilot as soon as a vacancy opened.

The Day My Destiny Changed

On November 20, 1974, four months after I started with Lufthansa, I joined an eighteen-person crew on a flight from Frankfurt to Johannesburg, South Africa. The plane was a Boeing 747, still a relative novelty after being in service only five years. We stopped over in Nairobi, Kenya, where we refueled and taxied into position for takeoff. I took an empty crew seat over the left wing and belted myself in.

The plane thundered down the runway, the nose lifted, and I felt the thump of the landing gear breaking contact with the tarmac. Everything seemed normal as we began our ascent, but then the plane hesitated. As a pilot, my stomach fluttered as I realized we were stalling. Moments later the massive ship slammed into the earth, tail first.

A deafening, grinding crash was followed by stillness. I was in front of the coach section and had survived the impact

my stomach fluttered as I realized we were stalling. Moments later the massive ship slammed into the earth, tail first.

unharmed. The left wing was on fire and the windows were melting so I jumped out of my seat and opened the door in front of the right wing.

I headed into the first-class cabin to find that the deck had collapsed into the baggage hold. People were screaming. The next minute or so seemed to collapse into an instant. I started grabbing arms, helping people up and out of the tangle, carrying those who couldn't walk as fast as I could move. The smell of jet fuel and smoke was intense and terrifying. We'd just topped off our tanks, so I knew it was just a matter of moments before the entire plane became engulfed in flames.

On my last, hurried trip down the aisle to make sure I hadn't missed anyone, I was about to turn and evacuate myself when I heard a faint cry from under some rubble. I lifted a seat fragment and saw a bleeding, elderly man gasping for breath. I pulled him up from beneath the debris and dragged him down the aisle and out of the plane. Just as we struggled out the emergency exit, I felt the heat and concussion of an explosion on the other side of the plane. Anyone still trapped in the wreckage was doomed.

The injured man and I got about a hundred yards from the wreckage when I turned and spotted a woman standing in the remains of the exit doorway I'd just left, waving frantically and screaming. Her husband was lying next to her, seriously injured. She needed help getting him out the door.

I sprinted back as a massive column of black smoke

turned day into night. I shouted instructions to her as we manuevered her semiconscious husband down the chute and off the plane. We stumbled through the scattered wreckage for about thirty yards when I felt a second, more intense wave of heat, and another concussion. The entire fuselage, where we'd been struggling moments earlier, was a boiling mass of flame.

It was a disaster for the history books: the first-ever fatal wreck of a Boeing 747. Ninety-eight people survived. Fifty-nine perished. Somebody counted a dozen people I'd helped escape. To me it was all a blur, and the shock was so intense it would be years before I could process it all.

Lessons From the Wreckage

CBS News anchor Walter Cronkite reporting the crash in 1974.

Newspapers around the world ran my photo next to pictures of the smoking wreckage under huge black headlines that emphasized the word "hero." It was embarrassing. In my mind, I was no more than a well-trained, quick-thinking member of a great crew with a world-class airline who'd been lucky enough to escape injury. Like other first responders, flight crews are trained to run toward trouble, not away from it. My duty as a crew member, and my instinct as a human being, was to pull as many people out of that wreckage as I could. Then, if possible, I would save myself.

Life became more precious, as did time. It had been a privilege to be able to guide those people out of the confusion and danger, and the experience gave me confidence in my instincts. The experience reshaped the way I looked at the world and my role in it.

One of the lessons was the value of planning and preparing for the worst. It's true that "it only happens to other people," until it happens to you.

One of my enduring images from that day was of a woman sitting on a smashed suitcase in the field by the runway, absorbed in searching for something in her purse, seemingly oblivious to the massive pillar of smoke where 59 people had just lost their lives.

I experienced a similar moment myself when, two hours after the crash, I was in a Nairobi drug store, shopping to replace my destroyed travel gear, and caught myself debating toothpaste brands. I realized that fixating on toothpaste was a way of avoiding coming to terms with having just witnessed and escaped death.

It would be another nine years before I gave up my career as an airline pilot and began my life as an investment advisor. When I did, I discovered that I could apply my insight into how I, and other people, respond in a crisis. Working with people to secure their financial futures gave me the satisfaction I got from helping others. With my instincts about money, it turned out to be a winning combination.

In the quarter-century since, I've pulled countless people out of the wreckage and confusion of their financial lives, and helped many find the happiness that comes from a healthy relationship with money, but which money alone cannot buy.

Along the way there were some I couldn't save. Some, like my father, had already exhausted their resources by the

NEWPORT MAN, 24, HERO IN JUMBO JET DISASTER

Coast Man Hero in Jet Crash

By GARY GRANVILLE
Of the Daily Pilot Staff

Survivors of a jumbo jet airliner crash in Kenya Wednesday credited 24-year-old Thomas Scott of Newport Beach with saving the lives of dozens of persons.

Scott, of 49 Royal St. George Road, was hailed as a hero by those he helped escape from a burning Lufthansa Boeing 747 jet that crashed while taking off from the Nairobi Airport.

"We all would have been dead if it hadn't been for him," a Dallas woman reportedly said in the wake of the first crash of a jumbo jet.

While 98 persons aboard the jet survived the crash, 59 were killed when it plunged into a marsh at the end of the runway, burned and then exploded.

Among the 98 survivors were many

PRAISED BY PASSENGERS
Heroic Steward Scott

747 JET CRASH IN NAIROBI—Smoke cloud rises over the first fatal wreck of a Boeing 747 since the jumbo jets went into service five years ago. The Lufthansa craft crashed shortly after takeoff.
Story on Page 1
(AP Wirephoto)

time they got to me. Others continued to make the mistakes that brought them to me in the first place and wouldn't heed my warnings.

Money can be the root of all happiness, but our culture encourages unrealistic expectations and unlimited temptations. Some of us have become addicted to buying now and gambling on being able to pay later. Some of us think there is a secret door to wealth and if we open enough doors, we'll find the right one. Some of us live in terror of poverty, which drives us to make terrible choices that lead to the place we most fear.

In the following pages you will read about some of these people, many of them clients I've helped achieve a wholesome relationship with money and a degree of happiness. You will no doubt identify with much of the faulty thinking that keeps so many from achieving their financial goals. Don't be too hard on yourself. Few people are born with a sixth sense about money. But it can be acquired.

2 How Much is Enough?

❝ Money, which represents the prose of life... is, in its effects and laws, as beautiful as roses.❞

—Ralph Waldo Emerson, 1844

Money is the root of all anxiety, and there is plenty of anxiety to go around these days. Just over half of Americans tell researchers that they are so discouraged about their inability to save that they avoid hearing, reading, or discussing the subject. That 2007 poll result, reported by Bankrate.com, also found that seven out of ten people are failing in their retirement savings goals because of other financial needs. Small wonder that insomnia has become epidemic.

For the past twenty-five years, I've been helping as many people as possible change their anxiety to contentment. That doesn't mean I help everybody get rich. It does mean I spend a great deal of my time helping clients develop a healthy, realistic relationship with their money.

In more cases than not, I find myself having to explain to people that they are less wealthy and secure than they believe. At the other end of the spectrum, I have actually had to convince people they were already well-to-do and give them permission to spend.

I once had a new client who was recently widowed. She had a conservative investment portfolio worth about $10 million, earning her about $500,000 a year. Her husband had also left her a pension of about $7,000 a month, along with a luxury, mortgage-free home. She was receiving Social Security benefits as well.

She complained to me that her friends were all going on cruises and vacations and she wished she could afford to join them. She wasn't pulling my leg. She'd grown up during the Depression and was so terrified of being broke she wouldn't spend a nickel she didn't have to. She bought her clothes in thrift shops and clipped supermarket coupons.

It took some convincing but I showed her that her expenses were lower than her income and she had enough money to live well for the rest of her life, no matter how many days she had left. I may not have cured her worrying altogether, but she did start to enjoy some of the pleasures she had been denying herself, including joining her friends on vacations.

The Human Factor

The trouble with money is the trouble with human nature, and especially so in our unique, free-market culture. Americans spend an inordinate amount of time obsessing about money. Popular programs like *Extreme Makeover, Who Wants to be a Millionaire?* and *Deal or No Deal* help perpetuate the myth that sudden prosperity can happen to just about anyone, and that if it does, all your problems are solved.

This mythology nurtures a competitive instinct: we are constantly measuring where we are in the financial pecking order. Ours is one of few cultures where it's not impolite to ask someone you've just met what they do for a living. We form conclusions about each other depending on the reply. Consciously or not, we make an immediate calculation of where we fit in the food chain relative to who we meet.

As a society, all this attention to money has made us wealthier than we've ever been, yet never more confused about how to manage that wealth. It's no surprise, what with the roar of voices trying to get our attention: mailboxes overflow with glossy brochures, television serves an endless stream of investment industry ads, and newspapers and magazines are full of stories and advice warning about scams or touting the strategy du jour.

Wealth/Food Chain

Job Status

The headlines are relentless and mind-bloggling:
"Forty Must-Own Stocks for Retirement!"
"When to Buy an Actively-Managed Fund"
"How Much Should You Pay for Advice?"
"A New Way to Assess a Mutual Fund"
"When to Postpone Social Security"
"Are You Saving Enough for Retirement?"
"How to Build a Million-Dollar Portfolio"
"Boomer Inheritance Hopes May Be a Bust"

How Wealth Is Lost

All the time and energy we spend fretting and talking about money, trying to hold on to what we've got and make more, is exhausting. I know, because I grew up in a household where money was frequently the subject of parental discord. My father had built with his own hands a successful Los Angeles-based elevator maintenance business that he sold at a relatively young age for a life-changing sum of money. And change his life it did.

He came from a line of entrepreneurs and proceeded to make a series of ill-conceived and ill-timed investments in ventures like vineyards and helicopter companies. He wanted to use his wealth to make some REAL money.

Nothing anyone could say to him could pull his head out of the clouds. Predictably, his fortunes slid from having lots of cash and a paid-for house to being forced to sell the house to pay off layers of mortgages and move himself and my mother into a condo.

But before you pass judgment on entrepreneurs like my father, consider an example from the opposite end of the spectrum. When I was a kid, my grandparents were friends with a couple who were known as one of the wealthy families in our southern California town. We were middle class, and it felt special that these wise, successful people chose to spend time with my family.

Years later, after I had established my career as an investment advisor, my mother called to tell me that Wilma, the widow of this couple, wanted to speak to me about her investments. Excited at the prospect of a new client—a close friend of the family at that—I called up Wilma and heard just about the saddest story I've encountered in all my years.

She was now living in a mobile home in a retirement trailer park. I was dumbfounded. What happened to the money? She explained that her husband had gotten sick and died in the 1980s at a time of record-high interest rates, when it was possible to earn twelve percent interest on an ordinary bank CD. (That seemed like a lot at the time, but after taking into account the high inflation and taxes, it was actually a poor investment.)

Excited at the prospect of a new client, I called up Wilma and heard just about the saddest story I've encountered in all my years

As he lay dying, Wilma's husband, fearful that his soon-to-be widow would be preyed upon by unscrupulous investment salespeople after he was gone, told her, "Just keep rolling the CDs over and you'll be fine. Don't let anyone try to talk you out of it."

After he died, interest rates began a long decline and Wilma's income from her CDs began to decline as well.

But she continued to live—and spend—as she always had. Nothing could get her to do anything but keep rolling over her CDs, each one yielding less than the last. Before long, she had to dip into principal to keep up her lifestyle.

Meanwhile, inflation was chewing away at her buying power. Between the ever-rising cost of living and the steady decline in income, Wilma lost her house and savings. The worst part was that by the time I got to her, there was nothing left to work with, nothing I could do to pull her from the wreckage. She was doomed to live out her life in a trailer trying to get by on Social Security. She ended up in exactly the situation from which her husband had hoped to protect her.

Money Is Your Stage

Over the past twenty-five years I've reviewed the financial lives of thousands of people and have worked with them to master their money. The metaphor I like to use that seems to resonate most strongly is borrowed from Shakespeare's play *As You Like It*:

"All the world's a stage,
And all the men and women merely players."

Your relationship with money is the stage on which your life unfolds. The stage should be a sturdy, well-built platform for everything you do, and the set should reflect everything you are. Your ability to be a good player—to perform your role in life with conviction—depends on the health of your relationship with money. The metaphor is rather simple. The performance is another matter.

Most people I meet for the first time are confused, misinformed, or conflicted about the big question: How much is enough? It's not because they're dim-witted. First of all, the answer is different for every person or family, and it's become a moving target as the number of years we can expect to live, and the period of time we plan to work, gets longer and longer.

The answer gets especially complicated for many people because their relationship with money is flawed by experience or expectation. I've had many new clients begin by telling me, "I want to build a nest egg of a million dollars for retirement."

"Why?" I ask.

"Well, isn't that how much a person needs these days to retire?" They are parroting something they read in a newspaper or magazine, or heard at the golf course or from a friend or relative.

"That depends," I say. "If you want to live on the beach in Malibu, it's not enough. If you plan to retire to a rural village in Mexico, it might be plenty."

The consistent theme, however, is that whatever they have, it's never enough. A client who earns $75,000 per year invariably tells me that if he or she could only make $100,000 per year, their money problems would be solved. I hear the same thing from someone earning $750,000 a year: they'll be sitting pretty as soon as they reach a million a year.

A couple I know had grown their wealth to more than $2 million in investments, in part by remaining in their modest home, sharing one car, and shopping at the local second-hand shop. The magic number for them was $4 million.

A client who is an entrepreneur earns $3 million per year and spends $3.5 million, but is unconcerned about his negative cash flow because he's doing so well (in his mind) that it's inevitable he'll soon be earning $6 million a year.

I've worked with corporate executives who've been dutifully squirreling away as much as they were allowed into their retirement plans for decades and have plenty of assets. But they still put in twelve-hour days because they're terrified they won't have enough for old age.

An estate lawyer in New York tells the story of a client who was rearranging his financial affairs following a Wall Street payday of $600 million. The lawyer asked his client, "Now that you're all set, what do you plan to do with your life?" The client responded, not missing a beat, "I'd like to see if now I can make some REAL money."

Too often, the answer to the question—how much is enough—is that there never is enough, and those who feel that way have an unhealthy relationship with money. It is their master when it should be their servant. My job, and the purpose of this book, is to show you how to fix that equation.

One of the great paradoxes in our conception of wealth and prosperity is that people who have a shortage of money enjoy one big advantage over the billionaires of the world. They believe that if they come into money somehow—through inheritance, the lottery, a lucky investment—life will become heaven on earth. This belief gives them hope.

> **People who have a shortage of money enjoy one big advantage over the billionaires of the world...hope.**

The billionaire, however, has learned the limits of wealth. Health, happiness, satisfying relationships—none of those things get better because one is or becomes wealthy. I've met a lot of miserable rich people and quite a few happy poor ones.

This book is about building a solid stage so you can choreograph the life you choose.

Ten Common Mistakes

I've identified ten common mistakes people make when dealing with their money and making investment choices:

1. Decisions based on the past, much like driving by watching the rear view mirror.
2. Thinking only of the short term.
3. Being stampeded by herd mentality.
4. Speculating instead of investing and not knowing the difference.

5. Being inconsistent—bouncing between complacency and panic.
6. Sticking their heads in the sand and refusing to learn about their investment options.
7. Adding to winners when it's time to sell, selling losers when it's time to buy.
8. Hugging one kind of investment, such as CDs, municipal bonds, technology stocks, real estate.
9. Being overconfident.
10. Using borrowed funds to get more bang for their buck.

Each of these mistakes stems less from ignorance and more from personality type and emotional states that cloud our judgment. Chances are very good that you fall into one of the following types of people I often meet in my business. Don't feel bad if you do. There are lots of others in the same boat.

Someone You Love Is A...

- *Hurry-Up Harry:* He wants to know where he should put his money this year. He's on the lookout for the short-term big score, chasing the latest fad, picturing the pot at the end of the rainbow.
- *Sedentary Sally:* She's unwilling to take any risk at all, she keeps her money in bank CDs, letting them just roll over every anniversary, feeling that at least she won't lose anything.

- *Liquidity Larry:* He's focused on converting as much of his wealth as possible into cash because, "You never know when you might need it."
- *Whirlwind Willie:* He's too busy earning a living or growing a business to take time to understand his finances and make informed investment decisions. If he works hard enough, "it'll take care of itself."
- *Home-Run Homer:* He has a wad of cash burning a hole in his pocket and wants to make a single big bet that'll make him rich overnight.
- *Carefree Carrie:* Oblivious to the ways she is squandering her future, she buys lottery tickets and convinces herself that "somehow, something will bail me out."
- *Real Estate Randy:* He doesn't trust anything he can't see and touch, so he believes there's only one place to put his money—in the ground and the buildings on it.

Think of the above characters as species, each of which can, in fact, thrive under certain specific environments, climates, and conditions. Real Estate Randy was a genius for a while, until the housing market crashed and he became a chump.

Like a salamander that needs a damp, tropical environment and is suddenly faced with a drought, extinction will be the likely outcome. In nature, most environmental changes occur over thousands of years, and real species of animals have time to adapt or migrate. In the world of finance, the environment can change suddenly and, like alpine flowers or desert cacti, we need to be able to survive the lean spells so we can flourish when conditions are good.

In the next pages, you'll get a chance to measure yourself against some common misconceptions and behaviors around money that may surprise, inspire, and even transform your life.

Money Boot Camp

❝❝ [T]he greatest harm done by vast wealth is...
when we let the vices of envy and hatred
enter deep into our own natures.❞

—Theodore Roosevelt, 1902

Many years ago, my girlfriend and I
moved into an older, middle-class, four-bedroom home with
a plan to give it an extreme makeover. I hired a contractor
and he went to town, helping us turn a wallflower suburban
home into an up-to-date, homey environment. When it came
time to talk about the kitchen, he said, "I need to know what
appliances you're getting so we can integrate them into the
design."

I figured you can't go wrong buying the best: they
last longer and enhance resale value. I told my girlfriend
that I thought we should get a Viking stove and a Sub-Zero

refrigerator. The cost of all this fancy equipment was going to be tens of thousands.

"Do they come in white?" she asked.

I was taken aback. "No! These are top-of-the-line appliances. The best of the best. Industrial quality. They only come in stainless steel."

"Well, I like white," she said dismissively. "That way I can see whether everything is clean."

This got me thinking. Not only am I no gourmet, nor even a hobby chef, but most of the time whatever I eat at home, when I eat at home, I can prepare in a few minutes in a countertop microwave oven you can buy for under $200. What did I need with a kitchen full of insanely expensive equipment that would sit idle? So we went with more modest equipment and I saved a bundle.

We had a similar discussion about the counter-tops. I was conditioned by social expectations to want expensive granite. She convinced me to go with tile, so we saved another $10,000.

This was an epiphany. Why waste money on something that's not going to make me any happier? It was money that could be put to use elsewhere, in a way that would bring me some real happiness. So instead of turning that middle-class house into a showcase, I invested in something I really care about—sailing. By saving money on appliances and other forms of plumage, I had the money to buy a 47-foot sailboat and keep it in the Caribbean, leasing it out when I wasn't using it.

This was an epiphany. Why waste money on something that's not going to make me any happier?

The Plumage Trap

This revelation made me realize how often people sabotage their financial future by spending money on what I have come to call plumage. A peacock has a beautiful tail to attract females so he can mate and pass on his genes. But that plumage also makes him highly visible and therefore vulnerable to predators. The peacock's genes are communicating to the female, "I am so smart that I have survived the predators in spite of showing off with this big, beautiful tail."

The same phenomenon holds among primates. If a new chimpanzee is introduced to an existing group, the other chimpanzees instinctively demonstrate their status with aggressive behavior. They make it clear that the new chimp is at the bottom of the totem pole, and the way to survive and get a chance to mate is by making sure everyone in the group knows how tough he is so he can move up the ladder.

Armed with my epiphany, I began to see how frequently humans exhibit this behavior—owning a fancy car or a large home, buying expensive clothes and jewelry. These are all ways in which we demonstrate our standing in the social pecking order. This is not a new phenomenon, but there is so much wealth in the world today, we have—or can borrow—the money to buy ever-larger, ever more colorful plumage.

I have no quarrel with the desire to surround oneself with the best of everything. I enjoy the luxuries of life as much as anyone else. But many people have trouble keeping their priorities in order. I've met untold numbers who have healthy household incomes and spend it all on expensive cars and vacation homes, tennis lessons and the high life, leaving nothing for an emergency or their post-career years.

A $500,000-A-Year Hopeless Cause

In the case of one such couple, the husband and breadwinner was a high-ranking executive with a large company. He had come to me for investment advice. They had the vacation home, the luxury cars in the garage, the country club membership, and all the rest. They spent everything he earned. Technically, they could afford to. But from my perspective, they were giving up so much more and taking on a lot of stress. "Stuff" has a way of owning you, instead of the other way around.

Like the peacock or the newest chimp in the crowd, he was showing off how well he was doing, how masterful he was. I couldn't help wondering, Do you think people love you more for this? Do you think that showing off your plumage improves your relationships with others? Of course not. It only makes them envious.

This man had been referred to me by one of his underlings who had a portfolio with me worth several million dollars, because for years he had been smart enough to invest the money he could have spent on plumage. Because my referring client had been so successful, I figured his boss must be wealthy.

So I was shocked when this executive, who was earning $500,000 a year, said all he had was a month or two of emergency cash, and $150,000 in his 401(k) at work. He was about to get a bonus of $150,000, but he had already made plans to spend it on more plumage—a yacht.

"What kind of income are you looking for in retirement?" I asked him.

"I'd like to net about what I do now, $300,000 a year after taxes."

I put my glasses and pen down. "You don't stand a chance." He gave me a blank look.

"Your only hope of even coming close is to take a large portion of your income, maybe $200,000 a year, and put it into the deferred compensation plan you have at work. You and your wife need to sit down and make a budget. You may have to unload some of your stuff."

The color drained from his face. It was as if I had just dumped a bucket of ice water on his head. He was in such a state of shock, he didn't argue. He knew he was in trouble, but this was the first time an expert had given him a definitive diagnosis.

There was nothing I could do for him. My reputation depends on my track record of helping people meet their goals and I could tell I would never be able to help this guy reach his. He had doomed himself and showed no sign he was ready to come to grips with his dilemma.

I felt bad for him so I said, "Look, if you're prepared to contribute to the plan at work as I suggested, and you want to visit me every couple of years, I'll try to guide you, as a favor." I was glad to give him free advice because he had been referred to me by a good client. Either way, I was sure I'd never see him again, and I was right.

Getting Rich At $11 an Hour

Although he was not my client, I think it's instructive to briefly tell the story of a man who was recently identified as a wealthy retiree when he made several large gifts to schools in southern New Jersey, where he had lived his whole life. Paul Navone, in his late seventies, had never earned more than $11 an hour and spent his sixty-two working years toiling in mills and factories.

He popped up on the media radar screen in January 2008 when he made a $1 million gift to a local community college and it was discovered he had also paid for an Olympic-sized swimming pool for a local Catholic prep school.

Navone started out his working career at age sixteen,

earning seventy-five cents an hour, did a tour of duty in the military, and never went to college. He lived with relatives until he'd saved the money to buy a house, and then bought a couple of modest rental properties. Eventually he decided to consult a stockbroker and over the years—shopping in thrift stores and avoiding management jobs "where you work longer hours for no more money"—he continuously saved. His financial adviser said Navone "stuck to a plan and reaped the benefits."

Navone owned no plumage—not even a television—and his friends had no idea he was rich until the press recently learned of and reported his big donations. Navone told his friends, "What am I supposed to do, wear a plaque on a string around my neck that says, 'I'm rich'?"

> **Navone told his friends, "What am I supposed to do, wear a plaque on a string around my neck that says, 'I'm rich'?"**

The press periodically reports such stories, and authors Thomas J. Stanley and William D. Danko chronicled some of them in their best-selling book, *The Millionaire Next Door*. Most of the millionaire households they profiled did not live the extravagant lifestyles that most people would assume.

Some of the best-known millionaires next door became the billionaires next door. Warren Buffett still lives in the house he bought in Omaha in 1955. The day Gerry Lenfest of Philadelphia sold his cable company to Comcast for $6.7 billion, a reporter came to the Lenfest's suburban home—the one they bought when they first married—for an interview. The reporter found Mrs. Lenfest in the kitchen on her knees with a brush and a pail of soapy water, scrubbing the floor. Like Mr. Navone, both billionaires have since given away the bulk of their fortunes.

The authors of *The Millionaire Next Door* found that the common thread among those they interviewed was that they lived below their means. As opposed to the "Income Affluent" (those with a high income, but little actual wealth, or low net-worth), the unsuspected millionaires were "Balance Sheet Affluent" (those with actual wealth, or high net worth).

For most Americans, living beneath their means is a foreign concept, the wisdom of which becomes clear only after it is too late..

For most Americans, living beneath their means is a foreign concept, the wisdom of which becomes clear only after it is too late.

Retirement Base Camp

Preparing for retirement should be approached like preparing to climb Mount Everest. At the base camp you get a feel for the mountain, get in shape, adapt to the climate, plan a strategy, and find a sherpa—an investment adviser or other guide. The sherpa doesn't just hand you a map and an ice pick and point at the trailhead. They need to go along to keep you from hurting yourself, and make sure you are properly equipped.

When you actually begin the retirement climb, you transition from living off your earned income to living off the retirement assets you've accumulated. For many this is a frightening prospect.

Everybody knows the dangers and the risks. All kinds of bad things can happen.

Your sherpa, your portfolio, and how well prepared it is for your post-earning years will determine whether you reach the summit in one piece.

As a sherpa, my conversation with clients begins with a discussion about lifestyle and life goals. "Describe what you see yourself doing in retirement. Tell me the places you want to visit. What activities are most important to you? What kind of cars do you want to drive?" And so on.

Once you establish how you plan to spend your time, the next step is to figure out what it's going to cost. I have that conversation with every potential client I meet and for most of them, it's the first time anyone has discussed their future financial lives from that perspective.

Too often, people get it backward. Like the executive in the hopeless situation, they start with an idea of how much money they want to earn each year, with the idea that the goal is to be able to continue living the way they have been. That's flawed thinking, and often disconnected from reality.

The Baby Busters

Baby boomers are just starting to wake up to the realization that they have torpedoed their financial futures. In some cases, like the corporate executive mentioned earlier, it's all about plumage. But in other cases, it's like trying to climb a mountain without a map, experience, equipment, or a guide.

Many people got lured into the real estate market when the stock market collapsed. As real estate boomed, they were lulled into believing that they were rich simply because the value of their properties kept going up. After all, everybody KNEW real estate never goes down—until it did.

I practically begged a few clients to take advantage of the boom and sell some of their properties, to sock away the profits in a more liquid investment. This was especially true for clients who had expressed an interest in retiring in the near future. But some of them wouldn't listen. They had it in their minds that real estate would keep going up forever, or that by selling too early they would miss an even bigger profit.

They failed to fasten their financial seatbelts and once the real estate market did collapse, there was no escape for them. They were trapped in their financial wreckage.

This is similar to what happens in a stock market bubble, and it is exactly what happened in the late 1990s when investors bought into the notion that the laws of economic gravity had been repealed. At least with stocks, you don't fall in love with them as much as I've seen some people fall in love with real estate.

Casual real estate speculators (as opposed to those who invest professionally in income-producing real estate) get the idea that their investment is safer, and they have more confidence in it because it's tangible. They can see it, touch it, and have a good idea of the value because they know what similar properties have sold for in the same neighborhood. But it's only an idea unless or until someone writes a check.

The value of stocks, on the other hand, are in part theoretical. Whereas the value of a house is based on what

someone will pay for it today, the price of a stock includes the calculation of what it will be worth in the future. In the investing business, this is called buying future cash flow, and it's where wealth is created in such a way that you can get at it when you need to. Unless the banking system completely collapses, you can sell most stocks with a snap of your fingers.

Clients who had fallen hopelessly in love with real estate during the housing bubble and kept borrowing against their equity to buy more made me nervous. When the downturn finally began in 2007, it required a bit of tongue-biting to keep from saying, "I told you so."

The housing crash didn't just hurt those with heavily mortgaged properties. Those who thought they were being safe by paying off their mortgages discovered that a big portion of their wealth was tied up in homes they couldn't sell—or could sell only by taking a big cut—and it became much harder to get a home equity loan to meet cash needs or emergencies.

Baby boomers who thought they were doing the safe thing by accelerating the payoff of their home mortgages discovered there is risk in every investment.

So even those baby boomers who thought they were doing the safe thing by accelerating the payoff of their home mortgages are discovering that there is risk in every investment and that locking your wealth up in your home—in one basket—limits your options.

Why Many Americans Need Money Sherpas

Our society is unique in its attitude about money and saving for retirement. On one side of the globe, in China, the household savings rate is phenomenal, with estimates ranging as high as fifty percent of gross domestic product (GDP).

On the other side of the globe, in many European countries, people don't feel the need to be savvy about their retirement plans because they pay huge taxes for government guarantees of a living pension.  Nevertheless, the household savings rate in France and Germany, for example, has been steady at about ten percent of their GDPs.

In America, we spend all we have, and more. Our household savings rate has been steadily declining since the late 1970s, from ten percent to a low of negative one percent. As a culture, we have become short-sighted and reckless with our wealth. We seem to have given up trying to be responsible, believing that some sort of miracle will come along and save us from destitution or that we'll somehow be able to fall back on Social Security.

There was a time, long ago, when it was possible in the U.S. to live a modest but dignified old age on Social Security. That possibility, based on the misperception that Social Security was supposed to guarantee a living pension, is long gone.

Social Security was invented during the Great Depression when unemployment was as high as twenty-five percent and poverty among senior citizens was greater than fifty percent. The strongest argument in favor of Social

Security was that it would remove a large number of older people from the workforce, opening up jobs for younger unemployed workers with children to feed. It was never envisioned as a European-style pension system. But that's how it came to be seen for many years.

The current anxiety about the future of Social Security is important, but not because the government owes us a living income in old age. It's important because it reveals for all to see that we are nation of people who are, on their own, confused about saving and investing. We avoid planning because we feel we have little control over our financial future. We hope for a stroke of luck: an inheritance, the one really good investment that makes us a ton of money, or a winning lottery ticket, literally and metaphorically.

It's as serious a problem as obesity, and as widespread. At least with obesity, everyone knows what it takes to get your weight under control. In the area of investing and finance, most people seem to have decided it isn't important, it's too overwhelming to think about, or they lay awake nights worrying about the future.

There is good reason to worry. The Social Security Administration estimates that a man who turned fifty in 2007 has a thirty percent chance of living another thirty-five years—longer than they have been adults—and nearly half of women aged fifty today are expected to reach that milestone. The percentages are sure to rise as preventive medicine and health care continue to improve.

But unlike obesity, which everyone can see, our financial problems are hidden from view and are a source for private embarrassment.

The Cost of Financial Shame and Guilt

People I meet in my business who have done well financially are proud of what they have accomplished and are eager to tell me about their financial lives. People who have stumbled and made mistakes often find it difficult to admit they fouled themselves up and it often takes some persuasion to get them to confess.

One of these was a well-respected CPA with offices near mine in Orange County, California, and with whom I often worked, helping each other's clients. Some of these were well-known celebrities in the entertainment business, so she got to see a good crosssection of the good, bad, and ugly of people's relationships with serious money.

She kept saying, "I don't have time." When she learned she had breast cancer, she said, "Things are up in the air. I need to get things together first."

After I had known her a few years, she gave me some of her money to invest. I appreciated her confidence but I try to make sure all my clients sit down with me and make a real financial plan. She kept saying, "I don't have time." When she learned she had breast cancer, she said, "Things are up in the air. I'm not quite sure what's going to happen. I need to get things together first."

I told her, "You don't need to get it together in order to make a plan. You make a plan, and then get it together."

She finally capitulated and I learned why she had been so reluctant to open her books to me. She was a closet financial disaster and embarrassed to have to admit it to a fellow professional. It was a tough thing for her to do, opening up her can of worms. Fortunately she opened up soon enough that I could help her get going in the right direction.

She lost her battle with cancer, but in the end she had more confidence that her kids would enjoy the benefit of her hard work.

You would think an accounting professional would have the knowledge and skills to be good with money. CPAs are always being asked, "What should I do with my money?" There are many examples of people who, one would think, should know better. Doctors and lawyers, for example, make a lot of money but are among the worst investors. A soon-to-be-retired doctor who came to me for help had only managed to save about $200,000 and declared that he and his wife needed $60,000 a year to live on, including their Social Security. He could save a life, but he couldn't add and subtract.

Choosing a Money Sherpa

People who foul up their financial futures aren't stupid. It's because they don't have a plan and they don't have a sherpa to guide them through it. They may not know how to

make a plan; it may not occur to them that they should have one; they may think it won't make any difference; or they may have sought help but the sherpa just pointed at the trailhead and wished them luck.

The way people choose their financial sherpas is much the way that people shop for a doctor or a lawyer—almost never. The financial guides we end up using are most often referrals by family or business associates.

Investment help, like medical care, is a need for which we rarely shop, even when there is a pressing need. Both, incorrectly, are viewed as commodities. When was the last time you compared your local hospital's inpatient mortality rate to those of other hospitals in your area? How many of us actually check the relative ranking of the medical school where our doctors got their training?

However we find them, once we feel we've found a good doctor or a good lawyer, we tend to stick with them. Price becomes a secondary issue. We expect to pay more for trustworthiness, reliability, and accessibility.

If people actually shop for investment help, it's less the adviser's trustworthiness they care about than, "What's it going to cost me?", "How much can you make me?", or "Just don't lose it." What shoppers for investment help usually find are people pushing products and one-size-fits-all packaged programs.

Like medical advice, financial advice is not just about the issue at hand, but about counseling and guidance. Barbara Kahn, a professor of marketing at Wharton School of Business, studied how consumers make important health care decisions and found that patients had no trouble identifying the most important factors—quality of life, survival rates, and cost—but they struggled to express them in a single value.

The choices that must be made around financial advice are somewhat similar to health care issues in that they are often unpleasant or anxiety-producing and difficult to express in a single value. But it's as simple as this: people want someone who can help them make good choices. They want someone who will not just listen to them but will work in partnership to help preserve what they have and grow it, today and tomorrow.

If you ask most advisers today, "What's your philosophy?" they will probably stutter before defaulting to a discussion about the firm's reputation, products, or superior customer service: "I carry my cell phone with me all the time." They may rattle off something they memorized from a training class or reel off the script they were given by the marketing department.

An adviser's philosophy should be clear and all about the client. Mine is to help people match their life goals to their financial goals. It's as simple as that. I enjoy saving people from their worst instincts and helping them reach the third act of life knowing their money won't run out before their lives do.

Being A Good Client

As mentioned earlier, in the process of choosing a financial adviser and starting the relationship, it's important for clients to be open about their finances and not hold back vital information, whether out of shame or fear of exploitation.

You are allowed and encouraged to interview investment professionals. If one of them says something you don't understand, you should set aside your fear of looking stupid and ask for an explanation.

Lack of communication is the single biggest problem between advisers and clients, and my solution is to check in with my clients once or twice a year. Most people need to have their hands held. They need the sherpa with them all the way to the summit. With certain clients, I know to be more watchful because they have a tendency to backslide and then not tell me about it.

Like dental care, people left to their own devices only go for financial help when something hurts. Like a good dentist, a good investment adviser reminds clients to have a periodic checkup, to identify potential problems before they turn into crises.

Your Money Isn't a "Product"

There are two basic ways investment advisers earn their keep. They either receive a commission on the amount of money you invest with them in certain products, such as mutual funds; or they charge a fee each year based on the value of the money they are managing for you. These two basic methods are as different as night from day, and I believe one is clearly better than the other.

Many investment advisers, especially those who work at national firms with hundreds of branches, are compensated by commission. When you buy one of their investment products, they immediately earn a commission, the percentage depending on the type of investment.

Whether or not the product makes you money in the long run will have no economic effect on the adviser who sold it to you.

Whether or not the product makes you money in the long run will have no economic effect on the adviser who sold it to you. If it loses money, the adviser may have a dissatisfied client, but he or she has been paid. The adviser who opts for the up-front commission has no motive to look after his or her clients to make sure they are on track and that their investments are doing well.

These advisers are not bad people. It's just the way the system works and unfortunately most salespeople are encouraged by the profit motive, and their bosses, to go for the quick buck.

The model I've been using for decades that is now widespread is called a fee-based arrangement. Instead of being paid a big commission up front, my clients pay one percent a year—pay as you go. This means I make less money at first, but I have an incentive to work hard so that my clients stay with me for the long haul, and if I do a good job and their investments grow, my reward is tied to theirs.

To me, a client's hard-earned money is not a product and I see my clients as partners in a long journey, not just one-time customers who might buy something from me today.

You Still Need a Plan

In much the same way that I choose the long-haul partnership approach with my clients, the key to the success of that partnership is a long-haul plan. Critics of the fee-based arrangement say an adviser could do nothing for their clients and just collect their annual fee without lifting a finger. There are regulations that prevent some of the potential abuses, and some investment advisers have been investigated by regulators for not being more active on their clients' behalf.

The real problem—regardless of how they get paid—is that many advisers never get around to truly helping clients put together a plan. Fee-based advisers understand that they will make more money in the long run as opposed to collecting up-front commissions on investment products. But many aren't evaluating goals and adjusting portfolios to keep up with changes in clients' financial lives. They fail to live up to the other side of the bargain and figure their clients will stick with them out of inertia.

My experience convinces me that many of my peers don't understand retirement planning. They don't even take the time to prepare their own retirement plans. Most offer planning only as a tool to get people to invest with them, without truly comprehending the effect their advice will have on their clients' financial future.

The most important aspect of a successful retirement is to have a realistic plan. The short-term performance of your investments is secondary. If you want to lose weight, you'd better have a diet plan. If you are going to put away money and have a goal to reach financially, you'd better have a plan.

The danger of having no plan or one that is poorly

The goal is to remove as much doubt or worry about the future, because worrying about money lets it master you, instead of making it serve you.

thought out is the single greatest fear investors express: they don't want to outlive their money. When you are fifty-five years old and you believe your money will last your statistical life expectancy of eighty-some years, that's so far away it's unimaginable. But we're living longer. What happens if you reach the late eighties in great shape, loving life, but with no money left? Because of this, I aim for plans that are realistic and have a good chance of providing income indefinitely. The goal is to remove as much doubt or worry about the future, because worrying about money lets it master you, instead of making it serve you.

Taking Charge and Responsibility

The most important message I hope readers take away from this book is that your financial future is your responsibility, not to be carelessly handed away to someone just because he or she has a fancy business card from a brand-name firm. You need to take charge, search for an adviser with integrity who demonstrates a commitment to sticking with you for the long haul, and one who knows how to put together a retirement plan that has the best chance of success, no matter how long you live.

It should be your number one goal to get money concerns off your conscience so you can enjoy playing your role on the stage of life.

PART **TWO**

Planning to Plan

4 Age, Rank, and Social Security Numbers

❝ There is no dignity quite so impressive and no independence quite so important as living within your means. ❞

—U.S. President Calvin Coolidge

As a Boeing 747 crew member who survived a catastrophic wreck, I took particular interest in a large National Transportation Safety Board study in 2001 that found that most passengers pay little or no attention to the flight attendant's predeparture safety instructions. Apparently a large number of passengers believe that if there's a crash, everyone always dies. But statistics tell a different story—passengers are five times more likely to survive a crash than to die in one. Paying attention could make, and often has made, the difference between life and death.

In my career as an investment adviser, I have performed a similar role in the financial lives of thousands of people. As part of my work, I have often given the "pre-departure safety instructions" to clients who I later discovered weren't paying attention, and they wound up paying a price for it.

One in particular had all his wealth tied up in real estate, some of it residential, as the market was exploding in 2002–2003. Prices had risen fast and he understood the logic of my argument and his wife's urging that he should take some of his eggs out of that one basket. He was wealthy on paper but land poor, dragged down by multiple mortgages, with anemic cash flow because everyone in the world was doing the same thing he was—buying houses and trying to rent them out. It was hard to find and keep tenants.

He was wealthy on paper but land poor, dragged down by multiple mortgages...because everyone in the world was doing the same thing he was—buying houses and trying to rent them out.

The worry, the financial stress, the endless days of driving around checking on his buildings, taking care of emergency repairs, and performing basic maintenance—all of it was taking its toll on the quality of his life and the patience of his family. He loved the game, but it was time to take some money off the table. My advice was based on financial common sense but colored by my observation that his family was unhappy with the long hours and constant tension.

I told him there was an IRS rule—a 1031 exchange—that would allow him to sell some of his properties and defer the capital gains tax if he reinvested the money in a similar investment, such as commercial real estate. I pointed out that

office buildings and shopping centers tend to produce more reliable income.

"That's a great idea!" he declared. "I'm ready. Let's do it."

I came up with a program that I thought would suit him, but when I called to discuss it, he interrupted to breathlessly tell me about a hot new luxury home he had his eye on that looked like a good deal. He thought he could swing the purchase by borrowing against the rising value of his existing properties. The fancy term for this is leveraging an asset, and it works great when prices are rising, which they had been for some time. But that was about to change, and I gave him my honest advice—don't do it—knowing he had already decided to go ahead.

Fortunately for him, the new property deal didn't go through because soon after, the housing market began to cool off. Then it imploded. The easy, speculative mortgage money, the kind my client depended on, dried up. The tide of eager buyers retreated, and he was left high and dry to survive the downturn as best he could.

This is the Real Estate Randy I describe in my list of investor species in Chapter Two. He only trusted what he could see and touch. He loved real estate and became emotionally attached to it, a common and often costly mistake.

Horse-Before-Cart Syndrome

For money to be a good servant, you need to become master of yours. Life goals should be the prominent consideration. Financial goals should serve life goals. Most people tend to think in reverse: if I can just accumulate a nest egg, then I'll have the freedom to live my life the way I want.

But life is expensive. It moves faster every day and the world is full of temptations. As a society we procrastinate and find endless excuses why we can't reach that financial goal we've decided is the magic number—a number that's often wrong.

Like the corporate executive I sent away, most people find this dilemma overwhelming. It's the "everyone dies in a plane crash" mentality. From every angle we're besieged with financial advice, advertisements, news, and analysis. We've heard it all a hundred times before, we feel hopeless or confused, and we quit listening. At the other end of the spectrum are those driven by fear or impatience into rash or ill-conceived investments, hoping for a big hit or the promise of high returns. My father's example is always there to remind me. The big score rarely works out the way you hoped.

Planning is essential because no matter how much money you have, it'll never feel like enough. It's a well-documented aspect of human nature. For this reason, the conversation I try to have with every client from the first time we meet, and once a year thereafter, revolves not around dollar goals but life goals. Once I know what those are, I can help clients evaluate whether and how we can come up with a plan that gives them the best chance of the dollars being there to support it.

The financial industry executive who faced a reduced lifestyle in retirement in spite of earning $500,000 a year was unable or unwilling to have that conversation, so I couldn't help him. Happily, there are many I have been able to help. For some it was easier than others.

One of my clients was a business leader who'd dutifully socked away twenty percent of everything he earned his whole life. His father had taught him, "Always pay yourself first." He had made some money in the 1980s in real estate and had managed his money well by taking his profits and diversifying through mutual funds he chose after a lot of studying and comparing.

I met him in a scuba diving class, and when I told him what I did for a living, he commented, "I'm going to retire soon and I've accumulated a chunk of change. But I don't want to be reading *The Wall Street Journal* and watching CNBC the rest of my life. I just want to go scuba diving in exotic places without having to think about it."

❝ I'm going to retire soon... But I don't want to be reading The Wall Street Journal and watching CNBC the rest of my life.❞

This conversation evolved over time into a client relationship when he asked me to put together a financial plan that would make it possible for him to travel the world, exploring the oceans. First we worked backward: How much would it cost him to live that life? How often would he travel and what lifestyle did he want to live when he returned home from his travels?

By the time we got done, we had built a financial plan that was realistic and gave him greater confidence he would have the means to pursue his passion. It meant keeping a modest home in the States, and staying in less-swanky hotels when he traveled. But he had a vision for himself, so these were minor concessions compared to the freedom—both physical and emotional—that he got in return.

To have your money under control, you must be clear about your goals and then go about achieving them in a methodical fashion.

His story is one I often tell to illustrate the idea that financial independence is not measured by your bank balance. Before I talk with people about preserving and accumulating money, I want to know what the money's for. In order to have your money under control, you must be clear about your goals and then go about achieving them in a methodical fashion.

Retirement Is Being Retired

Everywhere you turn, the investment industry talks to you about retirement. It's a term that baby boomers are in the process of retiring from their vocabulary, but the industry persists in using it. Our values have changed since the days when Dad worked at the same company for thirty years and then he and Mom moved to Florida to await the grim reaper in tropical comfort.

Today, the majority of Americans expect to work to age seventy, even if they don't have to; expect their lifestyles and expenses to remain about the same; and plan to finish out their lives either in their current homes or within twenty-five miles.

One of the more fascinating findings in recent polls on retirement attitudes is that most people place greatest emphasis on health, both mental and physical, and very little on financial independence. The flaw in this thinking is that if you don't take care of your financial independence, you risk greater stress, which leads to poorer health at a time when you may be least able to afford the best care.

Increasingly, baby boomers view the concept of retirement as alien, in part because most believe they'll never be able to afford to quit working, and because retirement is what their parents did when they got ready to die. And many did, mostly from inactivity.

Thurgood Marshall, the first African American to serve on the U.S. Supreme Court, told a reporter that he could not imagine doing anything else but serving on the court. He said that if he quit, he would probably die of boredom. When he finally retired in 1991 at the age of eighty-three, he said, "I'm getting old and coming apart." He died eighteen months later.

You Aren't Alone

If you recognize in some of these stories your own bad calls and misconceptions about money, don't feel too bad—you've got plenty of company. For example, ask any veteran investment adviser which clients are the clumsiest investors and they will invariably reply: accountants, lawyers, and doctors.

Among those, my experience is that accountants have the hardest time. Like engineers, they seem to focus on details instead of the big picture and are more willing than you'd imagine to speculate instead of investing. Accountants are like the cobbler who has no shoes.

Doctors and lawyers are smart and they know it, which tends to get in the way of their investment judgment. They tend to be stubborn. They make good incomes so they feel that no matter how badly they manage their finances, there will always be money coming in. These busy professionals have neither time nor patience to sit still and plan their financial futures. They get tips or investment offers from patients, clients, and colleagues, as well as a parade of investment sales people who prey on doctors and lawyers. These otherwise intelligent and successful professionals

 allow themselves to be victimized by patients or clients who turn out to be scam artists, or by brokers and advisers working for the big Wall Street firms who steer them into unsuitable investments that will pay big commissions.

There are so many ways wealth is squandered. In the investment world there is the well-documented phenomenon referred to as "shirtsleeves to shirtsleeves in three generations." It has been estimated that as much as seventy percent of

wealth is dissipated within three generations of its creation.

One of the most frequently cited examples is the Vanderbilt family. Cornelius Vanderbilt, who first built the Vanderbilt empire in shipping and then railroads, died in 1877 leaving an estate that, adjusted for inflation, was three times larger than Bill Gates's estimated wealth.

When 120 Vanderbilt heirs got together for a reunion almost a century later, there wasn't a single millionaire among them.

During a period when a growing number of people are experiencing sudden

When 120 Vanderbilt heirs got together for a reunion, there wasn't a single millionaire among them.

wealth—from entrepreneurs to professional athletes—stories of squandered good fortune are becoming more common. There are, by some estimates, more than nine million households in the U.S. with a net worth of $1 million or more—not including the value of their primary residence. Americans are adept at creating value and wealth, but often have a hard time holding on to it.

A Big Payday Is Not Wealth

Too many people think wealth comes from a large income or a big payday. It's not how much you earn or accumulate, it's what you do with what you earn or accumulate. There are, as I've noted, people who have earned very low salaries their entire lives but who wound up millionaires because of their lifelong saving and investing habits. On the other hand, there are those who have high-paying jobs but who have nothing to show other than fancy houses and expensive toys.

In southern California, where my offices are, there are many stories of people who made a killing in the entertainment industry, or in the stock market, only to go broke a couple of years later. When I have clients who've had a run of good luck, I work hard to steer them away from thinking they've arrived, and try to get them to see that the financial journey never ends.

One of my clients, for example, had done extraordinarily well in a retail business. He has an entrepreneurial mind and when he sold his business for many millions, he was only in his forties and the big payday unleashed a beast in him. He went on a spending spree, buying a very expensive home, private jet time, and all the rest of the symbols of wealth.

Clients like these make me nervous and in his case, the jury is still out as I write this. I'm afraid that if I can't get him under control, he will overspend and find himself on the short end of the stick. He is living in a state of financial euphoria, thinking he has unlimited wealth and doesn't have to worry.

I worry because I've seen a lot of good fortune turn into sad cases.

I worry because I've seen a lot of good fortune turn into sad cases. But when I can manage it, I get a great sense of satisfaction from helping people avoid throwing away their hard-earned financial freedom and from rescuing people from their financial wreckage.

5 The Basic Ingredients

❝ Poverty is not a scarcity of actual money, but a scarcity of vision.❞

—Dan Sullivan, Noted Business Coach and Speaker

One of the most successful money managers of the 1990s was a portfolio manager in San Francisco who had been featured in the financial media as a visionary. By 1999 he had made huge profits for his clients thanks to his early investment in technology stocks related to the Internet.

At the time everyone was talking about the "new" economy, but being a more conservative investor, I had stayed away from investing my clients' money in most of the dot-com companies because they weren't making anywhere near the kind of profits that would justify their stock prices. My clients—whose friends were bragging at cocktail parties about how much money they were making—started asking me, "Tom, why don't we own some of these stocks? Look how much money we would have made."

After reading an article about this portfolio manager, I decided to give him a call and find out if he had some sort of secret sauce. I figured he must be a lot smarter than I and that he must have a brilliant strategy to take his profits and get out of those dot-com stocks. I wanted to see what I could learn and evaluate whether his fund might be good for some of my clients.

I called him in January of 2000 and asked him what he saw in the future. He told me that he had no plans to get out of technology because "the valuations aren't that high compared to the growth that's coming with the Internet. I'm in this for the long haul, and anybody who isn't is going to be left behind."

Everyone was in a state of euphoria and I returned home depressed thinking I was a dinosaur who needed a new profession.

My heart started pounding. Here was a guy considered one of the top portfolio managers in the world telling me that I had really blown it and missed out on the biggest stock market boom in history. Everyone was in a state of euphoria and I returned home depressed thinking I was a dinosaur who needed a new profession because the world had clearly passed me by.

But on further reflection, looking at companies valued in the billions that hadn't yet earned a nickel, I wasn't convinced—and a good thing, too. The whole stock market began to collapse a few months later, and many of those dot-com stocks this portfolio manager owned burned to the ground. Over the period of about a decade, he had gone from best to worst.

I still don't think I was ever as intelligent as he was, so what was the difference? I believe he fell into the same trap as the Real Estate Randy who becomes infatuated with his real estate. Even though the San Francisco portfolio manager was a professional, he fell in love with his stocks and began to believe what people were saying about him: that he was a genius. His exuberance was irrational, the same emotion that keeps people in relationships long after they've gone bad.

When the honeymoon is over and the romance has died, we hate to give up, and we persuade ourselves that if we try hard enough, we can get back to that euphoric state. The difference is that it may be possible to repair a broken relationship but once a speculative, high-risk investment has gone to the dogs, your money's gone and it's never coming back.

A Kiss Is Still a Kiss

I am a history buff and have always been a value investor. I look for true bargains and then wait for the rest of the world to discover them. What is a true bargain? A great example is oil in 1998. At the same time that the mob was chasing the AOLs and Amazon.coms, oil was trading at just under $11 a barrel and many oil company stocks were trading at twenty-year lows. Occidental Petroleum at one point was paying a dividend of about twenty percent.

A company whose dividend ratio gets that high is one whose stock has fallen because investors have lost confidence in its ability to continue paying the dividend. Occidental was struggling but it owned a valuable commodity, and anyone could see that the world was not about to quit its addiction to oil.

In other words, an idea whose profitability had yet to be tested (Amazon) was being valued at ten times a company that had half a billion in cash in the bank and many billions of dollars worth of petroleum reserves in the ground. Money madness! A dollar invested in some of those beaten-down oil stocks in 1998-1999 would have grown to about $10 today—before dividends. That's an annualized return of twenty-six percent.

During the dot-com mania, my fellow advisers and I would go to conferences where money managers talked about the great future for growth companies. I asked these people, "Don't you think valuations are out of sight and that we are due for a major correction?" I got laughed out of the room. My philosophy, and history, proved me right. The fundamental things apply as time goes by.

Talking Clients Off Ledges

It's one thing to be laughed at by your colleagues for sounding like a dinosaur, but it's quite another to manage clients who have been whipped into a speculative frenzy by the media hype and the enviable stock market returns of friends and relatives. One of the things I did was buy and give to my clients copies of *Irrational Exuberance*, a book published in early 2000 by Yale economist Robert J. Shiller, warning about the speculative bubble of the stock market. Shiller later also correctly predicted the collapse of the real estate market bubble.

The title phrase was borrowed from Federal Reserve Chairman Alan Greenspan's December 1996 speech in which he posed the question, "How do we know when irrational exuberance has unduly escalated asset values, which then become subject to unexpected and prolonged contractions?" His speech roiled markets around the globe for awhile, but the speculative frenzy continued for another three years before it all fell apart.

At my regular checkup meetings with clients, I explained my strategies and the fundamentals of successful long-term investing. I lost a few clients who felt I wasn't being aggressive enough, but the majority stayed with me because I educated them. I took my role as sherpa seriously and I made it clear to everyone that I had studied history carefully. I also explained that real money is made by buying assets everyone else is selling and selling assets that everyone else is buying.

> **Real money is made by buying assets everyone else is selling and selling assets that everyone else is buying.**

The Templeton Story

Of all the smart people in the relatively short history of stock market investing, few can rival John Templeton, who nearly seventy years ago began an investing career that has yet to be rivaled. Ten years after the Crash of 1929, with the news of Hitler's invasion of Poland, Templeton was a young man working for a seismic exploration company in New York.

He had worked years earlier for a stock brokerage and he had such a powerful instinct that it was a good time to invest that he went to his boss and asked to borrow $10,000 to put into the stock market. His boss listened to Templeton's argument that the coming war in Europe would bring an end to the Depression and introduce a period of high economic activity, and he agreed to lend the money.

Templeton went to a former colleague at his old brokerage firm and placed orders to buy one hundred shares of every stock on the New York Stock Exchange that was trading at $1 a share or less. About a third of them were insolvent, and thus very cheap. The broker tried to talk him out of it but Templeton was determined.

Before the war ended, he sold his motley $10,000 collection of stocks for the princely sum of $40,000 (equal in buying power to about $600,000 in 2007). Only four of the companies he originally invested in had actually gone out of existence. He had discovered the power of thinking globally, diversifying, and—most important of all—buying when everyone else was selling.

Templeton didn't invent the mutual fund for which he is most famous, but he did prove the power of contrarian thinking. Forty years later, Templeton's fund had racked up an average annual return of about fourteen percent, well above the performance of the market as a whole.

Templeton was still a pioneer in the 1970s when he opened his first fully global mutual fund that invested in markets around the world. Once again, he was way ahead of the crowd. Templeton was smart, creative, and had the kind of basic common sense that's made people like himself and Warren Buffett extremely wealthy while keeping a lid on their risk.

Templeton, who passed away in 2008 at the age of ninety-five, joked in a 2004 interview, "I have put [my] philosophies into a simple statement: Help people. When people are desperately trying to sell, help them and buy. When people are enthusiastically trying to buy, help them and sell."

This outlook persuaded him to buy Ford Motor Company stock cheap in the late 1970s when everyone else was eager to sell, and then to sell it for a big profit later when everybody wanted to

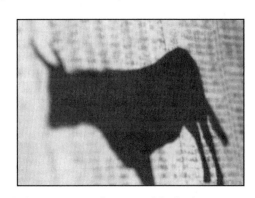

buy. His strategy and objectivity made it possible for him to predict the bull market of the 1990s, the market crash that followed and—just before he died—the bursting of the housing bubble.

The Myth of Averages

One of the biggest misconceptions people have about investing is based on fuzzy math and statistics. New clients who came to me in 2002—after the market crashed—began by announcing, "I lost a bundle. My portfolio is down fifteen percent."

But I pointed out to them, "Actually, that's not so bad when you consider that the Dow Jones Industrial Average[1] has fallen by thirty-three percent and the NASDAQ[2] has fallen seventy-six percent." People tend to think of their money in absolute terms instead of measuring how they're doing relative to the markets as a whole or relative to inflation or many other important yardsticks.

In fact, it is the primary responsibility of a good investment adviser to resist the urge to go for the big score and instead to manage your money to avoid as much risk as possible. The key to successful long-term investing is to do better than the market when things are bad, and to do well when things are good. Virtually no one is able to buy at the bottom and sell at the top.

As one of the arguments for the power of long-term investing, experts point to the growth in stock indexes over thirty or more years. But who buys and holds an investment for thirty years? In fact, Dalbar, a fund data company, found that between 1984 and 2002, a typical mutual fund shareholder's real returns were just 2.6%, lower than the inflation rate and considerably less than the return on the S&P 500 Index[3], because they bought after prices had already risen and sold after they had fallen.

Footnotes 1, 2, 3: See end of chapter for definitions.

Expect The Unexpected

This is perhaps the most important lesson I try to teach new clients: at some point in your investing career, you'll wake up to find that the financial markets have flown into an air pocket and the value of your portfolio has taken a big hit. This will cause you to break out in a cold sweat and your natural fear reaction will kick in, screaming at you to sell. Fear is a natural instinct—fight or flight—but not part of a successful investment program.

I tell clients to expect the unexpected. No one gets it right all the time, and no investment goes straight up. I spend a lot of my time training people how to be patient investors, to resist the urge to act in panic, or to hold on to an investment because they can't admit they made a mistake. In fact, I have trained my clients so well that when the market collapses, many of them call me to ask if it's a good time to buy.

It's important to recognize that anywhere you park your money involves some degree of risk. We can manage the risk

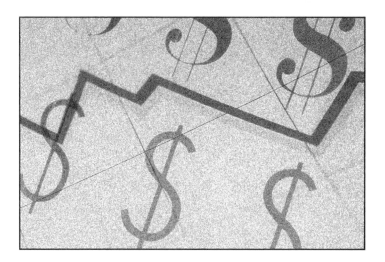

of loss in our homes by carrying insurance against fire and other calamities. But we cannot eliminate risk altogether, as people discovered when the real estate market collapsed. Real estate never goes down, until it does. In fact, simply owning residential real estate is not a good investment relative to inflation.

The Ten Percent Truth

Whether you make ten percent a year in stocks will depend on when you bought and when you sold.

The stock market mythology is that stocks earn on average about ten percent a year. This is technically true—over some decades of time, the average annual return from investing in stocks has been about ten percent although the actual long-term average annual return of the stock market from 1926 to 2008 (as measured by Standard & Poor's) comes out to an inflation-adjusted 6.2 percent, with dividends reinvested but before taxes and transaction costs.

Along the way we have gone through periods when the stock market falls apart, as it did in 2000 through 2002 after the technology bubble of the 1990s. A similar phenomenon took place in the late 1960s. The Dow Jones Industrial Average hit a high of about 1,000 back then, and it took nearly fifteen years to break through that old high and stay there.

Whether you make ten percent a year in stocks will depend on when you bought and when you sold. You might have lost fifty percent, or you may have earned 100 percent. Out of nearly sixty possible twenty-year slices of the stock market that have elapsed since the Crash of 1929 (as in, you bought the Dow Jones Industrial Average and held it for any continuous block of twenty years), your average annual rate of return could have been as low as three percent and as high as eighteen percent.

If you happened to hit an average of ten percent a year, a $100,000 initial investment would have grown in twenty years to about $675,000. If you were unlucky and caught the low-end slice, you'd only have $185,000, and at the high end you'd have as much as $2.7 million. This is before the erosion of inflation and the cost of taxes, so on the low end you not only would have failed to make any progress in the buying power of your dollars, you'd have lost some.

The ten-percent-a-year claim for stocks is irrelevant to real-life investors. In the real world, people have financial crises and health issues and become susceptible during anxious times to the investment industry's sales pitches. In the real world, the statistics are quite dismal.

If you had been patient and calm between 1986 and 2005, your average return on the S&P 500 Index would have been a respectable 11.90 percent. But according to Dalbar Inc., a leading financial services research firm, the average actual returns of investors over the same time was an anemic 3.9

percent. Dalbar reported that the difference was caused by investors' emotions driving their choices—selling after prices had already fallen and buying after they'd risen.

Another study titled "Dumb Money," conducted by professors at Yale and the University of Chicago, found that between 1983 and 2003, the hottest mutual funds—those experiencing the greatest inflows of new money from investors—performed much worse than mutual funds that investors were dumping. This phenomenon's referred to as investing by looking in the rearview mirror.

People tend to buy funds, stocks, and other tradable assets on the basis of PAST performance, which means they tend to buy them after most of the money has been made in that particular cycle, and they tend to sell after prices have fallen. Left to their own devices, most people are inclined to follow the crowd—even off a cliff.

Investment Follies

One of the things I observe about new clients is that in spite of all the information available about sound investing, it's very hard for the average person to discern whether a financial professional is competent and caring, or to evaluate the risk of any particular investment.

People recognize that they need help but they lack the tools to find the help they need and make good choices. Each year investing choices offered by the industry seem to become more complicated and therefore more confusing. People have a tendency to compound the problem with bad instincts.

People recognize that they need help but they lack the tools to find the help they need and make good choices.

For example, one of the questions people tend to focus on when evaluating a mutual fund investment is, "How much is this going to cost me?" A fund company charges fees to cover expenses, pay salaries, and make a profit for the firm. The key measure of cost is called the expense ratio—the percentage of your assets that is paid to the fund company in fees each year.

According to fund tracker Morningstar, the average expense ratio for 12,000 mutual funds in 2008 was 1.48 percent. That doesn't sound too bad but it can be a misleading number by itself. Some experts suggest measuring expenses as a percentage of mutual fund returns rather than just the value.

An example of deliberate confusion was a new savings account launched by a major bank in 2008 that offered a 5 percent interest rate instead of the average rate on savings accounts of nearly zero. That sounds like a great deal, made to seem even better when the bank said customers could earn a bonus of up to $300 depending on the size of their balance at the end of the year.

The bank invested tens of millions in a marketing campaign, and signed up lots of new customers for checking accounts tied to these new savings accounts.

But anyone who did a little bit of research would have learned that you could only deposit up to $100 a month into this new savings account, plus $1 for each debit-card transaction and online bill payment from your checking account. Also, the 5% was just a teaser rate for the first year. The rate dropped after that.

People are confused not only by industry hype, but also by nice clothes, fancy business cards, and brand-name educations. Emily Pronin, a Princeton University professor, ran an experiment, funded by the NASD Investor Education Foundation, in which she showed subjects one of two photos of an investment adviser, and asked them how much of a hypothetical $1,000 they would entrust with him to invest. For one photo, her model wore a suit. In the other, he dressed in casual clothing.

The man in the suit got an average of $535 and the subjects rarely checked his background. The same man in casual clothing got only $352, and subjects were more likely to check his background.

Pronin found that this halo effect was one of three biases that cause investors to make mistakes. The other two were being overly optimistic about financial prospects in retirement and making snap investment decisions. Pronin had done earlier studies that found people feel better when they make quick decisions. But when handling your money, quick decisions are usually bad ones because they are driven by emotion instead of information.

A Piece of Cake

In many ways, the basics of investing are a yawn. There are three flavors: equity (stocks, real estate, business ownership), debt (bonds and similar interest-bearing instruments), and cash equivalents (bank accounts, gold, commodities, collectibles, and so on). Almost every kind of investment you can possibly think of falls into one or more of these categories, whether it's a stock, mutual fund, variable annuity, unit investment trust, exchange traded fund or closed end fund, to name a few.

> When handling your money, quick decisions are usually bad ones because they are driven by emotion instead of information.

To make a boring subject just a little bit more interesting, I talk to clients about it as a baking analogy. When you bake breads, cakes, or cookies, you use flour, eggs, and butter. Nearly all baked goods contain those ingredients. Some also use sugar, yeast, and other ingredients. But the basics never change.

All the complicated investment products that are out there are all made up of the ingredients: equity, debt, and cash. If you understand these ingredients, you can understand how having an investment plan and strategy works better than throwing darts or rolling dice. And the best way to tell if an investment adviser is knowledgeable is to be knowledgeable yourself.

From my side of the desk, I can do the best job for those clients who have already tried doing it themselves or have taken the time to get educated about investments. It makes the whole conversation easier, and I'm in a better position to align their financial goals with their life goals.

Having read this far, the next time you read an article about mutual fund rankings, or see an ad from a mutual fund company bragging about their average annual return or their low fees, you'll know to ask the right questions. Because in the investment world, what you see is often not what you get.

DEFINITIONS FROM PAGE 92:

1. The **Dow Jones Industrial Average** (also referred to as the DJIA, Dow 30, or "The Dow") is an index created in the nineteenth century by Dow Jones & Co co-founder Dow Jones and is computed from the stock prices of 30 of the largest and most widely held public companies in the U.S.

2. The **Nasdaq Composite** is a stock market index computed from thje prices of more than 3,000 the common stocks and similar securities listed on the NASDAQ stock market. It is highly followed in the U.S. as an indicator of the performance of growth companies.

3. The **S&P 500** (Standard & Poor's 500 Index) is a value weighted index published since 1957 by Standard & Poor's, a division of McGraw-Hill, of the stock prices of 500 large public companies actively traded in the U.S. on the New York Stock Exchange or NASDAQ. After the Dow Jones Industrial Average, the S&P 500 is the most widely followed index.

6 Stories from the Front

> **❝ The importance of money flows from it being a link between the present and the future.❞**
>
> —John Maynard Keynes, British economist

Many of the people I meet who come to me for financial advice tell me they have had a bad experience elsewhere, and they are anxious to avoid getting burned a second time. A minority have tried to do it themselves and many of those tend to be in their thirties and early forties, introduced to the stock market over the Internet during the day-trading craze of the 1990s.

Those who had left another stockbroker or investment adviser—or wanted to—often had fallen prey to over-optimistic expectations, hadn't taken the time to educate themselves beyond scanning the fine print, ignored good advice, followed bad advice, or made poor investment choices.

It is common in the investment industry for a client to call her or her adviser asking for an opinion about some hot new investment—right after they've bought it. That's like buying a house and then having it appraised to see if you paid too much or too little. If you feel a blush coming on, you know who you are and you know what I mean.

The expectation problems clients report having elsewhere often involve volatility and poor communication. It's part of my job to make clear to clients that account balances will fluctuate and portfolio values will sometimes fall instead of rise. Nothing goes up in a straight line. On Wall Street the expression is, "The stock market climbs a wall of worry."

If you are prepared mentally and strategically for the ups and downs of markets, then you can ignore them, or at least ride them out with less stress than someone who is unprepared and more likely to react emotionally. When the market does drop, I don't wait for the phone to ring. I call my clients to let them know I'm on top of things, as well as my assessment of what's going on, whether I think any action should be taken, and my best estimate for the future. Individual and family clients, in particular, often need a calm voice to

keep them from panicking and making flawed decisions.

Professional investors, on the other hand, understand the mechanics of markets, and understand that performance is relative. Rather than focusing on whether or not they made money, they are interested in how well their adviser manages the bad times.

Among my clients, for example, is an insurance company that invests some of its reserves with me. They can't afford to take risks with their money. In a quarter when the stock market fell seven percent, but their investments with me fell only three percent, I got a hearty pat me on the back for a job well done.

Even though they were down, they were four percent ahead of the crowd and ... four percent closer to being in the black again.

They understood that even though they were down, they were four percent ahead of the crowd, and when the market would go back up, they would be four percent closer to being in the black again.

The average nonprofessional investor has no frame of reference for the argument that a three percent loss is a win. They look at it in absolute terms and if they don't say it, they often think it: "Who needs you? I can lose money all by myself."

But all forms of investments are evaluated in the context of the market in general and the cost of inflation and taxes. These last two are usually overlooked by people but part of wise money management is avoiding these hidden losses. For example, a money market fund paying two percent at a time when inflation is 3% and your tax rate is thirty percent is a money-losing proposition. You are losing one percent in your buying power from inflation, and another half percent to taxes.

Never Judge a Boy by His Bank Balance

Early in my practice as an adviser I adopted the attitude that I would take on anyone I felt I could truly help; and as a result, I had some interesting experiences. One that left a strong impression was a highschooler who had attended a talk I gave and came to me afterward asking for help with his savings of $2,000.

I love to talk about money and how it works, and I remember being young and an ardent saver myself.

Although it was a small sum, I love to talk about money and how it works, and I remember being young and an ardent saver myself. So I was happy to spend several hours explaining to this high school student the world of investment. He was too early in his life to make an investment or retirement plan, and his $2,000 was only going to generate a couple of dollars a year for my efforts and time. But I was impressed by his intelligence and curiosity, so I took his account and put his money to work in a mutual fund.

About two weeks later, I received a call from the boy's father. "You helped my son. I have half a million dollars. Can you help me, too?" That was a big lesson in the power of educating people about money and investments. It's rarely done, and even more rarely is it done well. It was a powerful lesson not to judge people by their bank balances, and it made me aware of how hungry people are for honest advice and a

caring attitude.

Ever since that experience, I haven't turned anyone away if they have a real interest and I can help. There is no one-size-fits-all solution, and there is no perfect financial planner or investment adviser for every investor. But clients have a right to know why financial professionals recommend particular investments, and how they are compensated for selling them.

No Time To Worry About Investments

Even most casual investors accept the wisdom that they should avoid putting all their eggs in one basket—the concept of diversifying your investments to minimize risk. But too many people who have had retirement plans at work, who thought that investing in the company they worked for was a good idea, ignored the wisdom and paid the price.

A typical situation arises when an employee works for a company a long time and has all of his or her retirement funds invested in company stock. During the 1990s when many private companies were going public, longtime employees became rich on paper overnight.

Either because they believe their company is going to continue to grow, or they don't want to get socked by a big tax bill by taking their profit, or perhaps just paralyzed by indecision, many people subsequently watched as their stocks sank along with the market. That was what happened to many employees of Enron. They thought the stock was going higher and they hung on to the bitter end.

missed opportunities are emotionally devastating, and can feel like crushing defeats.

Missed opportunities like that are emotionally devastating, and can feel like a crushing defeat. These losses occur for a lot of reasons, but they clearly illustrate the danger of concentrating all your wealth in one investment.

A good investment adviser—and a good investment plan—can change your life by protecting you from your worst instincts. Life is short and you shouldn't spend it worrying about your investments.

You Can't Perform Surgery On Yourself

Another trap I have seen people fall into is when successful entrepreneurs who have helped start and build up companies decide they are smart enough to put together their own investment plans. But being good at growing a business is not necessarily great training for becoming a sophisticated investor.

Nevertheless, many entrepreneurs try doing it themselves and may do it well for a period of time, but rarely are the results consistent and the ups and downs can be nerve-wracking and exhausting. Equally exhausting is the search for the right financial planner. Some offer plans that adhere to a certain model. Some claim an advantage because their firm is large and has experts on hand on each type of investment. Some use existing programs that you pour your funds into and the portfolio managers diversify it according to a formula.

The most important factor ought to be finding a person you feel comfortable with, who takes the time to get to know you and what you want, and will also take the time to fully explain your choices in language you can understand. You should feel comfortable with the person managing your money, much the same way you feel confident when you've got a doctor, lawyer, or car mechanic you trust.

The Rearview Mirror Trap

People get so emotional about money that they develop irrational prejudices and even grudges that interfere with good judgment later in life. For example, many  people who began their investing careers in the late 1960s lost a lot of money in mutual funds during the 1970s and swore they'd never invest in another mutual fund, even though doing so would have been to their benefit. People who lost money in dot-com stocks may never invest another penny in high technology, even if it's an appropriate choice.

Bad investing experiences can be especially traumatic for those who grew up in modest circumstances. They are often riddled with guilt or self-hatred for having lost wealth they'd acquired working at good jobs they were able to get because their mothers and fathers slaved to earn the money so they could go to college. It's hard to make clear-headed choices when your decision-making is informed by such strong emotions and pre-conceived ideas.

Whomever you choose as an investment adviser, it should be a person you have confidence will be with you through thick and thin, whose success is tied to yours, and who sees his or her job to protect you and to make sure you've got your financial seatbelt securely fastened, just in case.

PART **THREE**

Elements of Success

The Purpose-Driven Portfolio

❝ A wise man should have money in his head, but not in his heart.❞

—Jonathan Swift, 18th Century Irish writer

Over the quarter-century that I have been a wealth and investment adviser, I have come to think of myself as more than a financial planner. Money supports life, so managing money by extension means managing life. I've become a life planner. That means life goals come first, and the financial plan is designed to support the life goal, not the other way around.

As a life planner, I always want to know WHY clients want to build up and preserve wealth. I pass no judgments about how lavish or modest their goals, just so long as they have them and they make common sense.

"Why?" is the most important question I ask, and it is also the one most people have the greatest trouble articulating. Most people don't think very far into the future. They worry themselves sick about it, but they don't plan for it.

Most people don't think very far into the future. They worry themselves sick about it, but they don't plan for it.

My best clients are those who instinctively think long term, as opposed to those who are caught up in the day-to-day distractions of life and business and the constant background noise of news and gossip. But sometimes these long-termers have trouble switching at retirement from accumulating stored wealth to enjoying the freedom they've earned. That's one of those times when I become a life planner.

One of these clients was in the process of retiring from a successful professional services business that his son was taking over, so I arranged to visit him to review his portfolio. He had done very well over the years, building a solid financial stage. Now I wanted to learn what role he saw for his third and final act, so we could adjust his investments to support that role.

He told me that his wife wanted them to sell the older family home and move into a single-level new home where they could grow old in comfort and convenience, without worrying about stairs or maintenance. But he was resistant to the idea of spending the money, even though he had more than enough. He didn't think it was a good investment. I thought that was an odd way to think for a man in his early seventies, and a shame for his wife if he stuck to his guns. But I kept my mouth shut.

Then he got up from his desk to sketch out on a dry-erase board attached to the wall the details of some investment property he was looking into. He has had a lifelong feel for real estate, and I believed him when he said, "It'll be worth a fortune in twenty or thirty years."

But I couldn't help chuckling. I answered his questioning look with a question: "You're over seventy years old. Where are you going to be if you're ninety or a hundred?"

Marker poised in midair, his puzzled look vanished, replaced by recognition and shock. He never thought about how long he was going to live! It was as if nothing had changed for him, even though everything had. Maybe he thought he was going to be able to keep doing what he was doing until they found him slumped over his desk. Either way, what's the point of building wealth if you aren't going to do something with it, whether it's erect a castle or donate it all to charity?

Plan and Plan Again

Most of the people I work with share an essential dilemma—without a sense of purpose, without some sort of vision, people and institutions tend to make choices that hurt their interests. The best investment advice and adviser in the world can't protect you from yourself if you fail to plan, don't listen, or let your judgment become fogged by greed or other emotions.

Very few people I meet have thought out their post-career or retirement years, even down to not knowing when they want to retire. Those who enjoy their work often expect to continue to do it into their seventies. Those who didn't enjoy their careers tend to want to retire early and take it easy the rest of their lives.

Even if you love what you do and you think you'll want to do it until you keel over, I advise people to be flexible. Your life goals today may not be your life goals in five years. You should be reviewing your investment situation yearly, making sure you've left enough room for the possibility you or your circumstances might change.

I do this for myself, reviewing my retirement plan several times a year. Among my life goals, I've long assumed that I'd continue helping people with their money affairs as long as I'm able and still enjoy it. But what if an opportunity comes along that causes me to change my mind and throw in the towel early? What if my family situation were to change dramatically? I want my investments to reflect these potentially shifting goals. Too often, people make a plan and never look at it again, thinking the future has been settled. They forget that the present is everchanging.

The Cost of Procrastination

Failure to keep your financial plan in sync with your life plan can often lead to nightmares for survivors. Many people who left behind significant estates would roll over in their graves if they knew what actually happened to their money.

One such client many years ago had built up a successful business. There were some people in his life he didn't trust who, in the event of his death, would have a claim on his wealth. He was adamant that these people should get nothing.

many people who left behind significant estates would roll over in their graves if they knew what actually happened to their money.

He shared a common trait with most entrepreneurs in that he needed to control more than he could reasonably manage, and he could never find time to make and execute a financial plan to meet his goals. One day he had a serious heart attack and needed urgent surgery. His attorney went to the hospital and tried to get him to make some decisions to protect his interests from those unwanted hands.

"Sure, sure," my client said. "Come see me after the surgery. I'll just be sitting around anyway."

He died on the operating table. All those people who he wanted to get nothing? They got everything.

Another client who sold building machinery systems for office buildings suffered from the worst kind of distraction. When he could find time to come into my office to talk about planning his investments, he left his cell phone on and it kept ringing in the middle of our discussion.

He would take the calls and in one case I heard him sealing a deal that I knew would generate about $7,000 in annual revenue. It was impossible to get him to focus on his investments. It was a shame because if he had devoted a few minutes to hearing me out, we could have been able to make some changes that would have given him the potential to earn many times what that contract would generate. All without lifting a finger.

Extreme Behaviors

You'd think that money in government, nonprofits, and other institutions is carefully managed... But too often this isn't so.

The purpose of investing is to create excess or stored wealth for the owner of an account, whether it be an individual, a profit-sharing plan, a nonprofit, or something else. I've discussed individual behavior in detail, but it's not much different for institutions. You'd think that large sums of money in government, nonprofit organizations, and other institutions are carefully managed, closely monitored, and invested wisely and profitably. But too often this isn't so.

I've sat on the boards of nonprofits for whom I was a valuable resource for managing their assets. No one could pull the wool over their eyes or sell them something they didn't need. I was surprised to discover that my fellow directors on the board of a church I had agreed to help had no concrete purpose or goals for what they wanted to do with their excess funds.

The mission was undefined. It was just a rainy-day fund.

Instead of deciding what they wanted to do with this money and mapping out a plan that included adding to it over the years, they decided not to decide. I tried to work with the other directors to get them to see the value of putting money in diversified investments including stocks, but just when I would win an ally, his or her term would be up and they'd be replaced by someone who brought their own experiences and prejudices.

A new director came on the board and declared that the church shouldn't be investing in stocks and so they kept it all in bank CDs, which can't even keep up with inflation.

In a similar vein, a small insurance company whose reserves I was managing provided me with its investment policy statement, a standard document that is supposed to describe the goals and restrictions on how the money is to be managed. They had used a form they got somewhere else that was so ludicrous, I told them it needed to be completely rewritten. It said they wanted their cake and to eat it, too—I was supposed to make them a lot of money but not take any risk. It was impossible to do and I told them that. But they didn't care.

The CFO was unschooled in investments yet he had to approve every transaction. All he knew was that if a transaction involved a stock he'd heard of, like GE or Exxon Mobil, it must be okay and he wouldn't question me. But if it was something he didn't recognize, he'd call and ask what it was. After a short explanation, he'd give his blessing and hustle me off the phone. He was going through the motions without understanding the rationale behind the decisions.

I do my best for clients regardless of their knowledge, but

it is more satisfying and successful when people are engaged in the process of defining their goals and setting a course to reach them.

Plain Stupidity

Because it happened in my backyard, it's worth mentioning the sad tale of the Orange County government debacle of 1994. County Treasurer Robert Citron, who had been in his job for many years, was responsible for $20 billion of taxpayer funds. He had become something of a celebrity because he had made some very successful investment decisions.

Merrill Lynch & Co. was the county's investment adviser and they had sold him a lot of complicated investment products that were very sensitive to the rise and fall of interest rates. These were products similar to the derivative investments at the center of the sub-prime mortgage meltdown that began in 2007.

Citron's apparent financial genius and his habit of wearing turquoise jewelry earned him the nickname "Sun God." Over a period of ten or so years, he consistently earned the county a healthy ten percent on their money, and did very well in 1992 and 1993 as interest rates fell.

At the time I looked at what Citron was doing and it didn't make sense to me, but I decided he must know something or have something up his sleeve. I figured I just wasn't sophisticated enough to understand.

It all came apart in 1994 when interest rates went against Citron's speculative investments. When the dust had settled, Orange County became the largest municipal bankruptcy in history, and Merrill Lynch had to cough up $400 million. Citron ended up going to jail.

The most astonishing aspect of the case didn't come out until a couple of years later when it was revealed that Citron consulted an astrologer to help him make investment decisions. Furthermore, Merrill Lynch's salesman who sold Citron many of the securities used in his investments knew about Citron's quirk but never raised a red flag. Of course, he had no incentive to do so. Blowing the whistle on Citron would have meant the end of his commission gravy train.

The problem, as it turned out, was that for a while the astrologer was right. This proves the adage that anyone can look like a genius for awhile. A stopped clock is right twice a day.

The Orange County disaster is a reminder to the humblest among us that without a plan and without a strategy, even the mighty are susceptible to human nature's worst instincts. No matter how smart we are, or how much common sense we have, people still have the urge to walk up to the roulette table and plunk all their money down on red.

Choosing Your Personal CFO

**❝ No one would remember the Good Samaritan
if he'd only had good intentions.
He had money as well.❞**

—Margaret Thatcher, Former British Prime Minister

The moments of greatest satisfaction
in my work occur when I feel I have helped clients make
educated decisions about their financial futures. But once in
a while, I am reminded that the right choice at the time it's
made doesn't always look so right in retrospect.

One of my most embarrassing experiences involved
a client I'd known for many years who, before becoming
a client, had a tendency to get lured into questionable
investments that promised big returns but ended up losing
him money. He'd had a string of losses and his only asset that
hadn't gone sour was a profit sharing plan at his job.

When I convinced him to let me help, I discovered to my horror that ninety-five percent of his profit-sharing plan was invested in a single company: the penny stock of a gold mine in Canada. A gold mine, the saying goes, is a hole in the ground with a liar on top. Canadian mining stocks—many of which trade at under a dollar a share and are thus known as penny stocks—have long had a notorious reputation in the investment industry as the currency of gamblers and con artists. They prey on the same instincts that drive people to feed slot machines—maybe the next coin will hit the jackpot. Like the slots, the odds are stacked against you in penny stocks.

I did some research on my client's gold-mining stock

and discovered, to my surprise, that the CEO of the company appeared to be running it by the book. But he was barely competent beyond that. The company held some old, unexploited mining claims in South America of indeterminate value.

It's a mistake to keep serious money that you'll need later in one stock, let alone in a highly speculative gold mine. I convinced him to unload it and put his money to work in a diversified portfolio. I think I was more relieved than he was. Penny stocks are so thinly traded, they can lose all their value overnight.

Soon after he sold his gold-mining shares, the terrorist attacks of September 11, 2001 took place. Gold began to rise, as it usually does during international crises. The gold mining company was bought out by another gold producer at a big premium over the price my client received. I felt terrible. It was as if I'd found him at the roulette wheel in Las Vegas with all his money on the number nineteen, and I talked him into taking it off the table just before the ball landed on nineteen.

It doesn't matter whether it's General Electric or a penny stock, it's risky to keep all your eggs in one basket.

My client forgave me, and as bad as I felt, I knew my advice was sound. It doesn't matter whether it's General Electric or a penny stock, it's risky to keep all your eggs in one basket. I'd rather see someone give up the tiny chance of a big score and instead put their money where they have a better chance of a steady series of small wins.

Greater confidence in the future is based on predictability, and predictability is what everyone wants in their financial future. A 2007 poll by Harris Interactive reported ninety-seven percent of baby boomers cite guaranteed income for life as their top retirement goal.

Beyond Honesty

One of the most common mistakes people make in their financial lives is the way they pick their investment advisers. They tend to focus on what they most fear: getting cheated. They forget that there's more to it than honesty. As a result, they are commonly unhappy with the advice they get.

According to a 2007 survey by Spectrem Group, a think

tank that studies the attitudes and habits of the wealthy, half of investors worth $25 million and more think they can do a better job of managing their money than their advisers. The survey found that only half were satisfied with the knowledge of their advisers or their ability to deal with complex problems. As one commenter put it in a post on *The Wall Street Journal* web site, "I do not personally believe that an adviser can tell me anything that I do not know through my own observations and instincts."

Half of investors worth $25 million and more think they can do a better job of managing their money than their advisers.

It's true that the many financial advisers are product salespeople, more interested in short-term gain than long-term relationships. But there are plenty of people in the investment industry who walk the straight and narrow and who truly enjoy helping others protect and grow their wealth. But to be a good investment adviser you need more than solid ethics and good intentions.

For starters, "Just don't screw me!" is a low standard to set when thinking about hiring an adviser, but that's what many people do. Like finding a dentist or a lawyer, people often turn to an adviser at a time of crisis or change, both good (a windfall) and bad (a big loss).

Because humans want simple, quick solutions in life, we often go with the recommendation of a friend or relative. Or we put faith and financial future in the hands of a young relative who is just starting out in the investment business.

The instinct seems sensible: help a hungry up-and-comer who you believe is honest.

There are young people who have a gift for financial and life advice, but most seasoned advisers with a couple of decades of experience will tell you, "I wouldn't hire the person I was at that age. I didn't have a clue." Some of the worst investment traps people fall into are those peddled by advisers to their friends and relatives.

I advise clients to smile politely and ignore the recommendations of friends and relatives or at least endeavor to evaluate them the same way you would a total stranger. Someone you trust may recommend someone they trust, but you still have to do your homework. Ignorance and naivete are no defense.

Who Versus How Much

A good investment adviser is someone who doesn't just sell you products but who becomes a life partner helping you make choices that are consistent with your personality and goals as well as your resources and circumstances. It's not about how much you have and how much you think you need, it's about who you are and what you want to achieve in the future.

When I'm starting to work with new clients, once I have the financial facts, I want to learn about their lives. I ask and listen. What is your vision of your future? Are there any particular goals you've set for retirement? If not, is there a date by which you would like to be financially independent of having to work? What are your financial goals? Do you have kids to educate? Do you have a dream of owning a vacation home? Do you want to get an RV and travel the country, or take cruises? How do you see your life unfolding?

An investment adviser should be asking you all those questions and more. Life is a journey. It begins in the practicality of now, and it ends at the inevitability of death. Planning is crucial for that journey to turn out the way you want. But many people start out by telling me, "Things are up in the air right now. We really don't know where we're headed or what we want to do."

"*Your Dreams*"

They've got it backwards. The reason things are up in the air is because they don't have a goal.

"If things are really up in the air," I tell them, "let's put together a wish list and a 'what if' benchmark. Let's assume you are going to live thirty more years. Let's throw in some what-ifs so you have an idea where you are. What if you get sick? Lose your job? Want to move and can't sell your house?" And so on.

If you make this exercise an annual ritual, you will begin to get a sense of your direction, capabilities, and possibilities.

Your Chief Financial Officer

If the CEO of a company wants to launch a new product, build a new plant, or staff a new department, he has to check in with his chief financial officer (CFO) to see if it's realistic and fits into the budget. My clients are the CEOs and I am their CFO. Just as in companies, sometimes the CEO's great ideas get shot down by the CFO.

One of my clients, the widow of a successful businessman, was in the "distribution" phase of her life, living off her investments, when she called and said she wanted an additional $1,000 of monthly income. I evaluated her portfolio and didn't like the effect that taking out that much additional money would have on the predictability of her money outlasting her life, given inflation and a host of what-ifs.

> **My clients are the CEOs and I am their CFO. Just as in companies, sometimes the CEO's great ideas get shot down by the CFO.**

Using a specialized computer program, I calculated that she could take out up to an additional $400 a month without diminishing the predictability of her financial future. I try not to lecture clients, but I do want them to know how their choices may affect their lifestyles.

I apply that same rigor to my own life. It's why, even though I could afford a luxury home, I chose to stay in a more modest middle-class house and fix it up. It's why I don't own a second home. I can't see the sense of spending money on a second mortgage and upkeep for a house I'd only use now and then.

This has allowed me to indulge one of my passions,

sailing. But I came close to making a mistake like the one I avoided when my girlfriend wanted plain white kitchen appliances instead of the most expensive in the world. I had been chartering a large boat in the Caribbean for about two months each year, and my dream was to own my own boat outright so I could go sailing anytime I felt like it, anywhere I felt like it.

A good investment advisor can help you fight the tendency to live your life and spend your resources proving to others how happy and successful you are.

When I finally decided to act on my dream, I found a boat I liked and made arrangements to buy it. As the date to close the transaction approached, it hit me that I probably wouldn't spend more time sailing than I had when I was chartering. I live in southern California, so getting to the boat would be an effort. Besides, I keep myself busy with work and family life. I calculated that for ten months of the year the boat would sit idle, so I leased it out when I wasn't using it and ended up making money.

A good investment advisor can help you fight the tendency to live your life and spend your resources proving to others how happy and successful you are. As I've said, I pass no judgment on the desire to surround yourself with luxuries, so long as you've taken care of the basics first.

Getting To Happiness

> **❝ People with ten million dollars are no happier than people with nine million dollars. ❞**
>
> —Hobart Brown, American artist

My conviction that money can be the root of all happiness has nothing to do with money and everything to do with a person's attitude toward it and understanding how it works. Money itself is an abstract idea, an artificial construct that can make reality possible but cannot guarantee it. Which would you rather be shipwrecked with on a deserted island, a ton of gold or a ton of food?

In the award-winning 2000 film *CastAway*, starring Tom Hanks, a Federal Express executive is the sole survivor of a plane crash who finds himself marooned on a remote, uninhabited island with the clothes on his back and a pile of soggy Federal Express packages. All the money in the world can't keep him alive, but a pair of ice skates give him a cutting tool to break open coconuts and build a shelter, and a designer dress made of gauzy material gives him a net for catching fish.

One of the most extreme examples of the fragile usefulness of money took place during the Ruhr Valley Crisis of 1923 in Europe. Germany, staggering under an enormous reparations debt burden to France and England, propped up its economy by printing paper money at such a high rate that inflation got completely out of control. During the worst of it, prices for staples like bread and coal rose hourly.

Germany's currency became so devalued that at one point it was cheaper to burn it than to spend it buying coal. There were reports of people found starved to death in their homes, surrounded by bales of banknotes that weren't enough to buy a loaf of bread.

People think too much about dollars and not enough about the rationale behind them.

These are extreme examples of a phenomenon I often encounter in my discussions with prospective clients. People think too much about dollars and not enough about the rationale behind them. So many conversations begin with people telling me how many dollars they want to live on in retirement. The flaw with this thinking has been well explored in these pages, but it's such an important concept, it's worth hammering on one last time.

It's All Relative

Your financial choices should be driven by your life choices. If they are, your decisions will be based on your specific situation, not on an abstract notion tied to numbers of dollars.

For example, during the bubble in real estate prices, many people found themselves sitting on sudden new wealth as the value of their homes soared. Many of my clients were asking me if they should sell, take the money, and run; or hold on, hoping for an even higher price later.

Among my clients were a retired couple who planned within a few years to move from California to Montana. It was a dream they had nurtured for a long time. They were unsophisticated investors and when they asked me what to do, I recommended they sell, put the money away in a safe place, and rent until they were ready to buy their retirement home in Montana. That way they'd have greater confidence of having the money they needed to make their dream a reality.

I had a hunch that real estate prices were close to peaking and that a day of reckoning would come for those inflated home values. But I knew that even if I was wrong and they

left a few dollars on the table, removing the uncertainty about their future was worth it. They did as I suggested and when the real estate crash occurred, they had dodged a bullet. If they hadn't sold, their dream would have been snuffed out.

I had other clients with no plans to move anytime soon, and when they wanted to know if I thought they should sell their houses and capture the extra wealth, I posed a few simple questions.

"Do you like your house?"

"Yes, we love our house," they said. "We put a lot into it and we're really happy here. We love the neighborhood and we like our neighbors."

Next I asked, "Can you afford the mortgage payments?"

"Yes, the payments are no problem and our jobs are secure."

"Then why would you sell?" I said. "It doesn't sound like having a few extra dollars will make you any happier. Life is not just about dollars. It's about lifestyle."

> **"Why would you sell? It doesn't sound like having a few extra dollars will make you any happier. Life is not just about dollars. It's about lifestyle."**

The "What If?" Test

In my role as a financial guide, I strive to teach my clients how to think rationally, instead of focusing on what's going to return them the most money today. One way to test the rationality of your thinking is to give yourself the "What if?" test when considering any financial decision.

In the previous examples, the test works as follows: the

couple planning to retire to Montana wanted to know if they should sell their house now.

1. *What if they sell, and house prices keep going up?* They leave some money on the table but they have their dream retirement plan locked down. The money's in the bank.
2. *What if they do, and prices collapse?* Same as in Number 1, but they get the benefit of looking smart.
3. *What if they don't sell, and real estate prices soar higher?* They might be able to make more money, but there is no guarantee. Is it worth risking the dream?
4. *What if they don't sell and prices collapse?* The Montana retirement is gone.

The "What If?" test produces a clear result for this couple. They aren't going to live forever, and who can say how their health will hold up or predict the future direction of real estate prices? Having sold, they can relax and enjoy the present knowing the future is all tied up with a bow on top.

Most any major financial decision can be rationally assessed by applying the "What if?" test. What will happen to your investment portfolio if there's a severe market downturn? What if it's a prolonged down market? Will you have to change their lifestyle? Will you have to delay or forego retirement plans? If you are retired and the market crashes, will you be forced to go back to work?

There are no right answers to these questions. There

are only rational answers in the context of who you are and where you are in the cycle of life. Who you are includes factors such as how happy you are with your life today, like the clients who thought about selling their home even though they loved the house and the neighborhood. Selling was not a rational choice for them. They were happy. More dollars would not have made them happier, and leaving the home they loved would have robbed them of their contentedness.

If you are contemplating an investment, ask yourself, What if it goes to hell? Will you: a) slit your wrists; b) get horribly depressed; c) get drunk and create a scene in your broker's officer; or d) shrug your shoulders and chalk it up as a learning experience?

I have had a client for some time who has been a successful entrepreneur but has a tendency to invest in one speculative venture after another, with the unsurprising result that he usually loses some or all of his money. He often comes to me for advice about these investments and after showing him the risks, I make sure to tell him, "If you decide to go ahead, do it with the idea that you'll never see the money again. That way you'll never be surprised. If you can't stand the idea of losing it all, don't do it."

The Root of All Happiness

The message I have tried to convey here is to get your financial affairs in order so you can go out and live life to the fullest.

The biggest obstacle to success is your worst instincts. You can blame it on the stock market, the unpredictability of life, or anything else you want, but in the end the biggest problem is always going to be yourself, just as it is with dieting. If you don't watch what you eat; educate yourself on caloric intake, carbohydrates, protein, and so on; and neglect to exercise, you're going to fail.

> You can blame it on the stock market, the unpredictability of life, or anything else you want, but in the end the biggest problem is always going to be yourself.

To be a good investor, whether you have someone who helps you or not, it's important to be educated and engaged. You can't just stick your head in the sand and leave your money in bank CDs, and you can't throw the dice hoping to luck out with a big score.

When you get it right, money can become the root of all your happiness.

Lufthansa Flight 540
Made History

November 20, 1974
when it became
the world's first fatal crash
of a Boeing 747.
Here are a few details
of what happened,
and what it was like
to survive.

CORGI

THE STORY OF THE FIRST 747 JET DISASTER

WAKE UP, IT'S A CRASH!

A SURVIVOR'S ACCOUNT

EARL MOORHOUSE

WHAT DOES IT FEEL LIKE TO KNOW THAT THE AIRCRAFT YOU ARE FLYING IN IS CRASHING – THAT IN SECONDS YOUR LIFE MAY BE OVER? WHAT ARE THE THOUGHTS THAT FLASH THROUGH YOUR MIND? HOW DO YOU REACT?

Cover and back copy of survivor Earl Moorhouse's account of escaping the crash with his wife and children.

747 JET CRASH IN NAIROBI—Smoke cloud rises over the first fatal wreck of a Boeing 747 since the jumbo jets went into service five years ago. The Lufthansa craft crashed shortly after takeoff.

747 CRASH KILLS 59 IN KENYA, 98 SAVED

12 Americans on Lufthansa Flight Survive—1st Deaths on a Boeing Jumbo

By The Associated Press

NAIROBI, Kenya, Nov. 20—Fifty-nine persons on a West German jumbo jetliner died here today but the 98 others aboard survived when the plane crashed and burned shortly after take-off.

Most of the passengers were Germans, but the airline, Lufthansa, said the survivors included 12 Americans.

Ten American survivors were said to be members of a group that left Los Angeles last Sunday for a month-long tour of Africa.

Helmuth Wolff, the airline's manager in Nairobi, said that the other survivors were 67 Germans, 10 Britons, four Canadians, two South Africans, two Norwegians and one Belgian.

Seventy-three of the survivors were reported to be virtually unharmed and were resting at a hotel before resuming their trip. Twenty-three were admitted to hospitals, three in critical condition.

HOUSTON, Nov. 21 (Reuters)—A container of valuable lunar soil was apparently lost in yesterday's crash of a West German jetliner near Nairobi, it was learned today.

A spokesman for the Johnson Space Center here confirmed that a 1-by-3-inch container of soil from the moon was aboard the plane.

---

3 Californians Among 98 Jet Crash Survivors

BY DIAL TORGERSON
Times Staff Writer

NAIROBI, Kenya — Three Californians from the Los Angeles area—two of them crew members—were among the 98 survivors of the 157 passengers and crew of a Lufthansa Boeing 747 airliner that crashed and burned at Nairobi airport early Wednesday morning.

Tom Scott of Newport Beach, a steward, was hailed by passengers as a hero for his efforts to get survivors out of the wreckage of the plane, which lost power at about 200 feet after takeoff, struck a road embankment not far from the end of the runway, and split in two in a muddy field and was quickly engulfed in flames.

A fellow crew member who survived was stewardess Susan Mary Seaholm of Redondo Beach. The third Californian was Salome Zeiss of 757 Linda Vista, Pasadena, who was among the flight that had boarded the flight in Los Angeles for a month-long camera safari of Africa arranged by Club Universe tours. Twelve of the 13 members of the Club Universe tour survived, but the tour guide, Maya Galitzina from France, who was sitting in the rear of the plane, perished.

The plane had landed in Nairobi on a flight from Frankfurt, West Germany, and after refueling took off on its scheduled flight to Johannesburg, South Africa. It was the first fatal crash of a 747 since the big jumbos first came into commercial service five years ago.

One of the survivors, Mrs. Renate Kahn, 48, of Dallas, said that if it had not been for the heroic efforts of Scott, "we all would be dead." Her husband, Karl, and their daughter, Nancy, were among the survivors.

The other American survivors were identified as Mrs. Tillie Harmel and Gladys Golman, also of Dallas; Mr. and Mrs. Albert Oppenheimer of Baltimore, and Mrs. Edmund Senkier of Seattle.

Jurgen Freund, 34, another Lufthansa steward, also was credited with helping Scott get many passengers out of the tourist section.

"We had 35, maybe 40 seconds from when we hit until everyone was out," he said. "Then it was all in flames."

In first class, "the floor came up to meet us and split open," Mrs. Dawn Schultz of Duesseldorf recalled later. She and the others climbed over wreckage and tipped over seats and slipped through

Times map

the split to the ground and safety.

Gaetano Toffolatti, manager of an electrical firm working on an airport extension nearby, was one of the first on the scene. He came through a field littered with dead and dying; a dark-haired stewardess, face down in the mud; a man bleeding badly with his limbs shattered; a woman dead in her seat.

"I saw the co-pilot," he said. "He was cut badly but able to walk. Someone asked him what happened. 'We could not go up,' he said."

A blonde stewardess stood nearby, where the passengers who had escaped had quietly gathered, watching the first ambulances and fire engines arrive.

"It couldn't go up," she said, crying. "It just couldn't go up."

By the time the first fire trucks arrived the entire plane was burning. All firemen could do was remove the bodies after the fire was out. No one else escaped.

Of the 18 crew members, four of the cabin crew were believed to have died. All three members of the flight crew escaped serious injury.

747 Crew Are Praised For Saving Of Lives

NAIROBI, Kenya (AP) — Survivors of the Lufthansa jumbo jet crash praised the crew today and said without their quick action many more lives would have been lost.

Fifty-nine of the 157 persons aboard were killed when the West German airline's Boeing 747 lost power as it took off from Nairobi airport for South African Wednesday, plunged into a muddy field and exploded. It was the first fatal 747 crash.

"Looking at the scene, one would not expect too many survivors," a local civil aviation official said. "I think the crew reacted very fast at the first sign of trouble, and that accounts for the very large number of survivors."

Renate Kahn of Dallas, Tex., said an American steward, Tom Scott of Los Angeles, forced open an emergency door that two stewardesses were unable to wrench free, shouted "Out! Out! Out!" and got dozens of passengers moving toward the exit.

"We all would be dead if it hadn't been for him," said Mrs. Kahn. "Scott took an 89-year-old, deaf German man and dragged him out. He went back inside and checked the body of the plane until he was sure no one else could be rescued. He left only then. That's beyond the call, in my book."

A Lufthansa spokesman said the cause of the crash has not been determined. The plane, which had come from Frankfurt, was about 200 feet off the ground when it lost power and dropped back to the ground.

"The plane taxied and took off, and then there was an awful shudder," said John Bing, a travel agent from Johannesburg, who was unhurt. "Bric-a-brac in the passenger section flew in all directions with great momentum. The port wing caught fire, then the plane ditched."

Bing said the 54-year-old German pilot, Christian Krack, "made the most remarkable landing by any pilot ever. His skill saved lives."

Most of the passengers were German, but officials said 12 Americans were among the survivors. They reported 98 of the 139 passengers, including 13 of the 18 crew members, escaped, 73 of them virtually unharmed. Three of the injured were reported in serious condition.

THURSDAY
MORNING
FINAL

RACING RESULTS-ENTRIES

Los Angeles Times

LARGEST CIRCULATION IN THE WEST, 1,043,679 DAILY, 1,306,004 SUNDAY

Orange County Edition

VOL. XCIII   TWELVE PARTS—PART ONE   R   THURSDAY MORNING, NOVEMBER 21, 1974   212 PAGES   Copyright © 1974 Los Angeles Times   DAILY 10c

JET CRASH HERO

Survivors Laud Newport Beach Man

UNITED WAY, AID
Charity Drives: Merger Studied to Boost Take

BY ROBERT E. WOOD
Times Financial Editor

Metropolitan Los Angeles is widely recognized as virtually the largest tightwad among major U.S. metropolitan areas when it comes to many charitable donations.

Now a group of public-spirited citizens is quietly trying to improve the situation by consolidating the two biggest fundraising organizations in Southern California, United Way and AID-United Givers.

The merger could make millions of

REVIEW OF ISRAEL U.N. SEAT SOUGHT BY ARAB EMIRATE

BY DON SHANNON
Times Staff Writer

UNITED NATIONS — With signs pointing toward an Arab victory in the General Assembly debate on Palestine, the tiny Arab emirate of Qatar Wednesday proposed a review of Israel's continued membership in the world organization.

When the assembly voted 91 to 22 Nov. 12 to suspend South Africa's membership rights for the remainder of this session, there were foretastes of similar action against Israel. The suspension was based on the charges that South Africa's apartheid, or racial segregation, violated the U.N. Charter and the Declaration of Human Rights.

Jassin Trassif Jamal, Qatar's delegation, declared in his speech to the assembly:

"Zionism and the system of apartheid practiced in South Africa

CRASH SURVIVORS—Stewardess Susan Mary Seaholm of Redondo Beach and steward Tom Scott of Newport Beach were among three who survived 747 crash. Scott was hailed as hero in tragedy.

Steward Aboard 747 Leads Many Passengers to Safety

"We all would be dead if it hadn't been for him."

This was the reaction of Mrs. Renate Kahn, 45, of Dallas, one of the American survivors of the Lufthansa jumbo jet crash Wednesday in Kenya, to the heroism of Thomas Scott, 24, of Newport Beach, a steward aboard the ill-fated flight.

There were 56 survivors of the crash which killed 59 persons. (Story on Page 10.)

Scott was hailed by survivors as a hero for his efforts to get passengers out before the plane, which crashed on takeoff, exploded.

Mrs. Kahn and other survivors said Scott forced open an emergency door immediately after the crash, then he shouted "Out, out, out" and began to usher direct passengers down an escape chute to safety.

Another survivor, Lorna Moore-house, whose address was not known, said how tried, helped her

"The bottom of the first-class section collapsed right after the plane went down," Scott related in the telephone conversation with his family. "People were falling into the baggage compartment.

"I got all my passengers out of there and was still getting them out when I saw an old man who was bleeding. I was carrying him from the plane when I heard a rumble and the area I was in exploded behind me."

Please Turn to Page 11, Col. 1

Council Balks at Coal Contract; Long Walkout Possible

Door and slide used for escape   Survivors